CBS PROBLEMS and SOLUTIONS SERIES

Problems and Solutions in COMMUNICATION SYSTEMS

- This book is suitable for examinations of all Indian universities.
- Solutions of problems are given in most simplified manner.
- All types of problems are included and the solutions given in detail.
- To explain the basics lucidly, neat and well drawn line illustrations have been liberally added in the solutions. This volume contains more than 200 line diagrams.

CBS PROBLEMS and SOLUTIONS SERIES

Problems and Solutions in COMMUNICATION SYSTEMS

R GOPAL
Engineer

CBS Publishers & Distributors Pvt. Ltd.

New Delhi • Bengaluru • Chennai • Kochi • Kolkata • Mumbai
Hyderabad • Uttarakhand • Nagpur • Patna • Pune • Jharkhand

ISBN: 81-239-1146-7

First Edition: 2004
Reprint: 2007, 2008, 2013, 2018

Published by **Satish Kumar Jain** and produced by **Varun Jain** for
CBS Publishers & Distributors Pvt. Ltd.,
4819/XI Prahlad Street, 24 Ansari Road, Daryaganj, New Delhi - 110002
delhi@cbspd.com, cbspubs@airtelmail.in • www.cbspd.com
Ph.: 23289259, 23266861, 23266867 • Fax: 011-23243014

Corporate Office: 204 FIE, Industrial Area, Patparganj, Delhi - 110 092
Ph: 49344934 • Fax: 011-49344935
E-mail: publishing@cbspd.com • publicity@cbspd.com

Branches:
- ***Bengaluru:*** 2975, 17th Cross, K.R. Road, Bansankari 2nd Stage, Bengaluru - 70 • Ph: +91-80-26771678/79 • Fax: +91-80-26771680 E-mail: cbsbng@gmail.com, bangalore@cbspd.com
- ***Chennai:*** No. 7, Subbaraya Street, Shenoy Nagar, Chennai - 600030 Ph: +91-44-26681266, 26680620 • Fax: +91-44-42032115 E-mail: chennai@cbspd.com
- ***Kochi:*** Ashana House, 39/1904, A.M. Thomas Road, Valanjambalam, Ernakulum, Kochi • Ph: +91-484-4059061-65 Fax: +91-484-4059065 • E-mail: cochin@cbspd.com
- ***Kolkata:*** 6-B, Ground Floor, Rameshwar Shaw Road, Kolkata - 700014 Ph: +91-33-22891126/7/8 • E-mail: kolkata@cbspd.com
- ***Mumbai:*** 83-C, Dr. E. Moses Road, Worli, Mumbai - 400018 Ph: +91-9833017933, 022-24902340/41 • E-mail: mumbai@cbspd.com

Representatives:
- Hyderabad: 0-9885175004
- Patna: 0-9334159340
- Jharkhand: 0-9811541605
- Nagpur: 0-9021734563
- Pune: 0-9623451994
- Uttarakhand: 0-9716462459

Printed at:
J.S. Offset Printers, Delhi (India)

Preface

Communication Systems is one of the fundamental subjects for the students of electronics and telecommunication engineering. The author feels it a great pleasure in presenting this intricate subject through typical problems and their solutions.

This book covers all important and major topics taught at the undergraduate level in an engineering college. All the problems have been discussed at length, and detailed line diagrams given extensively to help the reader understand the basics and grasp the logic. This book is suitable for preparing for all university examinations and also to face the competitions. This feature is expected to help the reader in visualising the patterns of problems and the extent and level of difficulty in solving the questions likely to be encountered in the examination, and thus tackling the problems with confidence and success.

Although every care has been taken to ensure accuracy, yct some errors might have crept in. The author will be grateful if these are brought to his notice so that these could be rectified in the subsequent printings and editions of the book. Readers are requested to send their suggestions for further improvement and revision to me through the publishers at the following e-mail address: cbspubs@del3.vsnl.net.in.

R GOPAL

Contents

Chapter 1

Representation of Signals and Systems

Problem 1.1:

(*a*) Find the Fourier transform of the half-cosine pulse shown in Fig. P 1.1 (a).

(*b*) Apply the time-shifting property to the result obtained in part (*a*) to evaluate the spectrum of the half-sine pulse shown in Fig. P. 1.1 (b).

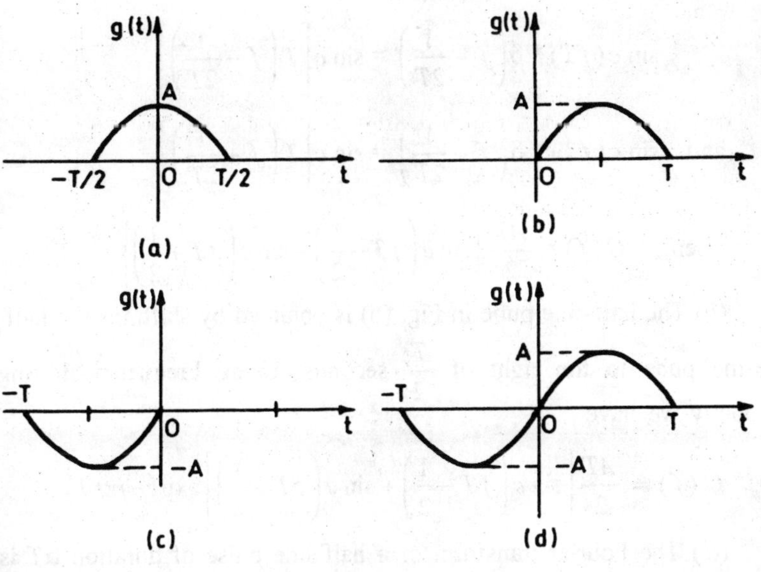

Fig. P. 1.1

(*c*) What is the spectrum of a half-sine pulse having a duration equal to aT?
(*d*) What is the spectrum of the negative half-sine pulse shown in Fig. P 1.1 (c)?
(*e*) Find the spectrum of the singla sine pulse shown in Fig. P 1.1 (d).

Solution:

(*a*) The pulse $g(t)$ is the product of rect$\left(\frac{t}{T}\right)$ and the sinusoidal wave $A\cos\left(\frac{\pi t}{T}\right)$. As

$$\text{rect}\left(\frac{t}{T}\right) \rightleftharpoons T\ \text{sin}\,c\,(fT)$$

$$A\cos\left(\frac{\pi t}{T}\right) \rightleftharpoons \frac{A}{2}\left[\delta\left(f-\frac{1}{2T}\right)+\delta\left(f+\frac{1}{2t}\right)\right]$$

Then, using convolutional property

$$G(f) = [T\ \text{sinc}\,(fT)] * \left\{\frac{A}{2}\left[\delta\left(f-\frac{1}{2t}\right)+\delta\left(f+\frac{1}{2T}\right)\right]\right\}$$

Where * denotes convolution. Then

$$\text{sin}\,c(fT) * \delta\left(f-\frac{1}{2T}\right) = \text{sin}\,c\left[T\left(f-\frac{1}{2T}\right)\right]$$

and $$\text{sin}\,c(fT) * \delta\left(f+\frac{1}{2T}\right) = \text{sin}\,c\left[T\left(f+\frac{1}{2T}\right)\right]$$

Then, $$G(f) = \frac{AT}{2}\left\{\text{sin}\,c\left(fT-\frac{1}{2}\right)+\text{sin}\,c\left(fT+\frac{1}{2}\right)\right\}$$

(*b*) The half-sine pube in Fig. (b) is obtained by shiftings the half-cosine pube to the right of $\frac{T}{2}$ seconds. Using Frequency-shifting property we have

$$G(f) = \frac{AT}{2}\left[\text{sin}\,c\left(fT-\frac{1}{2}\right)+\text{sin}\,c\left(fT+\frac{1}{2}\right)\right]\exp(-j\pi fT)$$

(*d*) The Fourier transform of a half-sine pulse of duration αT is equal to

$$\frac{|\alpha| AT}{2}\left[\sin c\left(afT - \frac{1}{2}\right) + \sin c\left(afT + \frac{1}{2}\right)\right]\exp(-j\pi afT)$$

then, the Fourier transform of the negative half-sine pulse of the pulse in Fig. (*c*) is obtained by putting $a = -1$ and multiplying the result by -1, i.e.

$$G(f) = -\frac{AT}{2}\left[\sin c\left(fT + \frac{1}{2}\right) + \sin c\left(fT - \frac{1}{2}\right)\right]\exp(j\pi fT)$$

(*e*) The Fig. (d) can be considered as a sum of Fig. (*b*) and Fig. (*c*) then,

$$G(f) = \frac{AT}{2}\left[\sin c\left(fT - \frac{1}{2}\right) + \sin c\left(fT + \frac{1}{2}\right)\right]$$
$$[\exp(-j\pi fT) - \exp(j\pi fT)]$$
$$= -jAT\left[\sin c\left(fT - \frac{1}{2}\right) + \sin c\left(fT + \frac{1}{2}\right)\sin(\pi fT)\right]$$
$$= -jAT\left[-\frac{\cos(\pi fT)}{\pi fT - \frac{\pi}{2}} + \frac{\cos(\pi fT)}{\pi fT + \frac{\pi}{2}}\right]\sin(\pi fT)$$
$$= jAT[\sin c(2fT + 1) - \sin c(2fT - 1)]$$

Problem 1.2: Evaluate the Fourier transform of the damped sinusoidal wave

$$g(t) = \exp(-t)\sin(2\pi f_c t)\,u(t)$$

where $u(t)$ is the unit step function.

Solution: Given

$$g(t) = \exp(-t)\cdot\sin(2\pi f_c t)\,u(t)$$

As, $\sin(2\pi f_c t) = \frac{1}{2j}[\exp(j2\pi f_c t) - \exp(-j2\pi f_c t)]$

Using frequency-shiftings property, we have

$$G(f) = \frac{1}{2j}\left[\frac{1}{1 + j2\pi(f - f_c)} - \frac{1}{1 + j2\pi(f + f_c)}\right]$$
$$= \frac{2\pi f_c}{(1 + j2\pi f)^2 + (2\pi f_c)^2}$$

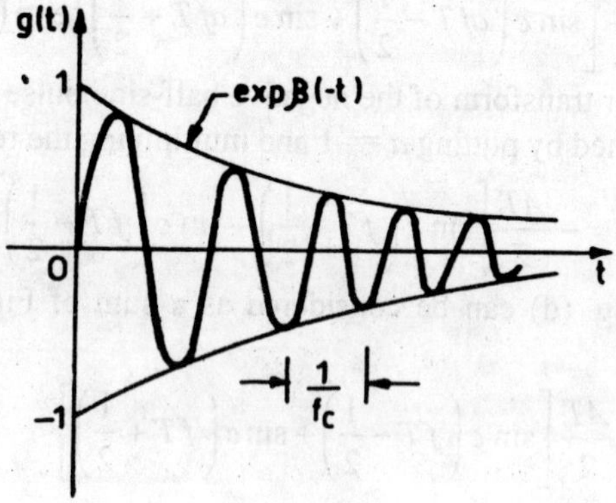

Fig. P. 1.2

Problem 1.3: Any function $g(t)$ can be split unambiguously into an *even part* and an *odd part*, as shown by

$$g(t) = g_e(t) + g_o(t)$$

The even part is defined by

$$g_e(t) = \frac{1}{2}[g(t) + g(-t)]$$

and the odd part is defined by

$$g_o(t) = \frac{1}{2}[g(t) - g(-t)]$$

(*a*) Evaluate the even and odd parts of a rectangular pulse defined by

$$g(t) = A \operatorname{rect}\left(\frac{t}{T} - \frac{1}{2}\right)$$

(*b*) What are the Fourier transforms of these two parts of the pulse?

Solution: (*a*) Even part,

$$g_e(t) = \frac{1}{2}(g(t) + g(-t))$$

For $g(t) = A \operatorname{rect}\left(\frac{t}{T} - \frac{1}{2}\right)$

$$g_e(t) = \frac{A}{2}\left[\operatorname{rect}\left(\frac{t}{T} - \frac{1}{2}\right) + \operatorname{rect}\left(\frac{-t}{T} - \frac{1}{2}\right)\right]$$

and, the odd part

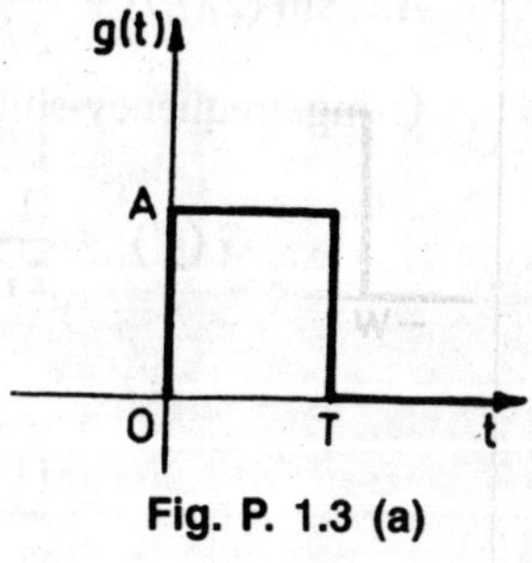

Fig. P. 1.3 (a)

$$g_o(t) = \frac{1}{2}[g(t) - g(-t)] = \frac{A}{2}\left[\text{rect}\left(\frac{t}{T} - \frac{1}{2}\right) - \text{rect}\left(\frac{-t}{T} - \frac{1}{2}\right)\right]$$

as shown below,

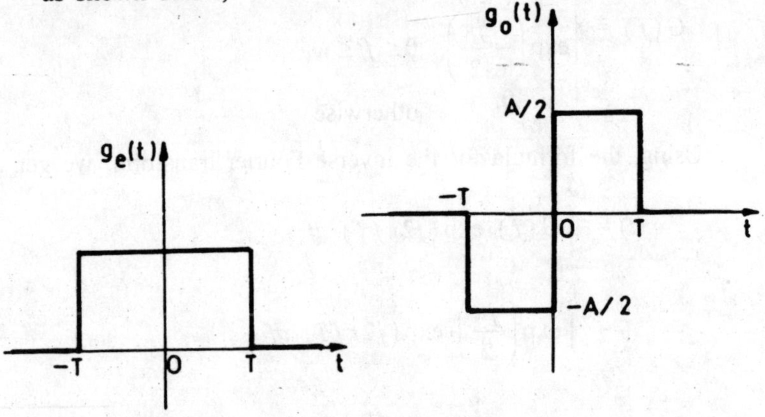

Fig. P. 1.3 (b) and (c)

(*b*) The Fourier transform for the even part

$$G_e(t) = AT \sin c(2fT)$$

and, the Fourier transform for the odd part

$$G_o(f) = \frac{AT}{2} \text{sinc}(fT) \exp(-j\pi fT) - \frac{AT}{2} \text{sinc}(fT) \exp(j\pi fT)$$

$$= \frac{AT}{j} \text{sinc}(fT) \cdot \sin(\pi fT)$$

Problem 1.4: Determine the inverse Fourier transform of the frequency function $G(f)$ defined by the amplitude and phase spectra shown in Fig. P 1.4.

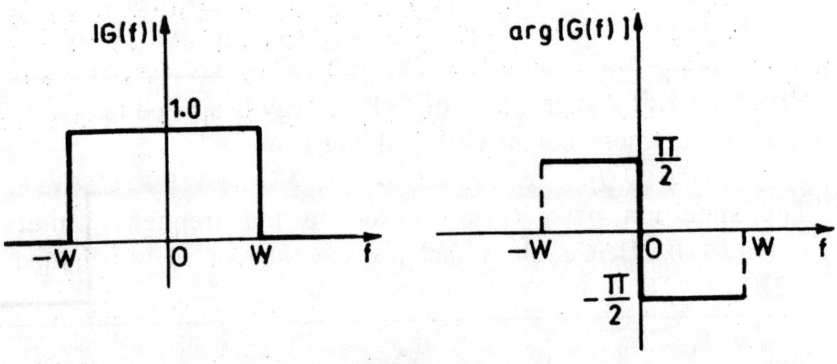

Fig. P. 1.4

Solution:

$$G(f) = \begin{cases} \exp\left(\frac{j\pi}{2}\right), & -w \le f \le 0 \\ \exp\left(-\frac{j\pi}{2}\right), & 0 \le f \le w \\ 0, & \text{otherwise} \end{cases}$$

Using, the formula for the inverse Fourier transform, we get,

$$g(t) = \int_{-\infty}^{\infty} G(f) \cdot \exp(j2\pi fT) \cdot df$$

$$= \int_{-w}^{0} \exp\left(\frac{j\pi}{2}\right) \cdot \exp(j2\pi fT) \cdot df -$$

$$\int_{0}^{w} \exp\left(-\frac{j\pi}{2}\right) \cdot \exp(j2\pi fT) \cdot df \qquad \text{...(1)}$$

then, replacing f with $-f$ in eqn (1) and interchanging the integration limits, we have

$$g(t) = \int_{0}^{w} \left[\exp\left(-j2\pi fT + j\frac{\pi}{2}\right) - \exp\left(j2\pi fT - j\frac{\pi}{2}\right)\right] df$$

$$= 2\int_{0}^{w} \cos\left(2\pi fT - \frac{\pi}{2}\right) df = 2\int_{0}^{w} \sin(2\pi fT)\, df$$

$$= \left[-\frac{\cos(2\pi ft)}{\pi t}\Bigg|_{0}^{w}\right] = \frac{2}{\pi t}\sin^2(\pi wt)$$

Problem 1.5: A signal $x(t)$ of finite energy is applied to a square–law device whose output $y(t)$ is defined by

$$y(t) = x^2(t)$$

The spectrum of $x(t)$ is limited to the frequency interval $-W \le f \le W$. Hence, show that the spectrum of $y(t)$ is limited to $-2W \le f \le 2W$.

Solution:

$$Y(t) = x^2(t) = x(t) \cdot x(t)$$

Since, multiplication in time domain is equivalent to convolution in frequency domain, then

$$Y(f) = \int_{-\infty}^{\infty} X(\lambda) \cdot X(f - \lambda) \cdot d\lambda$$

Here, $X(f)$ is the Fourier transform of $x(t)$ and $X(f)$ is zero in the interval $|f| > W$. Then

$$Y(f) = \int_{-W}^{W} X(\lambda) \cdot X(f - \lambda) \cdot d\lambda$$

It can be noted that $X(f - \lambda)$ is limited to $-W \leq f - \lambda \leq W$. When $\lambda = -W$, then $-2W \leq f \leq 0$ and when $\lambda = W$, then $0 \leq f \leq 2W$. Hence, $Y(f)$ is limited between $-2W \leq f \leq 2W$.

Problem 1.6: Evaluate the Fourier transform of the delta function by considering it as the limiting form of (1) a rectangular pulse of unit area, and (2) a sin *c* pulse of unit area.

Solution: Consider a rectangular pulse $g(t)$ of duration T and amplitude $\frac{1}{T}$, centered at $t = 0$, as shown below:

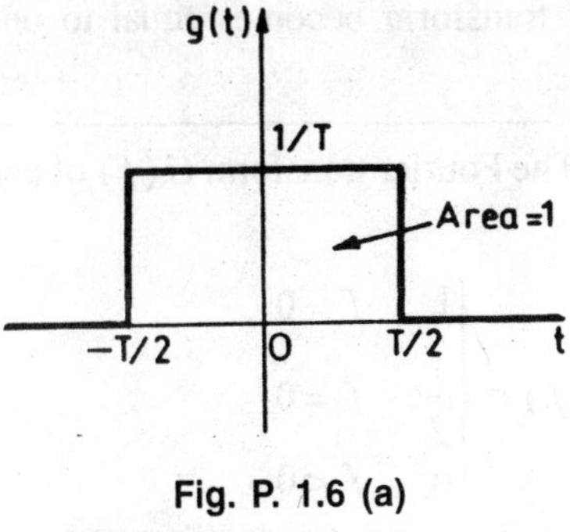

Fig. P. 1.6 (a)

The Fourier transform of $g(t)$ is

$$G(f) = \frac{\sin(\pi f T)}{\pi f T}$$

As the duration T approaches zero, $g(t)$ approaches a delta function, and so we find that in that time

$$\lim G(f) = \lim_{T \to 0} \frac{\sin(\pi f T)}{\pi f T} = 1$$

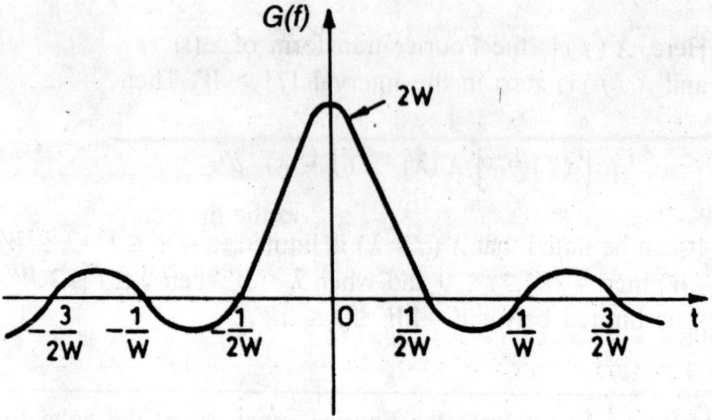

Fig. P. 1.6 (b)

The Fourier transform of $g(t)$ is

$$G(f) = \text{rect}\left(\frac{f}{2w}\right)$$

which has unit amplitude and width $= w$, centered at $f = 0$. As w approaches infinity, $g(t)$ approaches a delta function, and the corresponding Fourier transform becomes equal to one for all f.

Problem 1.7: The Fourier transform $G(f)$ of a signal $g(t)$ is defined by

$$G(f) = \begin{cases} 1, & f > 0 \\ \frac{1}{2}, & f = 0 \\ 0, & f < 0 \end{cases}$$

Determine the signal $g(t)$.

Solution: $G(f)$ in the form of unit step function is drawn as,

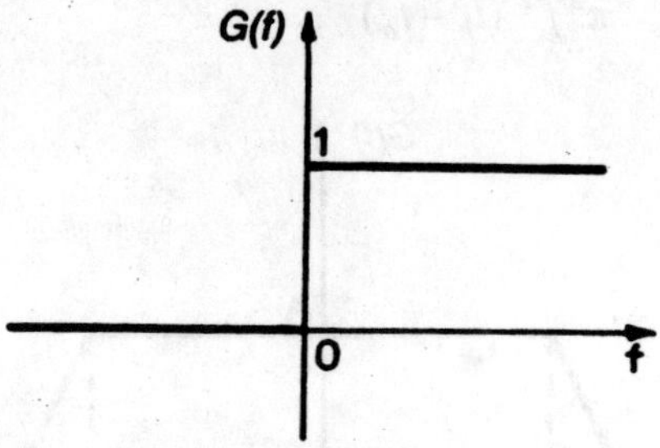

Fig. P. 1.7

Now, for a unit step function defined in the time domain, we have

$$u(t) \rightleftharpoons \frac{1}{j2\pi f} + \frac{1}{2}\delta(f)$$

Using duality property, we get

$$-\frac{1}{j2\pi t} + \frac{1}{2}\,\delta(t) \rightleftharpoons u(f) \qquad [\text{As } \delta(-t) = \delta(t)]$$

Hence, the time function $g(t)$, whose Fourier transform is specified, is expressed by,

$$g(t) = -\frac{1}{j2\pi t} + \frac{1}{2}\,\delta(t)$$

Problem 1.8: Consider a pulselike function $g(t)$ that consists of a small number of straignt-line segments. Suppose that this function is differentiated with respect to time t twice so as to generate a sequence of weighted delta functions, as shown by

$$\frac{d^2 g(t)}{dt^2} = \sum_i k_i \delta(t - t_i)$$

where the k_i are related to the slopes of the straight-line segments. (*a*) Given the values of the k_i and the t_i, show that the Fourier transform of $g(t)$ is given by

$$G(f) = -\frac{1}{4\pi^2 f^2}\sum_i k_i \exp(-j2\pi f t_i)$$

(*b*) Using this procedure, show that the Fourier transform of the trapezoidal pulse shown in Fig. 1.8 is given by

$$G(f) = \frac{A}{\pi^2 f^2 (t_b - t_a)} \sin[\pi f(t_b - t_a)] \sin[\pi f(t_b + t_a)]$$

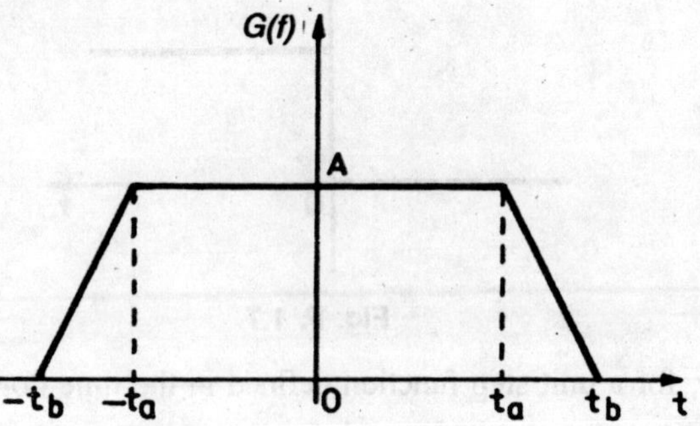

Fig. P. 1.8

Solution: (*a*) Taking the Fourier transform of both sides of

$$\frac{d^2 g(t)}{dt^2} = \sum_i k_i \delta(t - t_i), \text{ we get}$$

$$(j2\pi f)^2 G(f) = \sum_i k_i \exp(-j2\pi f t_i)$$

The, $$G(f) = \frac{-1}{4\pi^2 f^2} \sum_i k_i \exp(-j2\pi f t_i)$$

(*b*) Differentiating $g(t)$ twice, we get

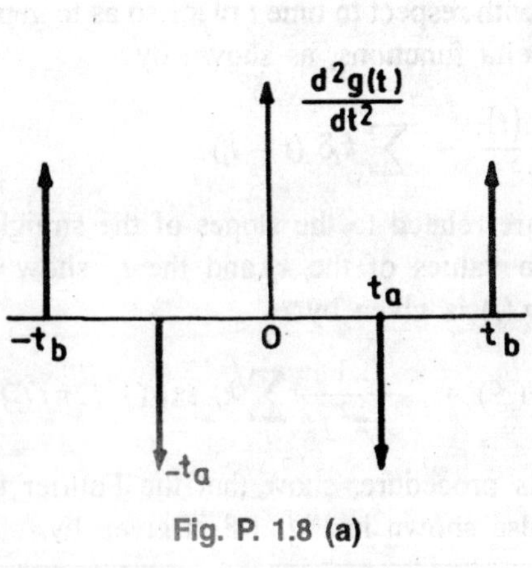

Fig. P. 1.8 (a)

$$\text{hence, } G(f) = \frac{-A}{4\pi^2 f^2 (t_b - t_a)} [\exp(j2\pi f t_b) - \exp(j2\pi f t_a) - \exp(-j2\pi f t_a) + \exp(-j2\pi f t_b)$$

$$= \frac{-A}{2\pi^2 f^2 (t_b - t_a)} [\cos(2\pi f t_b) - \cos(2\pi f t_a)]$$

$$= \frac{A}{\pi^2 f^2 (t_b - t_a)} \cdot \sin[\pi f (t_b - t_a)] \cdot \sin[\pi f (t_b + t_a)]$$

Problem 1.9: Consider the sin c pulse defined by

$$g(t) = A \sin c\,(zwt)$$

Determine the total energy of this signal and spectral density.

Solution: As

$$G(f) = F[g(t)] = \frac{A}{2w} \text{rect}\left(\frac{f}{zw}\right)$$

Then, energy spectral density of the sine pulse

$$\psi_g(f) = \left(\frac{A}{zw}\right)^2 \text{rect}\left(\frac{f}{zw}\right) \left\{ \because \text{rect}^2\left(\frac{f}{zw}\right) = \text{rect}\left(\frac{f}{zw}\right) \right\}$$

and energy of the signal,

$$E = \int_{-\infty}^{\infty} g^2(t)\, dt = \int_{-\infty}^{\infty} |G(f)|^2\, df = \left(\frac{A}{2w}\right)^2 \int_{-\infty}^{\infty} \text{rect}\left(\frac{f}{zw}\right) df$$

$$E = \left(\frac{A}{2w}\right)^2 \int_{-w}^{w} df = \frac{A^2}{2w}$$

Problem 1.10: Show that total area under the curve of sin $c^2(t)$ equals 1, i.e.,

$$\int_{-\infty}^{\infty} \sin c^2(t)\, dt = 1$$

Solution:

$$\int_{-\infty}^{\infty} \text{sinc}^2(t)\,dt = \int_{-\infty}^{\infty} |\text{rect}(f)|^2\,df = \int_{-\infty}^{\infty} \text{rect}(f)\cdot df = \int_{-1/2}^{1/2} df = 1$$

Hence, $$\int_{-\infty}^{\infty} \text{sinc}^2(t)\,dt = 1$$

Problem 1.11: The following expression may be viewed as an approximate representation of a pulse with finite rise time:

$$g(t) = \frac{1}{\tau}\int_{t-T}^{t+T} \exp\left(-\frac{\pi u^2}{\tau^2}\right) du$$

where it is assumed that $T \gg \tau$. Determine the Fourier transform of $g(t)$. What happens to this transform when we allow τ to become zero?

Solution: $g(t)$ can be expressed as,

$$g(t) = \frac{1}{\tau}\int_{t-T}^{0} \exp\left(-\frac{\pi u^2}{\tau^2}\right) du + \frac{1}{\tau}\int_{0}^{t+T} \exp\left(-\frac{\pi u^2}{\tau^2}\right) du$$

Then,

$$g_1(t+T) = \frac{1}{\tau}\int_{t}^{0} \exp\left(-\frac{\pi u^2}{\tau^2}\right) du = -\frac{1}{\tau}\int_{0}^{t} \exp\left(-\frac{\pi u^2}{\tau^2}\right) du$$

$$= -\frac{1}{\tau}\int_{-\infty}^{t} \exp\left(-\frac{\pi u^2}{\tau^2}\right) du + \frac{1}{2}\left[\frac{1}{\tau}\int_{-\infty}^{0} \exp\left(-\frac{\pi u^2}{\tau^2}\right)\cdot du - \frac{1}{2}\right] \quad ...(1)$$

Similarly,

$$g_2(t-T) = \frac{1}{\tau}\int_{0}^{t} \exp\left(-\frac{\pi u^2}{\tau^2}\right).\ du = \frac{1}{\tau}\int_{-\infty}^{t} \exp\left(-\frac{\pi u^2}{\tau^2}\right) du - \frac{1}{2} \quad ...(2)$$

Taking Fourier transform of $g_1(t+T)$ and $g_2(t-T)$,

$$G_1(f).\ \exp(j2\pi fT) = -\frac{1}{j2\pi f}\ \exp\ (-\pi\tau^2 f^2)$$

$$\left[\exp\left(-\frac{\pi t^2}{\tau^2}\right) \rightleftharpoons \tau\exp(-\pi\tau^2 f^2)\right]$$

$$\text{and } G_2(f)\cdot \exp(-j2\pi fT) = +\frac{1}{j2\pi f}\exp(-\pi\tau^2 f^2)$$

Thus,
$$\begin{aligned} G(f) &= G_1(f) + G_2(f) \\ &= \frac{1}{j2\pi f}\exp(-\pi\tau^2 f^2)\times \\ &\quad [-\exp(-j2\pi fT) + \exp(j2\pi fT)] \\ &= \frac{1}{\pi f}\exp(-\pi\tau^2 f^2)\cdot \sin(2\pi fT) \\ &= 2T\exp(-\pi\tau^2 f^2)\cdot \sin c\,(2fT) \end{aligned}$$

When $\tau \to 0$, $G(f)$ approaches the limiting value of $2T \sin c\,(2fT)$, which corresponds to the Fourier transform of rectangular pulse of unit amplitude and duration $2T$.

Problem 1.12: The Fourier transform of a signal $g(t)$ is denoted by $G(f)$. Prove the following properties of the Fourier transform:

(*a*) If a real signal $g(t)$ is an even function of time t, the Fourier transform $G(f)$ is purely real. If a real signal $g(t)$ is an odd function of time t, the Fourier transform $G(f)$ is purely imaginary.

(*b*) $$t^n g(t) \rightleftharpoons \left(\frac{j}{2\pi}\right)^n G^{(n)}(f) = (j)^n G^n(w)$$

where $G^{(n)}(f)$ is the nth derivative of $G(f)$ with respect to f.

(*c*) $$\int_{-\infty}^{\infty} t^n g(t)\,dt = \left(\frac{j}{2\pi}\right)^n G^{(n)}(0)$$

(*d*) $$g_1(t)\, g_2^*(t)\, dt \rightleftharpoons \int_{-\infty}^{\infty} G_1(\lambda)\, G_2^*(\lambda - f)\, d\lambda$$

(*e*) $$\int_{-\infty}^{\infty} g_1(t)\, g_2^*(t)\, dt = \int_{-\infty}^{\infty} G_1(f) G_2^*(f)\, df$$

Solution:

(*a*)
$$\begin{aligned} G(f) &= \int_{-\infty}^{\infty} g(t)\cdot \exp(-j2\pi ft)\cdot dt \\ &= \int_{-\infty}^{0} g(t)\cdot \exp(-j2\pi ft)\cdot dt + \int_{0}^{\infty} g(t)\cdot \exp(-j2\pi ft)\cdot dt \end{aligned}$$

$$= \int_{-\infty}^{0} g(t)\cos(2\pi ft)\cdot dt - j\int_{-\infty}^{0} g(t)\sin(2\pi ft)\cdot dt$$

$$+ \int_{0}^{\infty} g(t)\cos(2\pi ft)\cdot dt - j\int_{0}^{\infty} g(t)\sin(2\pi ft)\cdot dt$$

For even function,

$$g(t) = g(-t)$$

$$\text{or, } G(f) = -\int_{-\infty}^{0} g(-t)\cos(2\pi ft)\cdot dt - j\int_{-\infty}^{0} g(-t)\sin(2\pi ft)\cdot dt +$$

$$\int_{0}^{\infty} g(t)\cos(2\pi ft)\cdot dt - j\int_{0}^{\infty} g(-t)\sin(2\pi ft)\cdot dt$$

$$= \int_{0}^{\infty} g(t)\cos(2\pi ft)\cdot dt - j + \int_{0}^{\infty} g(-t)\sin(2\pi ft)\cdot dt$$

$$+ \int_{0}^{\infty} g(t)\cos(2\pi ft)\cdot dt - j\int_{0}^{\infty} g(t)\sin(2\pi ft)\cdot dt$$

$$= 2\int_{0}^{\infty} g(t)\cos(2\pi ft)\cdot dt \text{ which is purely real.}$$

For odd function,

$$g(-t) = -g(t),$$

$$G(f) = -\int_{\infty}^{0} g(-t)\cos(2\pi ft)\cdot dt - j\int_{0}^{\infty} g(-t)\sin(2\pi ft)\cdot dt$$

$$-\int_{-\infty}^{0} g(-t)\cos(2\pi ft)\cdot dt - j\int_{0}^{\infty} g(-t)\sin(2\pi ft)\cdot dt$$

$$= -\int_{0}^{\infty} g(t)\cos(2\pi ft)\cdot dt - j\int_{0}^{\infty} g(t)\sin(2\pi ft)\cdot dt$$

$$+ \int_{0}^{\infty} g(t)\cos(2\pi ft)\cdot dt - j\int_{0}^{\infty} g(t)\sin(2\pi ft)\cdot dt$$

$$= -2j\int_{0}^{\infty} g(t)\sin(2\pi ft)\cdot dt \text{ which is imaginary.}$$

(*b*) The Fourier transform of $g(t)$,

$$G(f) = \int_{-\infty}^{\infty} g(t)\exp(-j2\pi ft)\cdot dt \qquad \text{...(1)}$$

$$\text{then, } \frac{d^n G(t)}{df^n} = (-j2\pi)^n \int_{-\infty}^{\infty} t^n g(t)\exp(-j2\pi ft)\,dt$$

$$\text{or, } \quad t^n g(t) \rightleftharpoons \left(\frac{j}{2\pi}\right)^n \frac{d^n G(f)}{df^n}$$

(*c*) Putting $f = 0$ in eqn (1), we get

$$\int_{-\infty}^{\infty} t^n g(t)\, dt = \left(\frac{j}{2\pi}\right)^n G^n(o)$$

(*d*) Since,

$$g^*(t) \rightleftharpoons G_2^*(-f)$$

then,

$$g_1(t)\; g_2^*(t) \rightleftharpoons \int_{-\infty}^{\lambda} G_1(\lambda)\; G_2^*(\lambda - f)\cdot d\lambda$$

(*e*) Using part (*d*),

$$F\,[g_1(t)\; g_2^*(t)] = \int_{-\infty}^{\infty} g_1(t)\, g_2^*(t)\cdot \exp\,(-j2\pi ft)\; dt$$

$$= \int_{-\infty}^{\infty} G_1(\lambda)\, G_2^*(\lambda - f)\, d\lambda$$

Putting $f = D$ in the above equation, we get

$$\int_{-\infty}^{\infty} g_1(t)\; g_2^*(t)\; dt = \int_{-\infty}^{\infty} G_1(\lambda)\; G_2^*(\lambda)\cdot d\lambda$$

Problem 1.13: Evaluate the inverse Fourier transform $g(t)$ of the one-sided frequency function:

$$G(f) = \begin{cases} \exp(-f), & f > 0 \\ \frac{1}{2}, & f = 0 \\ 0, & f < 0 \end{cases}$$

Hence, show that $g(t)$ is complex, and that its real and imaginary parts constitute a Hilbert-transform pair.

Solution: As,

$$\exp(t)\, u(-t) \rightleftharpoons \frac{1}{1 - j2\pi f} \qquad \ldots(1)$$

where

$$\exp(t)\, u(-t) = \begin{cases} 0, & t > 0 \\ \frac{1}{2}, & t = 0 \\ \exp(t), & t < 0 \end{cases}$$

Using the duality property of the Fourier transform

$$\frac{1}{1 - j2\pi t} \rightleftharpoons \exp(-f) \cdot u(f) = G(f) \qquad \ldots(2)$$

Where

$$G(t) = \begin{cases} \exp(-f), & f > 0 \\ \frac{1}{2}, & f = 0 \\ 0 & f < 0 \end{cases}$$

From eqn (2), it follows that inverse transform of $G(f)$ is the complex time function,

$$g(t) = \frac{1}{1 - j2\pi t}$$

The real and imaginary parts are,

$$Re[g(t)] = \frac{1}{1 + (2\pi t)^2}$$

$$Im[g(t)] = \frac{2\pi t}{1 + (2\pi t)^2}$$

Problem 1.14: Determine the pre-envelope $g_+(t)$ corresponding to each of the following two signals:

(*a*) $g(t) = \sin c\,(t)$

(*b*) $g(t) = [1 + k\cos(2\pi f_m t)]\cos(2\pi f_c t)$

Solution: (*a*) $g(t) = \sin c\,(t) = \dfrac{\sin(\pi t)}{\pi t}$

then, $\hat{g}(t) = \dfrac{1-\cos(\pi t)}{\pi t}$

and, $g_+(t) = g(t) + j\hat{g}(t) = \dfrac{1}{\pi t}\{\sin(\pi t) + j\,[1 - \cos(\pi t)]\}$

$$= \frac{j}{\pi t}[1 - \cos(\pi t) - j\sin\pi t] = \frac{j}{\pi t}[1 - \exp(j\pi t)]$$

(*b*) $g(t) = [1 + k\cos(2\pi f_m t)]\cos(2\pi f_c t)$

$$= \cos(2\pi f_c t) + \frac{k}{2}\cos[2\pi(f_c + f_m)t] + \frac{k}{2}\cos \times$$
$$[2\pi(f_c - f_m)t]$$

then

$$\hat{g}(t) = \sin(2\pi f_c t) + \frac{k}{2}\sin[2\pi(f_c + f_m)t] + \frac{k}{2}\sin[2\pi(f_c - f_m)t]$$

thus, $g_+(t) = g(t) + j\hat{g}(t)$

$$= \exp(j2\pi f_c t) + \frac{k}{2}\exp[j2\pi(f_c + f_m)t] +$$
$$\frac{k}{2}\exp[j2\pi(f_c - f_m)t]$$

$$= [1 + k\cos(j2\pi f_m t) + \frac{k}{2}\exp(-j2\pi f_m t)\exp(j2\pi f_c t)$$

$$g_+(t) = [1 + k\cos(2\pi f_m t)]\cdot\exp(j2\pi f_c t)$$

Problem 1.15: Let $\hat{g}(t)$ denote the Hilbert transform of $g(t)$. Derive the following set of Hilbert-transform pairs:

$g(t)$	$\hat{g}(t)$
$\dfrac{\sin t}{t}$	$\dfrac{1-\cos t}{t}$
rect (t)	$-\dfrac{1}{\pi}\ln\left\lvert\dfrac{\left(t-\frac{1}{2}\right)}{\left(t+\frac{1}{2}\right)}\right\rvert$
$\delta(t)$	$\dfrac{1}{\pi t}$
$\dfrac{1}{1+t^2}$	$\dfrac{t}{1-t^2}$

Solution: (*a*) $g(t) = \dfrac{\sin t}{t}$

The Hilbert transfer of $g(t)$,

$$\hat{g}(t) = \frac{1}{\tau}\int_{-\infty}^{\infty}\frac{g(\tau)}{t-\tau}\cdot d\tau = \frac{1}{\pi}\int_{-\infty}^{\infty}\frac{\sin\tau}{\tau(t-\tau)}\cdot d\tau = \frac{1}{\pi t}\int_{-\infty}^{\infty}\left(\frac{1}{\tau}+\frac{1}{t-\tau}\right)\sin\tau\, d\tau$$

$$= \frac{1}{\pi t}\int_{-\infty}^{\infty}\frac{\sin\tau}{\tau}\cdot d\tau + \frac{1}{\pi t}\int_{-\infty}^{\infty}\frac{\sin\tau}{t-\tau}\, d\tau$$

Note that

$$\int_{-\infty}^{\infty}\sin c\,(t)\, dt = 1$$

then,

$$\int_{-\infty}^{\infty}\frac{\sin\tau}{\tau}\, d\tau = \pi$$

and, $$\int_{-\infty}^{\infty}\frac{\sin\tau}{t-\tau}\, d\tau = \int_{-\infty}^{\infty}\frac{\sin(t-\tau)}{\tau}\, d\tau$$

$$= \sin t\int_{-\infty}^{\infty}\frac{\cos\tau}{\tau}\, d\tau - \cos t\int_{-\infty}^{\infty}\frac{\sin\tau}{\tau}\, d\tau$$

$$= -\pi\cos t$$

Hence, $\hat{g}(t) = \frac{1}{t}(1 - \cos t)$

(*b*) $g(t) = \text{rect } t = \begin{cases} 1, & |t| < \frac{1}{2} \\ 0, & |t| > \frac{1}{2} \end{cases}$

The Hilbert transform of rect t is, $\hat{g}(t) = \frac{1}{\pi} p \int_{-\frac{1}{2}}^{\frac{1}{2}} \frac{1}{t - \tau} \, d\tau$

where p denotes the principal value of . When $t < -\frac{1}{2}$ the singularity in the integrand is below the range of integrational and the significant values of $t - \tau$ are negative. Then,

$$\hat{g}(t) = -\frac{1}{\pi}\left[\ln(t-\tau)\right]_{-\frac{1}{2}}^{\frac{1}{2}} = -\frac{1}{\pi}\ln\frac{\left(t-\frac{1}{2}\right)}{\left(t+\frac{1}{2}\right)}, \quad t < -\frac{1}{2}$$

For $t > \frac{1}{2}$,

$$\hat{g}(t) = -\frac{1}{\pi}\left[\ln(t-\tau)\right]_{-\frac{1}{2}}^{\frac{1}{2}} = -\frac{1}{\pi}\ln\left(\frac{t-\frac{1}{2}}{t+\frac{1}{2}}\right) \quad t > -\frac{1}{2}$$

When, $-\frac{1}{2} < t < \frac{1}{2}$, then

$$\hat{g}(t) = \frac{1}{\pi} \underset{\varepsilon \to 0}{lt} \left[\int_{-\frac{1}{2}}^{t-\varepsilon} \frac{d\tau}{t-\tau} + \int_{t+\varepsilon}^{\frac{1}{2}} \frac{d\tau}{t-\tau}\right]$$

$$= \frac{1}{\pi} \underset{\varepsilon \to 0}{lt} \left\{\left[-\ln(t-\tau)\right]_{-\frac{1}{2}}^{t-\varepsilon} + \left[-\ln(t-\tau)\right]_{t+\varepsilon}^{\frac{1}{2}}\right\}$$

$$= \frac{1}{\pi} \underset{\varepsilon \to 0}{lt} \left[-\ln\left(\frac{\varepsilon}{t+\frac{1}{2}}\right) - \ln\left(-\frac{t-\frac{1}{2}}{\varepsilon}\right)\right]$$

$$= -\frac{1}{\pi}\ln\left[\frac{\frac{1}{2}-t}{\frac{1}{2}+t}\right], \quad -\frac{1}{2} < t < \frac{1}{2}$$

Thus, $$\hat{g}(t) = -\frac{1}{\pi}\cdot\ln\left|\frac{t-\frac{1}{2}}{t+\frac{1}{2}}\right|$$

(*c*) $$g(t) = \delta(t)$$

and, $$\hat{g}(t) = \frac{1}{\pi}\int_{-\infty}^{\infty}\frac{\delta(\tau)}{t-\tau}\,d\tau$$

Using the shifting property,

$$\int_{-\infty}^{\infty} g(t)\,\delta(t-t_o) = g(t_o)$$

we have,

$$\hat{g}(t) = \frac{1}{\pi t}$$

(*d*) $$g(t) = \frac{1}{1+t^2}$$

then,

$$\hat{g}(t) = \frac{1}{\pi}\int_{-\infty}^{\infty}\frac{d\tau}{(1+\tau^2)(t-\tau)} = \frac{1}{\pi(1+t^2)}\int_{-\infty}^{\infty}\left(\frac{t+\tau}{1+\tau^2}+\frac{1}{t-\tau}\right)d\tau$$

But

$$\int_{-\infty}^{\infty}\frac{1}{1+\tau^2}\,d\tau = \pi, \quad \int_{-\infty}^{\infty}\frac{\tau}{1+\tau^2}\,d\tau = 0, \quad \int_{-\infty}^{\infty}\frac{\tau}{t-\tau}\,d\tau = 0,$$

Thus, $$\hat{g}(t) = \frac{t}{1+t^2}$$

Problem 1.16: Prove the following properties of the convolution process:

(*a*) The commutative property:

$$g_1(t) * g_2(t) = g_2(t) * g_1(t)$$

(*b*) The associative property:

$$g_1(t) * [g_2(t) * g_3(t)] = [g_1(t) * g_2(t)] * g_3(t)$$

(*c*) The distributive property:

$$g_1(t) * [g_2(t) + g_3(t)] = g_1(t) * g_2(t) + g_1(t) * g_3(t)$$

Solution: (*a*)

$$g_1(t) * g_2(t) = \int_{-\infty}^{\infty} g_1(\tau)\, g_2(t-\tau)\, d\tau$$

let $\tau = t - u$, then

$$g_1(t) * g_2(t) = \int_{-\infty}^{\infty} g_1(t-u)\, g_2(u)\, (-du)$$

$$= \int_{-\infty}^{\infty} g_2(u)\, g_1(t-u) \cdot du = g_2(t) * g_1(t)$$

(*b*) Let

$$g_a(t) = [g_2(t) * g_3(t)] = \int_{-\infty}^{\infty} g_2(\tau)\, g_3(t-\tau)\, d\tau$$

Then,

$$g_1(t) * g_a(t) = \int_{-\infty}^{\infty} g_1(u)\, g_a(t-u)\, du$$

$$= \int_{-\infty}^{\infty} g_1(u) \int_{-\infty}^{\infty} g_2(\tau)\, g_3(t-u-\tau)\, d\tau\, du$$

$$= \int_{-\infty}^{\infty}\int_{-\infty}^{\infty} g_1(u)\, g_2(\tau)\, g_3(t-u-\tau)\, d\tau\, du$$

next, let

$$g_b(t) = g_1(t) * g_2(t) = \int_{-\infty}^{\infty} g_1(u)\, g_2(t-u)\, du$$

then,

$$[g_1(t) * g_2(t)] * g_3(t) = \int_{-\infty}^{\infty} g_b(t) * g_3(t) = \int_{-\infty}^{\infty} g_b(\tau)\, g_3(t-\tau)\, d\tau$$

$$= \int_{-\infty}^{\infty}\int_{-\infty}^{\infty} [g_1(u)\, g_2(t-u)\, du]\, g_3(t-\tau)\, d\tau$$

$$= \int_{-\infty}^{\infty}\int_{-\infty}^{\infty} g_1(u)\, g_2(t-u)\, g_3(t-\tau)\, du\, d\tau$$

Replacing $\tau - u$ by τ, we obtain

$$[g_1(t) * g_2(t)] * g_3(t) = \int_{-\infty}^{\infty}\int_{-\infty}^{\infty} g_1(u)\, g_2(u)\, g_3(t-\tau-u)\, d\tau\, du$$

$$= g_1(t) * [g_2(t) * g_3(t)]$$

(*c*)

$$g_1(t) * [g_2(t) + g_3(t)] = \int_{-\infty}^{\infty} g_1(\tau)\, [g_2(t-\tau) + g_3(t-\tau)]\, d\tau$$

$$= \int_{-\infty}^{\infty} g_1(\tau)\, g_2(t-\tau)\, d\tau + \int_{-\infty}^{\infty} g_1(\tau)\, g_3(t-\tau)\, d\tau$$

$$= g_1(t) * g_2(t) + g_1 * g_3(t)$$

Problem 1.17: Show that the complex envelope of the sum of two narrow-band signals (with the same carrier frequency) is eqaul to the sum of their individual complex envelopes.

Solution: Suppose two narrow-band signals are $x(t)$ and $y(t)$ and their sum be $g(t)$. The complex envelope of $g(t)$ equals,

$$\tilde{g}(t) = g_+(t) \cdot \exp(-j2\pi f_c t) = [g(t) + j\,\hat{g}(t)]\, \exp(-j2\pi f_c t)$$

As, the Halibert transform is a linear transform, then

$$\tilde{g}(t) = [x(t) + y(t) + j\,\hat{x}(t) + j\,\hat{y}(t)]\, \exp(-j2\pi f_c t)$$

$$= x_+(t) \cdot \exp(-j2\pi f_c t) + y_+(t) \cdot \exp(-j2\pi f_c t)$$

$$= \tilde{x}(t) + \tilde{y}(t)$$

Problem 1.18: Consider a rectangular pulse $x(t)$ of unit amplitude and duration T, which is applied to an ideal low-pass filter of bandwidth B. Then, determine the response $y(t)$ of the filter.

Solution:

The impulse response of the filter is, $h(t) = 2B \operatorname{sinc}[2B(t - t_0)]$ then, response

$$y(t) = \int_{-\infty}^{\infty} x(\tau) \cdot h(t-\tau)\, d\tau = 2B \int_{-T/2}^{T/2} \frac{\sin[2\pi B(t - t_o - \tau)]}{2\pi B(t - t_o - \tau)} . d\tau$$

Define $\lambda = 2\pi B(t - t_o - \tau)$

Then, changing the integration variable from τ to λ, we have

$$y(t) = \frac{1}{\pi} \int_{2\pi B(t-t_o-T/2)}^{2\pi B(t-t_o+T/2)} \frac{\sin\lambda}{\lambda} . d\lambda$$

$$= \frac{1}{\pi}\left[\int_0^{2\pi B(t-t_0+T/2)} \frac{\sin\lambda}{\lambda} d\lambda - \int_0^{2\pi B(t-t_0-T/2)} \frac{\sin\lambda}{\lambda} d\lambda\right]$$

$$= \frac{1}{\pi}\left\{\sin\left[2\pi B\left(t - t_o + \frac{T}{2}\right)\right] - \sin\left[2\pi B\left(t - t_o - \frac{T}{2}\right)\right]\right\}$$

Where sine integral is expressed by

$$\sin(u) = \int_0^u \frac{\sin\lambda}{\lambda} . d\lambda$$

Problem 1.19: Consider an ideal band-pass filter of midband frequncy f_c, and bandwidth B as shown in Fig. P. 1.19 with $f_c > \frac{B}{2}$.

Determine the response of this filter to an *RF* pulse of duration T and frequency f_c defined as,

$$x(t) = A \operatorname{rect}\left(\frac{t}{T}\right) \cos(2\pi f_c t)$$

where $\quad f_c T \gg 1$

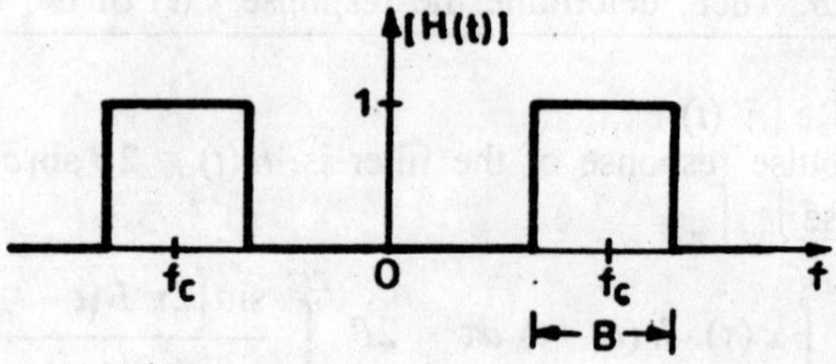

Fig. P. 1.19 (a)

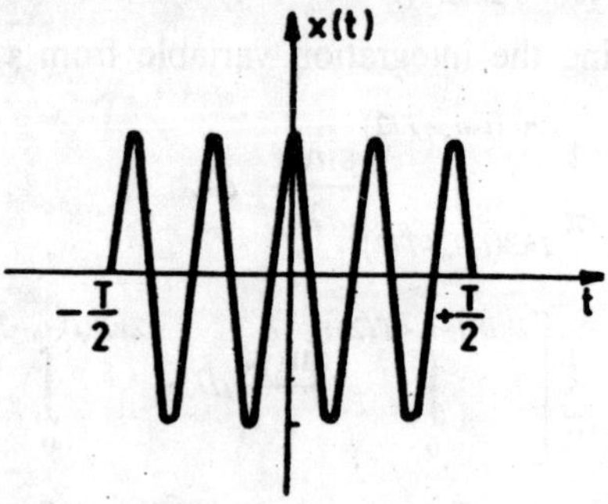

Fig. P. 1.19 (b)

Solution: The transfer function $\widetilde{H}(f)$ of the LPF is,

$$\widetilde{H}(f) = \begin{cases} \exp(-j2\pi f t_o), & -\frac{B}{2} < f < \frac{B}{2} \\ 0, & |f| > \frac{B}{2} \end{cases} \qquad ...(1)$$

The complex impulse response in this has only a real component as shown,

$$\widetilde{h}(t) = B \sin c\ [B(t - t_o)] \qquad ...(2)$$

and, the complex envelope of $x(t)$ is

$$\widetilde{x}(t) = x_+(t) \cdot \exp\{-j2\pi f_c t\}$$

$$= A \text{ rect}\left(\frac{t}{T}\right) \cdot \exp(j2\pi f_c t) \exp(-j2\pi f_c t) = A \text{ rect}\left(\frac{t}{T}\right)$$

The complex envelope output $\widetilde{y}(t)$ is,

$$\tilde{y}(t) = \frac{A}{\pi}\left\{si\left[\pi B\left(t+\frac{T}{2}-t_o\right)\right]-si\left[\pi B\left(t-\frac{T}{2}-t_o\right)\right]\right\}$$

and, the output

$$y(t) = \text{Re}\,[\tilde{y}(t)\exp(j2\pi f_c t)] = \tilde{y}(t)\cos(2\pi f_c t)$$

$$= \frac{A}{\pi}\left\{si\left[\pi B+\frac{T}{2}-t_o\right]-si\left[\pi B\left(t-\frac{T}{2}-t_o\right)\right]\right\}\cos(2\pi f_c t)$$

Which is sketched below,

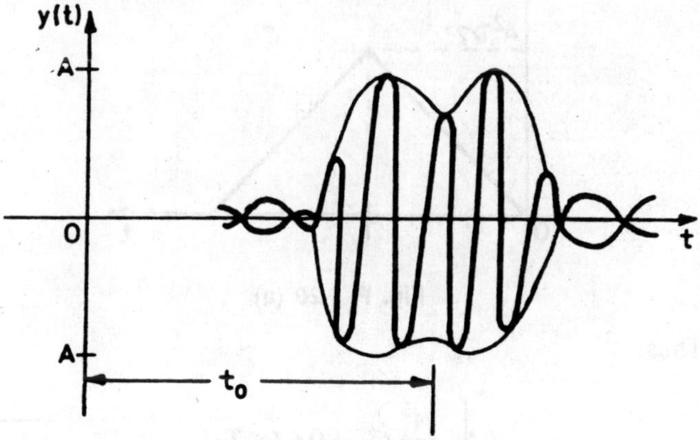

Fig. P. 1.19 (c)

Problem 1.20: The rectangular RF pulse

$$x(t) = \begin{cases} A\cos(2\pi f_c t), & 0 \le t \le T \\ 0, & \text{elsewhere} \end{cases}$$

is applied to a linear filter with impulse response

$$h(t) = x(T-t)$$

Assume that the frequency f_c equals a large integer multiple of $\frac{1}{T}$. Determine the response of the filter and sketch it.

Solution: The complex envelope of the RF pulse is

$$\tilde{x}(t) = \begin{cases} A, & 0 \le t \le T \\ 0, & \text{elsewhere} \end{cases}$$

The complex impulse response of the filter is

$$\tilde{h}(t) = \begin{cases} A, & 0 \le t \le T \\ 0, & \text{elsewhere} \end{cases}$$

The complex envelope of the filter output is,

$\tilde{y}(t) = \frac{1}{2}\tilde{h}(t) * \tilde{x}(t)$ is shown by the following diagram,

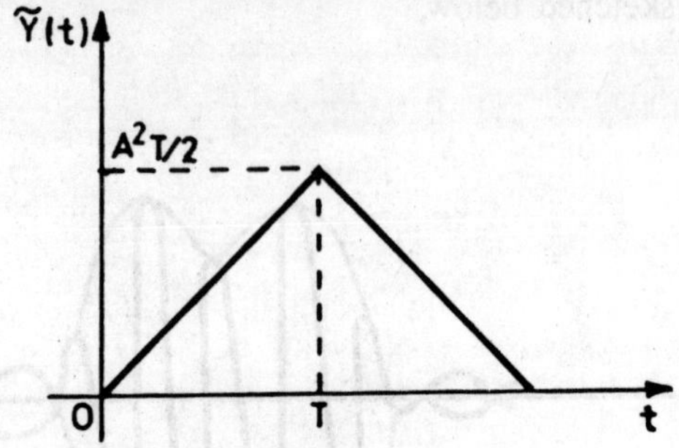

Fig. P. 1.20 (a)

Thus,

$$\tilde{y}(t) = \begin{cases} \frac{A^2}{2}t & 0 \le t \le T \\ A^2T - \frac{t}{2} & T \le t \le 2T \\ 0 & \text{elsewhere} \end{cases}$$

$$y(t) = \begin{cases} \frac{A^2}{2}t\cos(2\pi f_c t) & 0 \le t \le T \\ A^2\left(T - \frac{t}{2}\right)\cos(2\pi f_c t) & T \le t \le 2T \\ 0 & \text{elsewhere} \end{cases}$$

Chapter 2

Continuous Wave Modulation

Problem 2.1: A carrier wave of frequency 1 MHz is modulated 50 percent by a sinusoidal frequency 5 kHz. The resulting AM signal is transmitted through the resonant circuit of Fig. P. 2.1, which is tuned to the carrier frequency and has a Q-factor of 175. Determine the modulated signal after transmission through this circuit. What is the percentage modulation of this modulated signal?

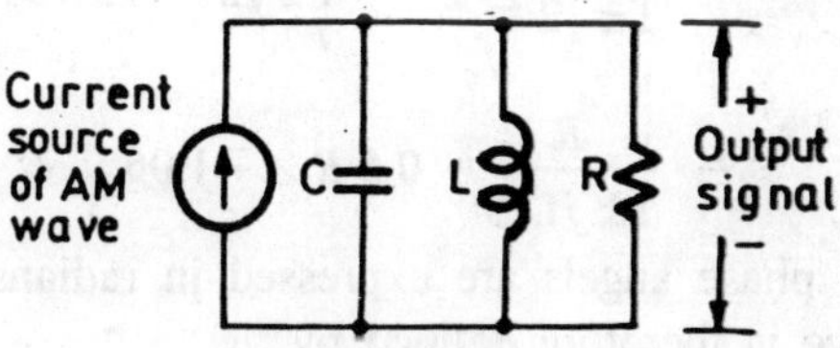

Fig. P. 2.1

Solution:

The transfer function of the resonant circuit of Fig. P 2.1 relating the output voltage *v*(*t*) to the input current *i* (*t*), is

$$H(f) = \frac{V(f)}{I(f)} = \frac{1}{\left(\frac{1}{R}\right) + j\left(2\pi fc - \frac{1}{2}\pi fL\right)}$$

$$= \frac{R}{1 + jQ(f - f_c)\dfrac{(f + f_c)}{ff_c}} \qquad ...(1)$$

Where $V(f) = F[v(t)]$ $I(f) = F[i(t)]$

$$f_c = \frac{1}{2\pi\sqrt{LC}}, \qquad Q = R\sqrt{\frac{C}{L}}$$

When $Q \gg 1$, we find that the frequencies of interest lie in the neighborhood of f_c, and so we may approximate Eq. (1) as follows

$$H(f) = \frac{R}{1 + j2Q(f - f_c)/f_c}, f > 0 \qquad ...(2)$$

The spectrum of the input AM wave $i(t)$ consists of a carrier at f_c, and two side frequencies at $f_c \pm f_m$, as shown by

$$\begin{aligned} i(f) &= A_c \cos(2\pi f_c t) \\ &\quad + \frac{\mu Ac}{2}\{\cos[2\pi(f_c + f_m)t] + \cos[2\pi(f_c - f_m)t]\} \\ &= A_c \cos(2\pi \times 10^6 t) + 0.25 A_c [\cos(2.01\pi \times 10^6) \\ &\quad + \cos(1.99\pi \times 10^6 t)] \end{aligned}$$

Therefore evaluating Eq. (2) at the frequencies fc and $f_c \pm f_m$, we get,

$$H(f_c) = R\angle 0$$

$$H(f_c \pm f_m) = \frac{R}{1 \pm j2\dfrac{Qf_m}{f_c}} = \frac{R}{1 \pm j2 \times 175 \times 5 \times 10^3 / 10^6}$$

$$= \frac{R}{1 \pm j1.75} = 0.5\,R\angle\mp 1.05$$

Where the phase angels are expressed in radians. The resulting output AM wave is therefore defined by

$$v(t) = A_c R \cos(2\pi \times 10^6 t) + 0.125 A_c R [\cos(2.01\pi \times 10^6 t - 1.05) + \cos(1.99\pi \times 10^6 + 1.05)]$$

The percentage modulation of this modulated wave is 25 percent.

Problem 2.2: For a *p-n* junction diode, the current i through the diode and the voltage v across it are related by

$$i = I_0\left[\exp\left(-\frac{v}{V_T}\right) - 1\right]$$

Where I_0 is the reverse saturation current, and V_T is the volt-equivalent of temperature defined by

$$V_T = \frac{kT}{e}$$

where k is Boltzmann's constant in joules per degree Kelvin, T is the absolute temperature in degrees kelvin, and e is the charge of an electron. At room temperature $V_T = 0.026$ volts.

(a) Expand i as a power series in v, retaining terms up to v^3.
(b) Let $v = 0.01 \cos(2\pi f_m t) + 0.01 \cos(2\pi f_c t)$ volts where $f_m = 1$ kHz and $f_c = 100$ kHz. Determine the spectrum of the resulting diode current i.
(c) Specify the band-pass filter required to extract from the diode current an AM signal with carrier frequency f_c.
(d) What is the percentage modulation of this AM signal?

Solution:

(a) Since $\exp(-x) = 1 - x + \frac{x^2}{2} - \frac{x^3}{6}$, we may express the diode current i, normalized with respect to I_0, as

$$\frac{i}{I_0} = \exp\left(-\frac{v}{V_T}\right) - 1 = -\frac{v}{V_T} + \frac{1}{2}\left(\frac{v}{V_T}\right)^2 - \frac{1}{6}\left(\frac{v}{V_T}\right)^3 \quad \text{...(1)}$$

(b) Given

$$\frac{v}{V_T} = \frac{0.01}{0.026}[\cos(2\pi f_m t) + \cos(2\pi f_c t)]$$

$$= 0.385\,[\cos(2\pi f_m t) + \cos(2\pi f_c t)] \quad \text{...(2)}$$

We find that substitution of Eq. (2) in (1) yields

$$\frac{i}{I_0} = -0.385\,[\cos(2\pi f_m t) + \cos(2\pi f_c t)] + 0.074\,[\cos(2\pi f_m t) + \cos(2\pi f_c t)]^2 - 0.0095\,[\cos(2\pi f_m t) + \cos(2\pi f_c t)]^3 \quad \text{...(3)}$$

Noting that

$$\cos^2\theta = \frac{1}{2}(1 + \cos 2\theta)$$

$$\cos^3\theta = \frac{3}{4}\cos\theta + \frac{1}{4}\cos 3\theta$$

$$\cos\theta\cos\phi = \frac{1}{2}[\cos(\theta + \phi) + \cos(\theta - \phi)]$$

we may rewrite eqn (3) in the form :

$$\frac{i}{I_0} = 0.074 - 0.406\,[\cos(2\pi f_m t) + \cos(2\pi f_c t)] + 0.037 \{\cos(4\pi f_m t) + \cos(2\pi f_c t)] + 2\cos[2\pi(f_c + f_m)t] + 2\cos(2\pi(f_c - f_m)t]\} - 0.0016\,[\cos(6\pi f_m t) + \cos(6\pi f_c t)] - 0.0071\,\{\cos[2\pi(f_c + 2f_m)t] + \cos[2\pi(f_c - 2f_m)t] + \cos[2\pi(2f_c + f_m)t] + \cos[2\pi(2f_c - f_m)t]\}$$

For $f_m = 1$ kHz and $f_c = 100$ kHz,

we thus find that the discrete amplitude spectrum of the diode current i (for $f \geq 0$) is as shown below:

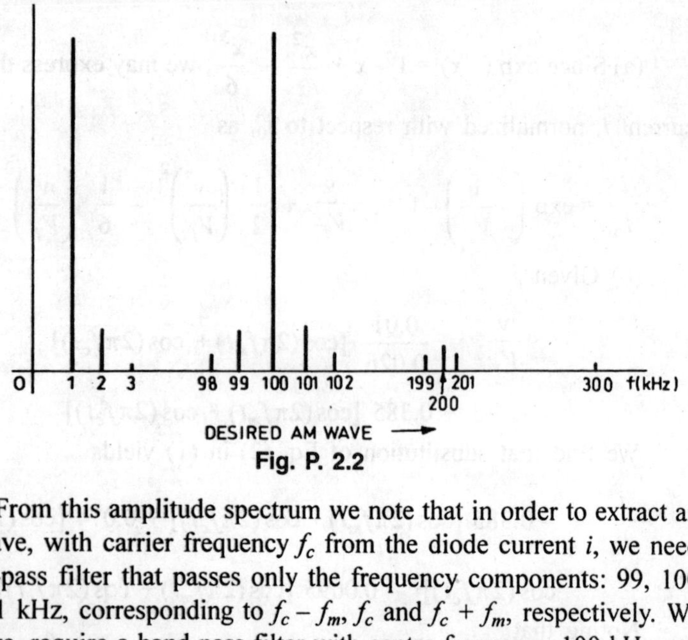

Fig. P. 2.2

(*c*) From this amplitude spectrum we note that in order to extract an AM wave, with carrier frequency f_c from the diode current i, we need a band-pass filter that passes only the frequency components: 99, 100 and 101 kHz, corresponding to $f_c - f_m$, f_c and $f_c + f_m$, respectively. We therefore, require a band-pass filter with centre frequency 100 kHz and bandwidth 2 kHz.

(*d*) The resulting band-pass filter output is

$$\frac{i}{I_0} \cong -\,0.406\cos(2pf_c t) + 0.148\cos(2pf_c t)\cos(2pf_m t)$$

$$= -\,0.406\,(1 - 0.362\cos(2\pi f_m t)\,(2\pi f_m t)\cos(2\pi f_c t)$$

The percentage modulation is therefore 36.2 percent.

Problem 2.3: Suppose that nonlinear devices are available for which the output current i_o and input voltage v_i are related by

$$i_o = a_1 v_i + a_3 v_i^3$$

where a_1 and a_3 are constants. Explain how these devices may be used to provide:

(*a*) a product modulator and

(*b*) an amplitude modulator.

Solution :

(a) Let the input voltage v_i consist of a sinusodal wave of frequency $\frac{1}{2} f_c$ (i.e., half the desired carrier frequency) and the message signal $m\ (t)$

$$V_i = A_c \cos(\pi f_c t) + m\ (t)$$

Now, the output current i_o is

$$\begin{aligned} i_o &= a_1 v_i + a_3 v_i^3 \\ &= a_1 [A_c \cos(\pi f_c t) + m(t)] + a_3 [A_c \cos(\pi f_c t) + m(t)]^3 \\ &= a_1 [A_c \cos(\pi f_c t) + m(t)] + \frac{1}{4} a_3 A_c^3 [\cos(3\pi f_c t) + \\ &\quad 3 \cos(\pi f_c t)] + \frac{3}{2} a_3 A_c^2 m(t) [1 + \cos(2\pi f_c t)] + \\ &\quad 3 a_3 A_c \cos(\pi f_c t)\ m^2(t) + a_3 m^3(t) \end{aligned}$$

Assume that $m\ (t)$ occupies frequency interval $- W \le f \le W$. Then, the amplitude spectrum of the output current i_o is as shown below:

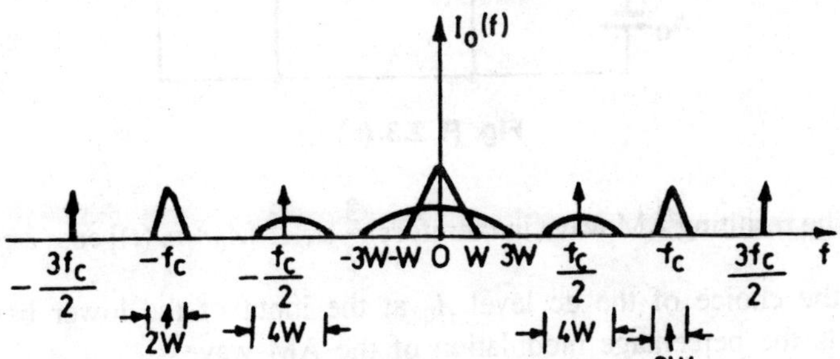

Fig. P. 2.3 (a)

From this diagram we see that in order to extract a *DSBSC* wave, with carrier frequency f_c from i_o, we need a band-pass filter with mid-band frequency f_c and bandwidth 2W, which satirby the requirement:

$$f_c - W > \frac{f_c}{2} + 2\,W$$

That is, $f_c > 6W$

Therefore, to use the given nonlinear devices a product modulator, we may use the following configuration :

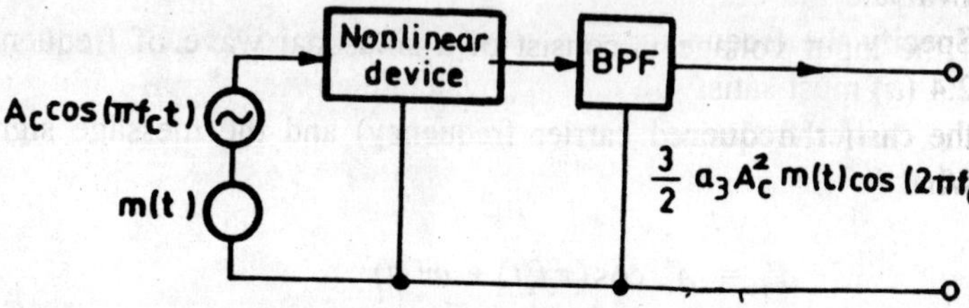

Fig. P. 2.3 (b)

(*b*) To generate an AM wave with carrier frequency f_c we require a sinusoidal component of frequency f_c to be added to the DSBSC generated in the manner described above. To achieve this requirement, we may use the following configuration involving a pair of the nonlinear devices and a pair of identical band-pass filters:

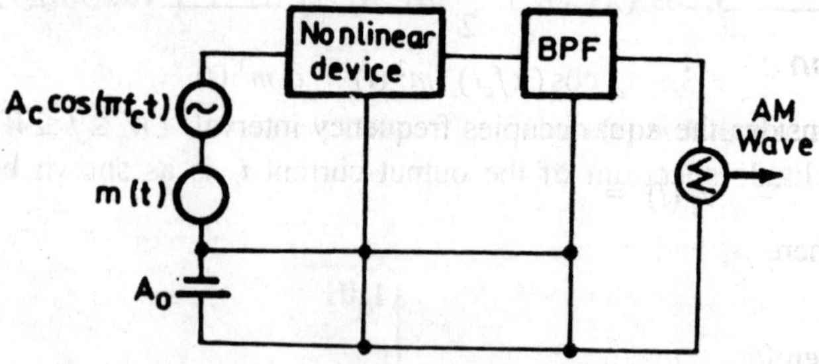

Fig. P. 2.3 (c)

The resulting AM wave in therefore $\frac{3}{2}\,a_3 A_c^2\,[A_0 + m\,(t)]\cos(2\pi f_c t)$.

Thus the choice of the dc level A_0 at the input of the lower branch controls the percentage modulation of the AM wave.

Problem 2.4: Fig. P. 2.4 (a) shows the circuit diagram of a *square-law modulator*. The signal applied to the nonlinear device is relatively weak, such that it can be represented by a square law:

$$v_2(t) = a_1 v_1(t) + a_2 v_1^2(t)$$

where a_1 and a_2 are constants, $v_1(t)$ is the input voltage, and $v_2(t)$ is the output voltage. The input voltage is defined by

$$v_1(t) = A_c \cos(2\pi f_c t) + m(t)$$

where $m(t)$ is a message signal and $A_c \cos(2\pi f_c t)$ is the carrier wave.

(a) Evaluate the output voltage $v_2(t)$.

(b) Specify the frequency response that the tuned circuit in Fig. P. 2.4 (*a*) must satisfy in order to generate an AM signal with f_c as the carrier frequency.

(c) What is the amplitude sensitivity of this AM signal?

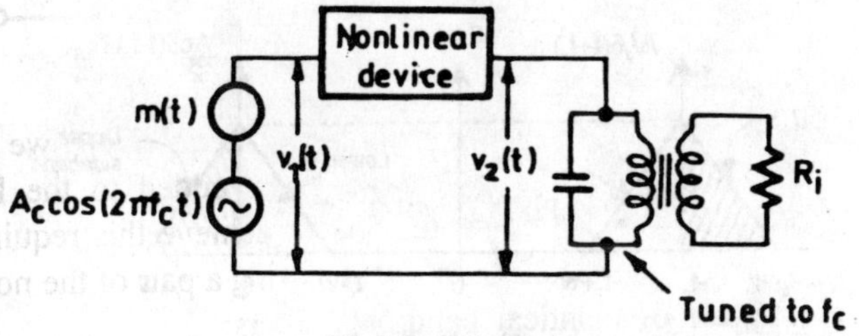

Fig. P. 2.4 (a)

Solution :

Consider the square law characteristic:

$$v_2(t) = a_1 v_1(t) + a_2 v_1^2(t) \quad ...(1)$$

Where a_1 and a_2 are constants. Let

$$v_1(t) = A_c \cos(2\pi f_c t) + m(t) \quad ...(2)$$

Therefore, substituting eqn (2) into (1), and explaining terms:

$$v_2(t) = a_1 A_c \left[1 + \frac{2a_2}{a_1} m(t)\right] \cos(2\pi f_c t) + a_1 m(t) + a_2 m^2(t) +$$

$$a_2 A_c^2 \cos^2(2\pi f_c t) \quad ...(3)$$

The first term in eqn (3) is the desired AM signal with $K_a = 2a_2/a_1$. The remaining three term are unwanted terms that are removed by filtering. Let the modulating wave $m(t)$ be limited to the band $-W \leq f \leq W$, as in Fig. 2.4 (*a*). Then from Eqn (3) we find that the amplitude spectrum $|v_2(f)|$ is as shown in fig. 2.4 (*b*). It follows that the unwanted terms may be removed from $v_2(f)$ by designing the tuned filter at the modulator output to have a mid-band frequency f_c & band width 2W, which satisfy the requirement that $f_c > 3W$.

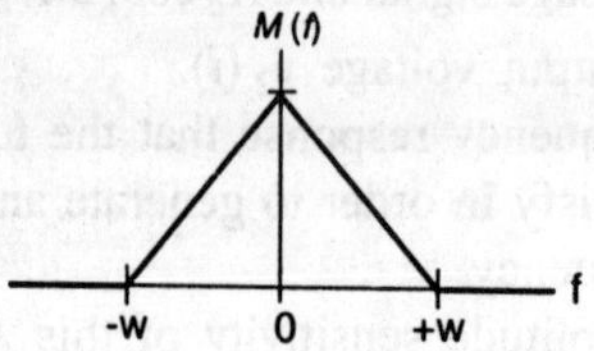

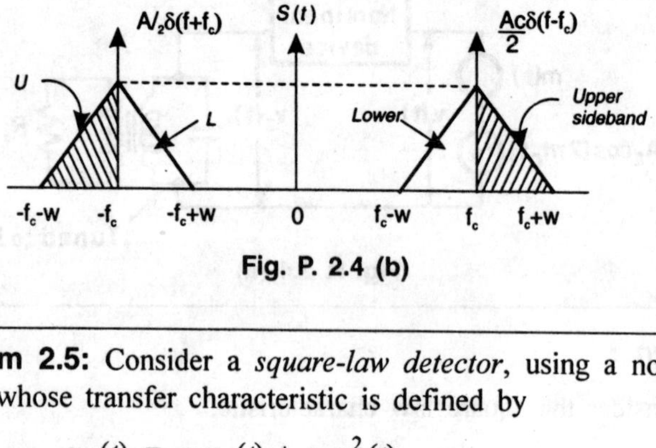

Fig. P. 2.4 (b)

Problem 2.5: Consider a *square-law detector*, using a nonlinear device whose transfer characteristic is defined by

$$v_2(t) = a_1 v_1(t) + a_2 v_1^2(t)$$

where a_1 and a_2 are constants, $v_1(t)$ is the input, and $v_2(t)$ is the output. The input consists of the AM wave.

$$v_1(t) = A_c\,[1 + k_a m(t)]\cos(2\pi f_c t)$$

(a) Evaluate the output $v_2(t)$.
(b) Find the conditions for which the message signal $m(t)$ may be recovered from $v_2(t)$.

Solution :

Let $\quad v_1(t) = A_c\,[1 + k_a m(t)]\cos(2\pi f_c t)$

Then the output of the square-law device will be,

$$v_2(t) = a_1 v_1(t) + a_2 v_1^2(t)$$
$$= a_1 A_c [1 + k_a m(t)] \cos(2\pi f_c t) +$$
$$\frac{1}{2} a_2 A_c^2 \; [1 + 2\, k_a m(t) + k_a^2 m^2(t)] \; \{1 + \cos(4\pi f_c t)\}$$

The desired signal, namely $a^2 A_c^2 k_a m(t)$, is due to the $a_2 v_1^2(t)$, hence, the name "*square-law detection*". This component can be extracted by means of a low-pass filter. This is not the only contribution within the baseband spectrum, because the term $\frac{1}{2} a_2 A_c^2 k_a{}^2 m^2(t)$ will give rise to a plurality of similar frequency components. The ratio of wanted signal to distortion is $2/k_a m(t)$. To make this radio large, the percentage modulation, that is, $|k_a m(t)|$ should be kept small compared with unity.

$$s(t) = A_c [1 + k_a m(t)] \cos 2\pi f_c t$$

$|k_a m(t)| < 1$ for all t, otherwise envelope distortion.

To avoid it, a one-to-one relationship should be maintained between the envelope of the AM wave and the modulating wave, for all value of t.

Problem 2.6: Fig. P. 2.6 shows the circuit diagram of a *balanced modulator*. The input applied to the top AM modulator is $m(t)$, whereas that applied to the lower AM modulator is $-m(t)$; these two modulators have the same amplitude sensitivity. Show that the output $s(t)$ of the balanced modulator consists of a DSB-SC modulated signal.

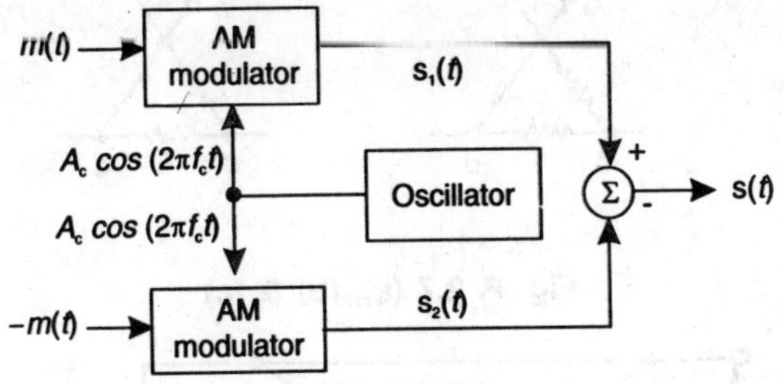

Fig. P. 2.6

Solution:

The two AM modulator outputs are

$$s_1(t) = A_c [1 + k_a m(t)] \cos(2\pi f_c t)$$
$$s_2(t) = A_c [1 - k_a m(t)] \cos(2\pi f_c t)$$

subtracting $s_2(t)$ from $s_1(t)$, we have

$$s(t) = s_2(t) - s_1(t) = 2\,kaA_c m(t)\cos(2\pi f_c t)$$

Which represents a DSB-SC modulated wave.

Problem 2.7: Figure 2.7 shows the circuit details of the ring modulator. Assume that the diodes are identical and the transformers are perfectly balanced. Let R denote the terminating resistance at the input end and output end of the modulator (assuming ideal 1 : 1 transformers). Determine the output voltage of the modulator for each of the two conditions described in Figs. P. 2.7 (b) and 2.7 (c). Hence, show that these two output voltages are equal in magnitude and opposite in polarity.

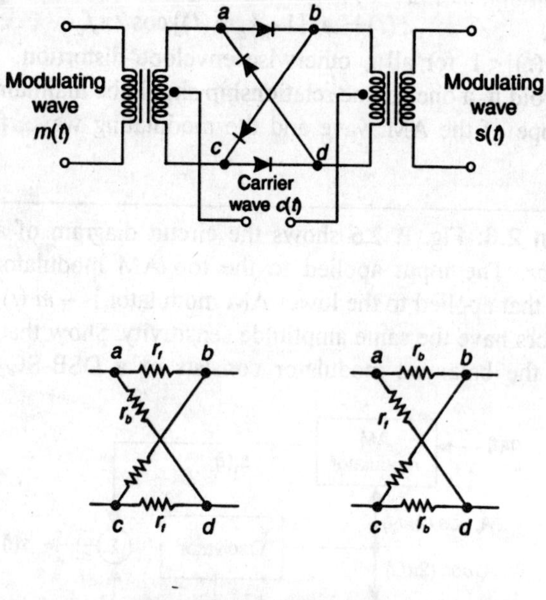

Fig. P. 2.7 (a), (b) & (c)

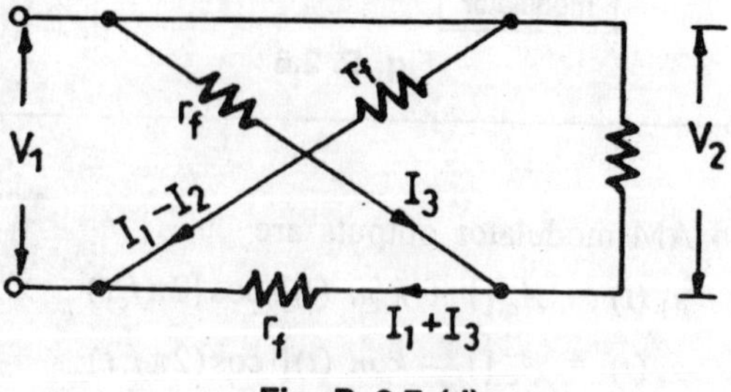

Fig. P. 2.7 (d)

Solution:

From Fig. P. 2.7 (a), we have

With V_1 applied to the input, we note the following relations :

$$V_1 = r_f I_1 + r_b (I_1 - I_2) = r_b I_3 + r_f (I_2 + I_3) = r_f I_1 + R I_2 + r_f (I_2 + I_3)$$

Solving for the output current I_2: $I_2 = \dfrac{\begin{vmatrix} r_f + r_b & V_1 & 0 \\ 0 & V_1 & r_b + r_f \\ r_f & V_1 & r_f \end{vmatrix}}{\begin{vmatrix} r_f + r_b & -r_b & 0 \\ 0 & r_f & r_b + r_f \\ r_f & R + r_f & r_f \end{vmatrix}}$

$$= V_1 \left\{ \frac{(r_f + r_b)(-r_b) + r_f (r_b + r_f)}{(r_f + r_b)\left(r_f^2 - (r_b + r_f)(R + r_f)\right) - r_f r_b (r_b + r_f)} \right\}$$

$$= V_1 \left\{ \frac{r_b - r_f}{R(r_b + r_f) + 2 r_b r_f} \right\}$$

The output voltage is therefore

$$V_2 = \frac{R(r_b - r_f)}{R(r_b + r_f) + 2 r_b r_f} V_1 \quad \ldots(1)$$

Consider next Fig. 2.7 (e):

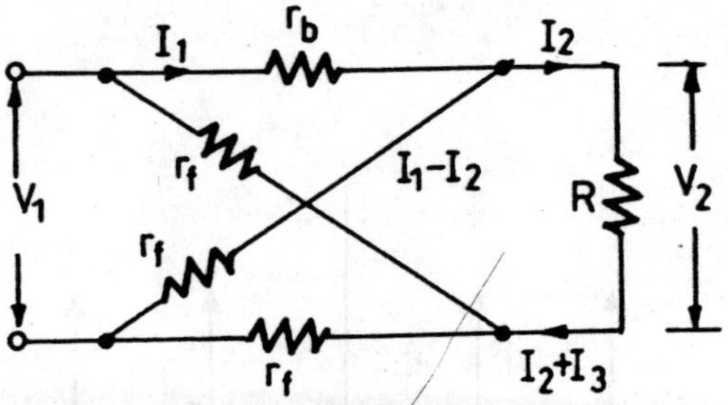

Fig. P. 2.7 (e)

For this later circuit, we have

$$V_1 = r_b I_1 + r_f (I_1 - I_2)$$

$$V_1 = r_f I_3 + r_b (I_2 + I_3)$$
$$V_1 = r_b I_1 + R I_2 + (I_2 + I_3)$$

Solving for the output current :

$$I_2 = \frac{\begin{vmatrix} r_b + r_f & V_1 & 0 \\ 0 & V_1 & r_b + r_f \\ r_b & V_1 & r_b \end{vmatrix}}{\begin{vmatrix} r_b + r_f & -r_f & 0 \\ 0 & r_b & r_b + r_f \\ r_b & R + r_b & r_b \end{vmatrix}} = V_1 \left\{ \frac{r_f - r_b}{R(r_b + r_f) + 2r_b r_f} \right\}$$

The output voltage for the second case is therefore

$$V_2 = \frac{r_f - r_b}{R(r_b + r_f) + 2r_b r_f} V_1 \qquad \text{...(2)}$$

Comparing Eqs (1) and (2), we see that the output voltages for Figs P. 2.6 (b) and 2.6 (c) are equal in magnitude and opposite in polarity.

Problem 2.8: DSB-SC modulated signal is demodulated by applying it to a coherent detector.

(a) Evaluate the effect of a frequency error Δf in the local carrier frequency of the detector, measured with respect to the carrier frequency of the incoming DSB-SC signal.

(b) For the case of a sinusoidal modulating wave, show that because of this frequency error, the demodulated signal exhibits *beats* at the error frequency. Illustrate your answer with a sketch of this demodulated signal.

Solution:

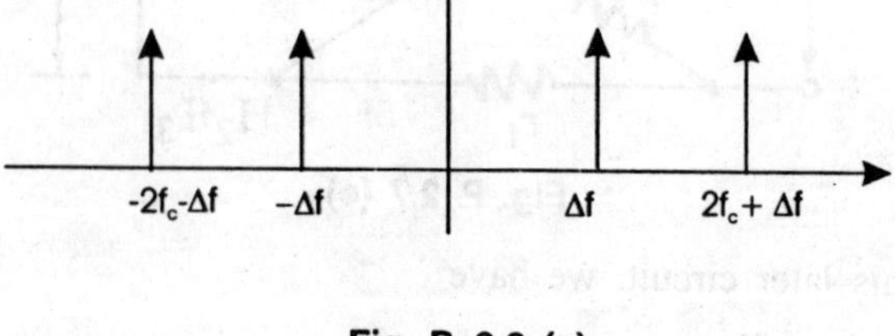

Fig. P. 2.8 (a)

(a) Multiplying the signal by the local oscillator gives :

$$s_1(t) = A_c m(t) \cos 2\pi f_c(t) \cos[2\pi(f_c + \Delta f)t]$$

$$= \frac{A_c}{2} m(t) \left[\cos(2\pi\Delta f t) + \cos[2\pi(f_c + \Delta f)t]\right]$$

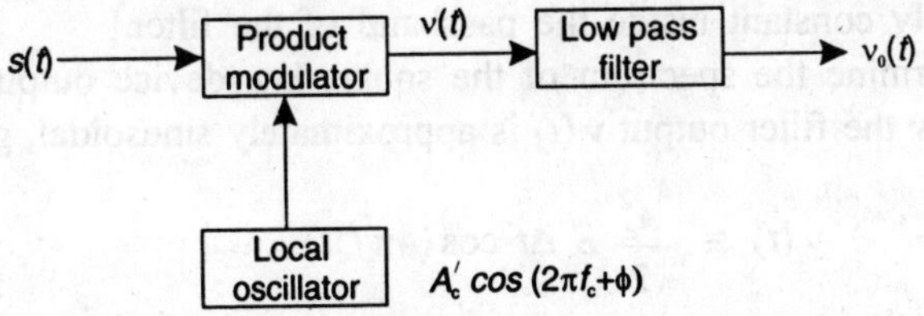

Fig. P. 2.8 (b)

Low pass filtering leaves :

$$s_2(t) = \frac{A_c}{2} m(t) \cos(2\pi\Delta f t)$$

Thus, the output signal is the message signal modulated by a sinusoid of frequency Δf.

(b) If $\quad m(t) = \cos(2\pi f_m t)$,

then $\quad s_2(t) = \dfrac{A_c}{2} \cos(2\pi f_m t) \cos(2\pi\Delta f t)$

$$= \frac{A_c}{4}\left[\cos[2\pi(f_m + \Delta f)t + \cos(2\pi(f_m - \Delta f)t)\right]$$

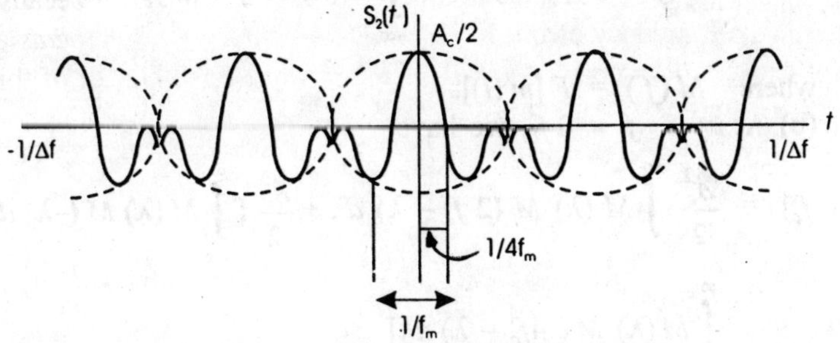

Fig. P. 2.8 (c)

> **Problem 2.9:** Consider the DSB-SC signal
>
> $$s(t) = A_c \cos(2\pi f_c t)\, m(t)$$
>
> where $A_c \cos(2\pi f_c t)$ is the carrier wave and $m(t)$ is the message signal. This modulated signal is applied to a square-law device characterized by

$$y(t) = s^2(t)$$

The output $y(t)$ is next applied to a narrow-band filter with a passband amplitude response of one, mid-band frequency $2f_c$, and bandwidth Δf. Assume that Δf is small enough to treat the spectrum of $y(t)$ as essentially constant inside the passband of the filter.

(a) Determine the spectrum of the square-law device output $y(t)$.

(b) Show the filter output $v(t)$ is approximately sinusoidal, given by

$$v(t) \cong \frac{A_c^2}{2} E\, \Delta f \cos(4\pi f_c t)$$

where E is the energy of the massage signal $m(t)$.

Solution :

(a)
$$f(t) = s^2(t) = A_c^2 \cos^2(2\pi f_c t)\, m^2(t)$$
$$= \frac{A_c^2}{2}[0.1 + \cos(4\pi f_c t)]\, m^2(t)$$

Therefore, the spectrum of the multiplier output is

$$Y(f) = \frac{A_c^2}{2}\int_{-\infty}^{\infty} M(\lambda)\, M(f-\lambda)\, d\lambda + \frac{A_c^2}{4}\Big[\int_{-\infty}^{\infty} M(\lambda)$$
$$M(f-2f_c-\lambda)\, d\lambda + \int_{-\infty}^{\infty} M(\lambda)\, M(f+2f_c-\lambda)\, d\lambda\Big]$$

where $M(f) = F[m(t)]$.

(b) At $f = 2f_c$, we have

$$Y(2f_c) = \frac{A_c^2}{2}\int_{-\infty}^{\infty} M(\lambda)\, M(2f_c-\lambda)\, d\lambda + \frac{A_c^2}{2}\Big[\int_{-\infty}^{\infty} M(\lambda)\, M(-\lambda)\, d\lambda +$$
$$\int_{-\infty}^{\infty} M(\lambda)\, M(4f_c-\lambda)\, d\lambda\Big]$$

since $M(-\lambda) = M^*(\lambda)$, we may write.

$$Y(2f_c) = \frac{A_c^2}{2}\int_{-\infty}^{\infty} M(\lambda)\, M(2f_c-\lambda)\, d\lambda + \frac{A_c^2}{4}$$
$$\Big[\int_{-\infty}^{\infty} |M(\lambda)|^2\, d\lambda + \int_{-\infty}^{\infty} M(\lambda)\, M(4f_c-\lambda)\, d\lambda\Big] \quad \ldots(1)$$

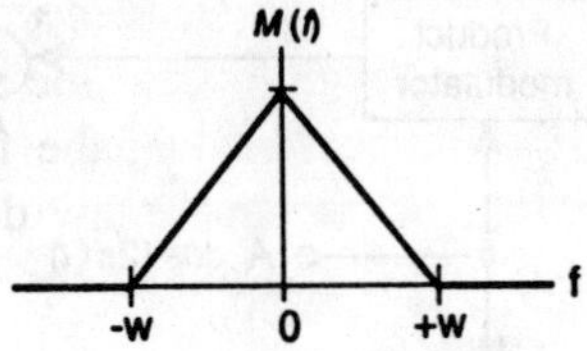

Fig. P. 2.9 (a)

With $m(t)$ limited to $-W \le f \le W$ & $f_c > W$, we find that the first and third integrals reduce to zero, and so we may simplify Eq. (1) as follows.

$$Y(2f_c) = \frac{A_c^2}{4} \int_{-\infty}^{\infty} |M(\lambda)|^2 \, d\lambda = \frac{A_c^2 E}{4}$$

where E is the signal energy (by Rayleigh's energy theorem). Similarly, we find that

$$Y(-2f_c) = \frac{A_c^2}{4} E$$

The bond-pass filter output in the frequency domain, is therefore defined by

$$V(f) = \frac{A_c^2}{4} E \Delta f \, [\delta(f - 2f_c) + \delta(f + 2f_c)]$$

Hence,

$$V(t) = \frac{A_c^2}{2} E \Delta f \cos(4\pi f_c t)$$

Problem 2.10: Consider the quadrature-carrier multiplex of Fig. P. 2.10. The multiplexed signal $s(t)$ produced at the transmitter output in Fig. 2.10 (a) is applied to a communication channel of transfer function $H(f)$. The output of this channel is in turn applied to the received input in Fig. P. 2.10 (b). Prove that the condition

$$H(f_c + f) = H^*(f_c - f), \; 0 \le f \le W$$

is necessary for recovery of the message signals $m_1(t)$ and m_2 at the receiver outputs; f_c is the carrier frequency, and W is the message bandwidth.

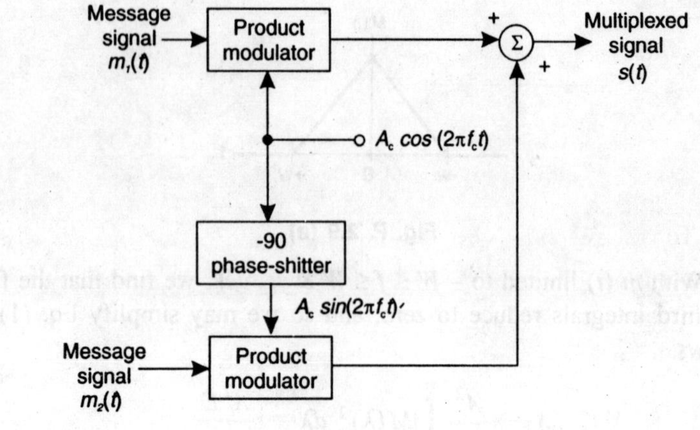

Fig. P. 2.10 (a)

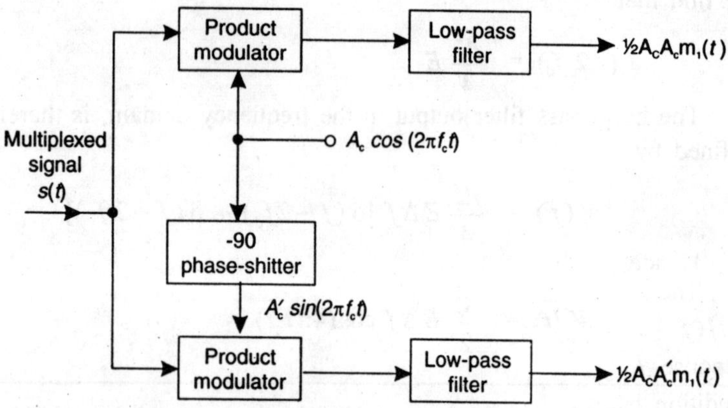

Fig. P. 2.10 (b)

Solution: The multiplied signal is

$$s(t) = A_c m_1(t) \cos(2\pi f_c t) + A_c m_2(t) \sin(2\pi f_c t)$$

therefore,

$$s(f) = \frac{A_c}{2}[M_1(f - f_c) + M_1(f + f_c)] + \frac{A_c}{2j}(M_2(f - f_c) - M_2(f + f_c)]$$

Where $M_1(f) = F[m_1(t)]$ and $M_2(f) = F[m_2(t)]$, the spectrum of the received signal is therefore

$$R(f) = H(f)\, s(f)$$

$$= \frac{A_c}{2} H(f)\,[M_1(f - f_c) + M_1(f + f_c)$$

$$+ \frac{1}{j} M_2(f - f_c) - \frac{1}{j} M_2(f + f_c)]$$

To recover $m_1(t)$, we multiply $r(t)$, the inverse Fourier transform of $R(f)$, by $\cos(2\pi f_c t)$ and then pass the resulting output through a low-pass filter, producing a signal with the following spectrum.

$$F[r(t)\cos(2\pi f_c t)] = \frac{1}{2}[R(f - f_c) + R(f + f_c)]$$

$$= \frac{A_c}{4} H(f - f_c)\,[M_1(f - 2f_c) + M_1(f) +$$

$$\frac{1}{j} M_2(f - 2f_c) - \frac{1}{j} M_2(f)] +$$

$$\frac{A_c}{4} H(f + f_c)\; M_1(f) + M_1(f + 2f_c)$$

$$+ \frac{1}{j} M_2(f) - \frac{1}{j} M_2(f + 2f_c)] \qquad ...(1)$$

The condition $H(f_c + f) = H^*(f_c - f)$ is equivalent to $H(f + f_c) = H(f - f_c)$; this follow from the face that for a real-valued pulse response $h(t)$ we have $H(-f) = H^*(f)$, Hence, substituting this condition in Eqn (1) we get,

$$F[r(t)\cos(2\pi f_c t) = \frac{A_c}{2} H(f - f_c)\,[M_1(f) + \frac{A_c}{4} H(f - f_c)$$

$$[M_1(f - 2f_c) + \frac{1}{j} M_2(f - 2f_c) +$$

$$M_1(f + 2f_c) - \frac{1}{j} M_2(f + 2f_c)]$$

The low-pass filter output, therefore, has a spectrum equal to $(A_c/2)\, H(f - f_c)\, M_1(f)$.

Similarly to recover $m_2(t)$, we multiply $r(t)$ by $\sin(2\pi f_c t)$ and then pass the resulting signal through a low-pass filter. In this case, we get an output with a spectrum equal to $(A_c/2)\, H(f - f_c)\, M_2(f)$.

Problem 2.11: Consider the SSB wave

$$s(t) = m(t)\cos(2\pi f_c t) - \hat{m}(t)\sin(2\pi f_c t)$$

where f_c is the carrier frequency, $m(t)$ is the message signal, and $\hat{m}(t)$ is its Hilbert transform, This modulated wave is applied to a square-law device characterized by

$$y(t) = s^2(t)$$

Show that the output $y(t)$ contains a frequency component at twice the carrier frequency but that is has a time-varying phase, which makes it impractical to recover the carrier by squaring.

Solution:

The square-law device output, with the SSB wave $s(t)$ as input, is given by

$$\begin{aligned} y(t) &= s^2(t) = [m(t)\cos(2\pi f_c t) - \hat{m}(t)\sin(2\pi f_c t)]^2 \\ &= m^2(t)\cos^2(2\pi f_c t) + \hat{m}^2(t)\sin^2(2\pi f_c t) \\ &\quad - 2\, m(t)\, \hat{m}(t)\cos(2\pi f_c t)\sin(2\pi f_c t) \\ &= \frac{1}{2} m^2(t)\, [1 + \cos(4\pi f_c t) \\ &\quad + \frac{1}{2}\hat{m}^2(t)\, [1 - \cos(4\pi f_c t) - m(t)\, \hat{m}(t)\sin(4\pi f_c t) \\ &= \frac{1}{2}[m^2(t) + \hat{m}^2(t)] + \{\frac{1}{4}[m^2(t) + \hat{m}^2(t)]^2 + \\ &\quad m^2(t)\, \hat{m}^2(t)]\}^{1/2} \cos(4\pi f_c t + \theta(t)] \end{aligned}$$

where $\theta(t) = \tan^{-1}\left[\dfrac{2m(t)\,\hat{m}(t)}{m^2(t) + \hat{m}^2(t)}\right]$

We see therefore that $y(t)$ represents a hybrid combination of amplitude and frequency modulation. The amplitude modulation may be removed by limiting and filtering. However, the phase modulation is unaffected by such an operation, which makes it impractical to recover the carrier wave by a squaring procedure.

Problem 2.12: A method that is used for carrier recovery in SSB modulation systems involves transmitting two pilot frequencies that are appropriately positioned with respect to the transmitted sideband. This is illustrated in Fig. P. 2.12 (a) for the case when only the lower side band is transmitted. In this case, the two pilot frequencies f_1 and f_2 are defined by

$$f_1 = f_c - W - \Delta f$$

and

$$f_2 = f_c + \Delta f$$

where f_c is the carrier frequency and W is the message bandwidth. The Δf is chosen so as to satisfy the relation

$$n = \frac{W}{\Delta f}$$

where n is an integer. Carrier recovery is accomplished by using the scheme shown in Fig. P 2.12 (b). The outputs of the two narrow-band filters centered at f_1 and f_2 are defined by, respectively,

$$v_1(t) = A_1 \cos(2\pi f_1 t + \phi_1)$$

$$v_2(t) = A_2 \cos(2\pi f_2 t + \phi_2)$$

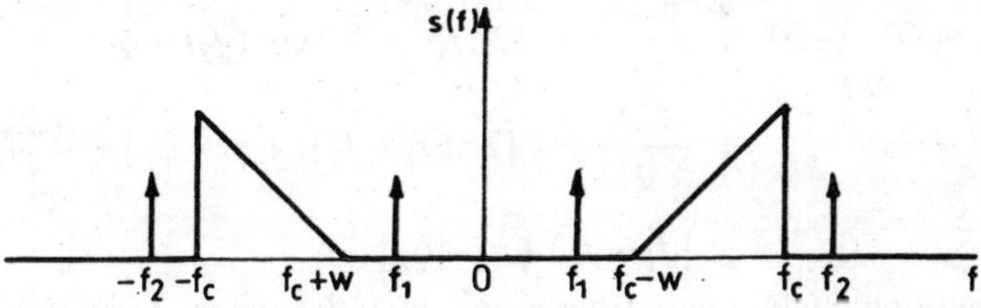

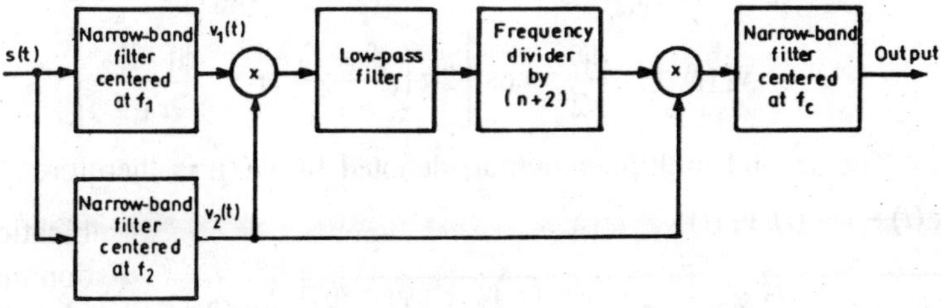

Fig. P. 2.12 (a) & (b)

The low-pass filter is designed to select the difference frequency component of the first multiplier output due to $v_1(t)$ and $v_2(t)$.
(a) Show that the output signal of the circuit in Fig. P. 2.12 (b) is proportional to the carrier wave $A_c \cos(2\pi f_c t)$ in the phase angles ϕ_1 and ϕ_2 satisfy the relation

$$\phi_2 = -\frac{\phi_1}{1+n}$$

(b) For the case when only the upper sideband is transmitted, the two pilot frequencies are defined by

$$f_1 = f_c - \Delta f$$

and

$$f_2 = f_c + W + \Delta f$$

How would you modify the carrier recovery circuit of Fig. 2.12 (b) in order to deal with this case? What is the corresponding relation between ϕ_1 and ϕ_2 for the circuit output to be proportional to the carrier wave?

Solution:

Multiplying $v_1(t)$ by $v_2(t)$, we get

$$v_1(t) \cdot v_2(t) = A_1 A_2 \cos(2\pi f_1 t + \phi_1)\cos(f_2 t + \phi_2)$$

$$= \frac{A_1 A_2}{2}\cos[2\pi(f_1+f_2)t+\phi_1+\phi_2]+\frac{A_1 A_2}{2}$$

$$[f_1 - f_2)+\phi_1-\phi_2]$$

Denoting the low-pass filter output by $v_3(t)$, we may therefore write

$$v_3(t) = \frac{A_1 A_2}{2}\cos[2\pi(f_1-f_2)t+\phi_1-\phi_2]$$

Denoting the frequency divider output by $v_4(t)$, we have

$$v_4(t) = \frac{A_1 A_2}{2}\cos\left[2\pi\left(\frac{f_1-f_2}{n+2}\right)t + \frac{\phi_1-\phi_2}{n+2}\right]$$

The second multiplier output, denoted by $v_5(t)$, is therefore

$$v_5(t) = v_2(t)\, v_4(t)$$

$$= \frac{A_1 A_2^2}{2}\cos\left[2\pi\left(\frac{f_1-f_2}{n+2}\right)t + \frac{\phi_1-\phi_2}{n+2}\right]\cos(2\pi f_2 t+\phi_2)$$

$$= \frac{A_1 A_2^2}{4}\left\{\cos\left[2\pi\left(\frac{f_1 - f_2}{n+2}\right)t + 2\pi f_2 t + \frac{\phi_1 + \phi_2}{n+2} + \phi_2\right]\right.$$

$$\left. + \cos\left[2\pi\left(\frac{f_1 - f_2}{n+2}\right)t - 2\pi f_2 t + \frac{\phi_1 - \phi_2}{n+2} - \phi_2\right]\right\} \quad ...(1)$$

we note that

$$\left(\frac{f_1 - f_2}{n+2}\right) + f_2 = \frac{f_c - W - \Delta f - (f_c + \Delta f)}{\left(\frac{W}{\Delta f}\right) + 2} + f_c + \Delta f = f_c$$

$$\frac{\phi_1 - \phi_2}{n+2} + \phi_2 = \frac{\phi_1 + \phi_2 / (1+n)}{n+2} - \frac{\phi_1}{1+n} = 0$$

We thus find that the first component of Eq. (1) has a frequency equal to f_c and zero phase, so that this component is passed by the narrow-band filter. On the other hand, the second component has a frequency that lies outside the passband of the filter, and so it is rejected. Therefore, the signal appearing at the output of the narrow-band filter is proportional to the carrier $A_c \cos(2\pi f_c t)$.

(b) To deal with the case when only the upper sideband is transmitted, we interchange the positions of the narrow-band filters centered at f_1 and f_2. We thus find that the second multiplier output is

$$v_5(t) = \frac{A_1^2 A_2}{2}\cos\left[2\pi\left(\frac{f_1 - f_2}{n+2}\right)t + \frac{\phi_1 - \phi_2}{n+2}\right]\cos(2\pi f_1 t + \phi_1)$$

$$= \frac{A_1^2 A_2}{4}\cos\left\{\left[2\pi\left(f_1 - \frac{f_1 - f_2}{n+2}\right)t + \phi_1 - \frac{\phi_1 - \phi_2}{n+2}\right]\right.$$

$$\left. + \cos\left[2\pi\left(f_1 - \frac{f_1 - f_2}{n+2}\right)t + f_1 + \frac{f_1 - f_2}{n+2}\right]\right\} \quad ...(2)$$

In this case, we note that the frequency of the first component in Eq. (2) is

$$f_1 - \frac{f_1 - f_2}{n+2} = f_1 - \frac{f_c - \Delta f - (f_c + W + \Delta f)}{(W/\Delta f) + 2} = f_c$$

The corresponding phase $\phi_1 - (\phi_1 - \phi_2) / (n + 2)$ is equal to zero if we choose $\phi_2 = -\phi_1 (n + 1)$.

Then, we find that the output signal at the narrow-band filter output has a frequency equal to f_c and a phase of zero. The second component in Eq. (2) has a frequency that lies outside the passband of the filter, and it is therefore rejected. Here again, the output of the carrier recovery circuit is proportional to $A_c \cos(2\pi f_c t)$.

Problem 2.13: Fig. P. 2.13 shows the block diagram of a *frequency synthesizer*, which enables the generation of many frequencies, each with the same high accuracy as the *master oscillator*. The master oscillator of frequency 1 MHz feeds two *spectrum generators*, one directly and the other through a *frequency divider*. Spectrum generator 1 produces a signal rich in the following harmonics: 1,2,3,4,5,6,7,8, and 9 MHz. The frequency divider provides a 100-kHZ output, in response to which spectrum generator produces a second signal rich in the following harmonics: 100, 200, 300, 400, 500, 600, 700, 800, and 900 kHz. The harmonic selectors are designed to feed two signals into the mixer, one from spectrum generator 1 and the other from spectrum generator 2. Find the range of possible frequency outputs of this synthesizer and its resolution.

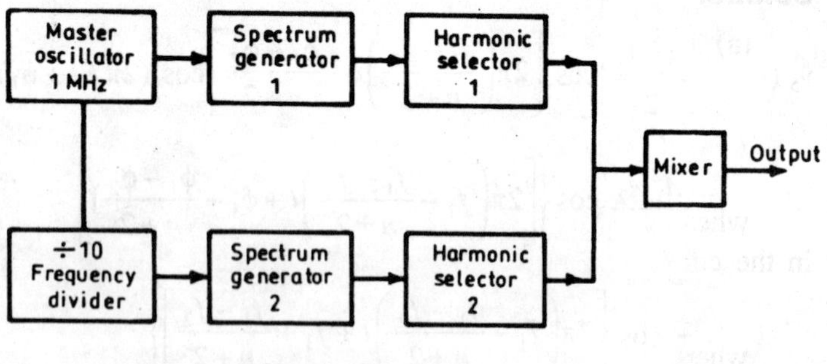

Fig. P. 2.13

Solution:

The mixer will produce an output signal of frequency equal to the sum or the difference of its two input signal frequencies. The range of sum or difference frequencies is from 100 kHz (difference of input frequencies 1 MHz and 900 kHz) to 9.9 MHz (sum of input frequencies 9 MHz). The resolution is 100 kHz.

Problem 2.14 : Consider a multiples system in which four input signals $m_1(t)$, $m_2(t)$, $m_3(t)$, and $m_4(t)$ are respectively multiplied by the carrier waves

$$[\cos(2\pi f_a t) + \cos(2\pi f_b t)]$$

$$[\cos(2\pi f_a t + \alpha_2) + \cos(2\pi f_b t + \beta_1)]$$

$$[\cos(2\pi f_a t + \alpha_2) + \cos(2\pi f_b t + \beta_2)]$$

$$[\cos(2\pi f_a t + \alpha_2) + \cos(2\pi f_b t + \beta_3)]$$

and the resulting DSB-SC signals are summed and then transmitted over a common channel. In the receiver, demodulation is achieved by multiplying the sum of the DSB-SC signals by the four carrier waves separately and then using filtering to remove the unwanted components.

(a) Determine the conditions that the angle α_1, α_2, α_3, and $\beta 1$, β_2, β_3, must satisfy in order that the output of the kth demodulator is $m_k(t)$, where k = 1,2,3,4.

(b) Determine the minimum separation of carrier frequencies f_a and f_b in relation to the bandwidth of the input signals so as to ensure a satisfactory operation of the system.

Solution:

(a) The multiplexed signal is

$$s(t) = \sum_{k=1}^{4} [\cos(2\pi f_a t + \alpha_{k-1}) + \cos(2\pi f_b t + \beta_{k-1})]\, m_k(t)$$

where $\alpha_0 = \beta_0 = 0$. The corresponding product modulator output in the coherent detector of the receiver is

$$v_i(t) = s(t)\,[\cos(2\pi f_a t + \alpha_{i-1}) + \cos(2\pi f_b t + \beta_{i-1})]$$

where i = 1,2,3,4. Therefore,

$$v_i(t) = \sum_{k=1}^{4} m_k(t)\,[\cos(2\pi f_a t + \alpha_{k-1}) + \cos(2\pi f_b t + \beta_{k-1})]\,[\cos(2\pi f_a t + \alpha_{i-1}) + \cos(2\pi f_b t + \beta_{i-1})]$$

$$= \sum_{k=1}^{4} m_k(t) \, [\cos(2\pi f_a t + \alpha_{k-1}) \, [\cos(2\pi f_a t + \alpha_{i-1})$$

$$+ [\cos(2\pi f_a t + \alpha_{k-1}) \cos(2\pi f_a t + \beta_{i-1})$$

$$+ [\cos(2\pi f_b t + \beta_{k-1}) \cos(2\pi f_a t + \alpha_{i-1})$$

$$+ [\cos(2\pi f_b t + \beta_{k-1}) \cos(2\pi f_b t + \beta_{i-1})]$$

$$= \frac{1}{2} \sum_{k=1}^{4} m_k(t) \, \{\cos(\alpha_{k-1} - \alpha_{i-1}) + (\beta_{k-1} - \beta_{i-1})$$

$$+ \cos(4\pi f_b t + \alpha_{k-1} + \alpha_{i-1}) + \cos(4\pi f_b t + \beta_{k-1} + \beta_{i-1}) + \cos(2\pi(f_a + f_b)t + \alpha_{k-1} + \beta_{i-1}] + \cos(2\pi (f_a - f_b)t + \alpha_{k-1} - \beta_{i-1}] + \cos[(2\pi(f_a + f_b)t + \alpha_{i-1} + \beta_{k-1}] + \cos(2\pi(f_a - f_b)t + \alpha_{i-1} - \beta_{k-1}]\}$$

The low-pass filter in the coherent detector of the receiver removes the six high freqency components of $v_i(t)$, leaving an output equal to

$$v_i'(t) = \frac{1}{2} \sum_{k=1}^{4} m_k(t) \, [\cos(\alpha_{k-1} - \alpha_{i-1}) + \cos(\beta_{k-1} - \beta_{i-1})]$$

The requirement on α_k and β_k is therefore:

$$\cos(\alpha_{k-1} - \alpha_{i-1}) + \cos(\beta_{k-1} - \beta_{i-1}) = \begin{cases} 2, & i = k \\ 0, & i \neq k \end{cases}$$

where i, k = 1, 2, 3, 4.

(b) The minimum separation between the carrier frequencies f_a and f_b must be such that $f_a - f_b - W$ is greater than W, where W is the largest bandwidth of the message signals $m_K(t)$, for k = 1,2,3,4. That is, $f_a - f_b > 2W$.

Problem 2.15: In this problem we study the idea of mixing in a superheterodyne receiver. To be specific, consider the block diagram of the mixer shown in Fig. P. 2.15 that consists of a product modulator with a local oscillator of *variable frequency* f_i, followed by a band-pass filter. The input signal is am AM wave of bandwidth 10 kHz and carrier frequency that may lie anywhere in the range 0.535 – 1.605 MHz; these parameters are typical of AM radio broadcasting. It is required to translate this signal to a frequency band centered at a fixed *intermediate frequency* (IF) of 0.455 MHz. Find the range of tuning that must be provided in the local oscillator in order to achieve this requirement.

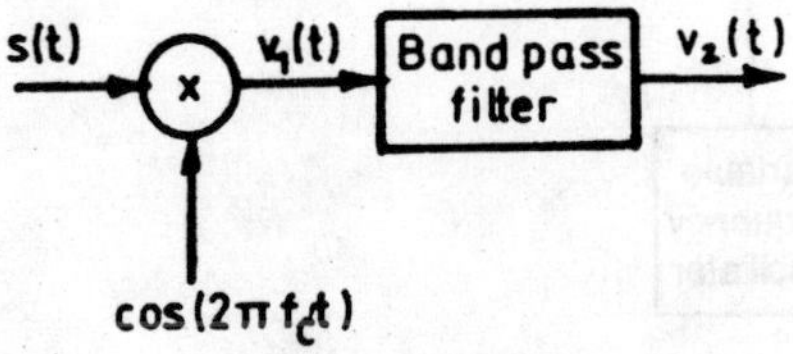

Fig. P. 2.15

Solution:

Consider an incoming narrow-band signal of bandwidth 10 kHz. and mid-band frequency which may lie in the range 0.535 – 1.605 MHz. It is required to translate this signal to a fixed frequency band centered at 0.455 MHz. The problem is to determine the range of tuning that must be provided in the local oscillator.

Let f_c denote the mid-band frequency of the incoming signal. and f_i denote the local oscillator frequency. Then we may write

$$0.535 < f_c < 1.605$$

and $$f_c - f_i = 0.4555$$

whcrc both f_c and f_i arc cxprcsscd in MHz. That is.

$$f_i = f_c - 0.455$$

When f_c = 0.535 MHz, we get f_1 = 0.08 MHz; and when f_c = 1.605 MHz, we get f_i = 1.15 MHz. Thus the required range of tuning of the local oscillator is 0.08 – 1.15 MHz.

Problem 2.16: Figure P. 2.16 shows the block diagram of a *heterodyne spectrum analyzer*. It consists of a variable-frequency oscillator, multiplier, band-pass filter, and root mean square (rms) meter. The oscillator has an amplitude A and operates over the range f_0 to f_0 + W, where f_0 is the mid-band frequency of the filter and W is the signal bandwidth. Assume that f_0 = 2W, the filter bandwidth Δf is small compared with f_0 and that the passband amplitude response of the filter is one. Determine the value of the rms meter output for a low-pass input signal $g(t)$.

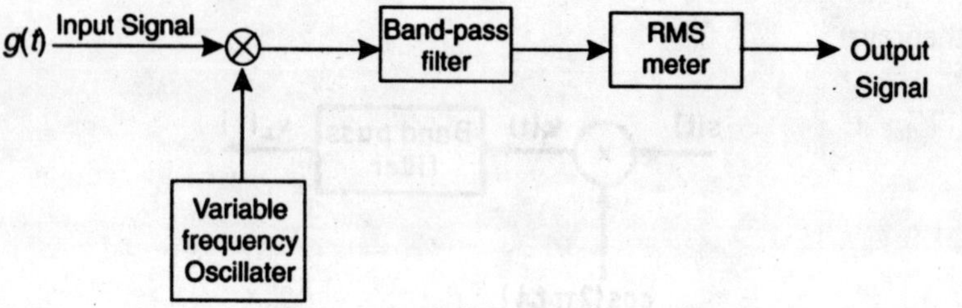

Fig. P. 2.16

Solution:

Let $s(t)$ denote the multiplier output, as shown by

$$s(t) = Ag(t)\cos(2\pi f_c t)$$

where f_c lies in the range f_0 to $f_0 + W$. The amplitude spectra of $s(t)$ and $g(t)$ are related as follows:

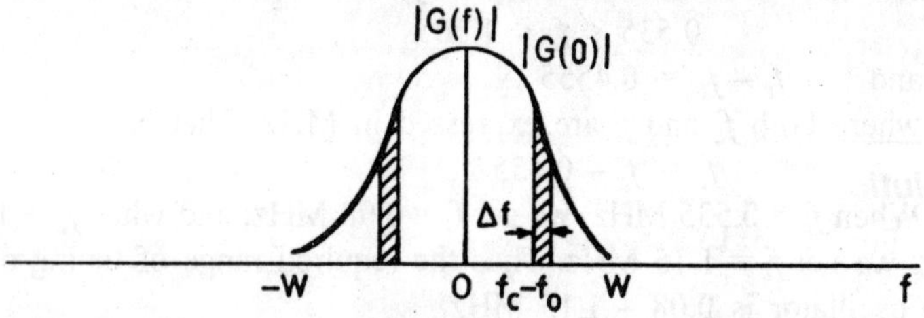

Fig. P. 2.16 (a)

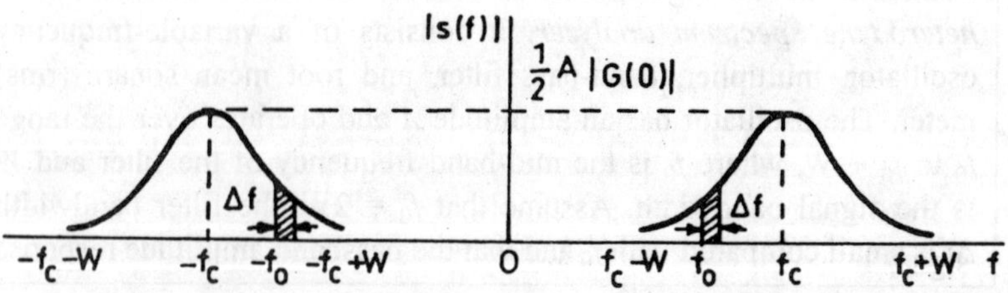

Fig. P. 2.16 (b)

With $v(t)$ denoting the band-pass filter output, we thus find that the Fourier transform of $v(t)$ is approximately given by

$$v(f) = \frac{1}{2} AG(f_c - f_0),\ f_0 - \frac{\Delta f}{2} \leq |f| \leq f_0 + \frac{\Delta f}{2}$$

The rms meter output is therefore (by using Rayleight's energy theorem)

$$V_{rms} = \left[\int_{-\infty}^{\infty} v^2(t)dt\right]^{1/2} = \left[\int_{-\infty}^{\infty} |V(f)|^2 df\right]^{1/2}$$

$$= [2\frac{1}{4}A^2 |G(f_c - f_0|^2)\Delta f]^{1/2} = \frac{A}{\sqrt{2}} |G(f_c - f_0)| \sqrt{\Delta f}$$

Problem 2.17: Sketch the PM and FM waves produced by the sawtooth wave shown in Fig. P. 2.17.

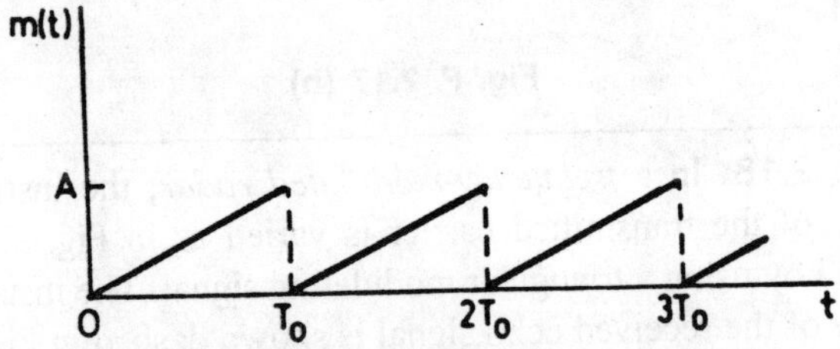

Fig. P. 2.17

Solution:

For the PM case,

$$s(t) = A_c \cos[2\pi f_c t + k_p m(t)].$$

The angle equals

$$\theta_1(t) = 2\pi f_c t + k_p m(t).$$

The instantaneous frequency.

$$f_i(t) = f_c + \frac{Ak_p}{2\pi T_0} - \sum_n \frac{Ak_p}{2\pi}(t - nT_0).$$

is equal to $f_c + Ak_p/2\pi T_0$ except for the instants that the message signal has discontinuities. At these instants, the phase shifts by $-k_pA/T_0$ radians.

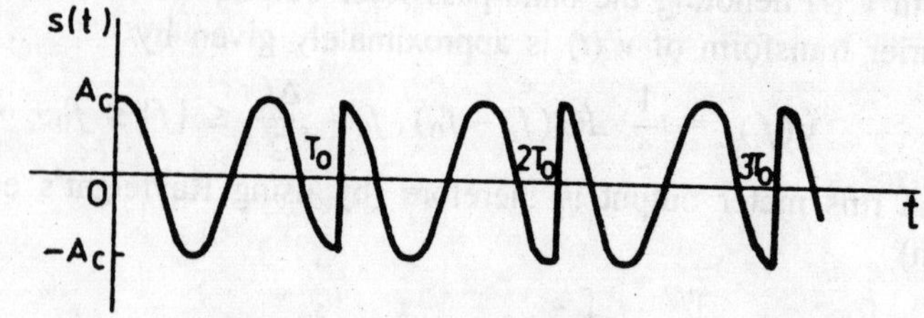

Fig. P. 2.17 (a)

For the FM case, $f_1(t) = f_c + k_f\, m(t)$

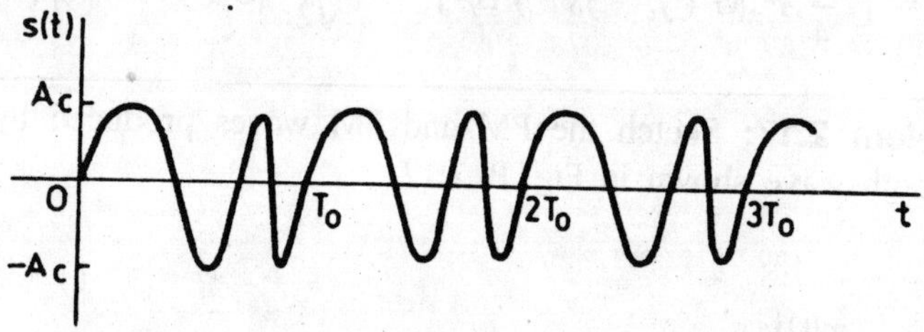

Fig. P. 2.17 (b)

Problem 2.18: In a *frequency-modulated radar*, the instantaneous frequency of the transmitted carrier is varied as in Fig. 2.18 which is obtained by using a triangular modulating signal. The instantaneous frequency of the received echo signal is shown dashed in Fig. P. 2.18, where τ is the round-trip delay time. The transmitted and received echo signal are applied to a mixer, and the difference frequency component is retained. Assuming that $f_0\tau \ll$ I, determine the number

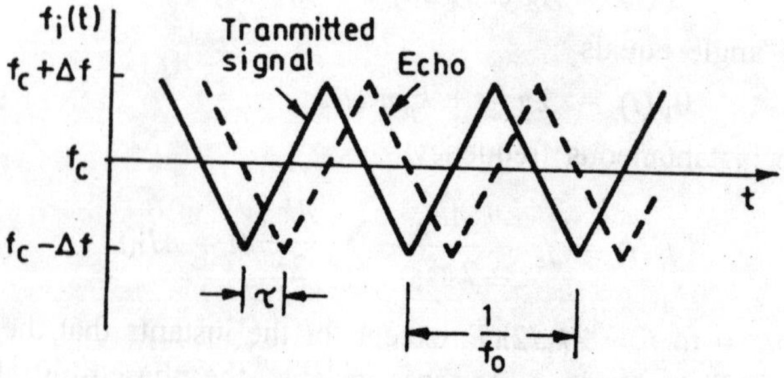

Fig. P. 2.18

of beat cycles at the mixer output, averaged over one second, in terms of the peak deviation Δf of the carrier frequency, the delay T, and the repetition frequency f_0 of the transmitted signal.

Solution:

The instantaneous frequency of the mixer is as shown below.

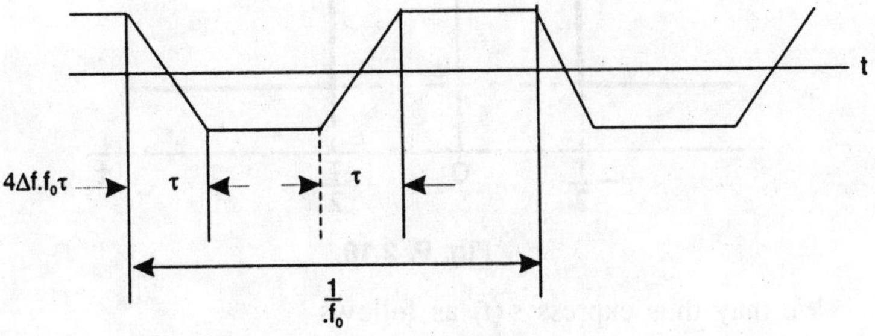

Fig. P. 2.18 (a)

The presence of negative frequency merely indicates that the Phasor representing the difference frequency at the mixer output has reversed its direction of rotation.

Let N denote the number of beat cycles in one period. Then, noting that N is equal to the shaded area shown above, we deduce that

$$N = 2\left[4\,\Delta f \cdot f_0\tau\left(\frac{1}{2f_0} - \tau\right) + 2\Delta f \cdot f_0\tau^2\right] = 4\,\Delta f \cdot \tau\,(1 - f_0\tau)$$

Since $f_0\tau \ll 1$, we have, $N = 4\,\Delta f \cdot \tau$.

Therefore, the number of beat cycles counted over one second is equal to

$$\frac{N}{1/f_0} = 4\Delta f \cdot f_0\,\tau.$$

Problem 2.19: The instantaneous frequency of a sine wave is equal to $f_c - \Delta f$ for $|t| \le T/2$, and f_c for $|t| > T/2$. Determine the spectrum of this frequency modulated wave.

Solution:

The instantaneous frequency of the modulated wave $s(t)$ is as shown below :

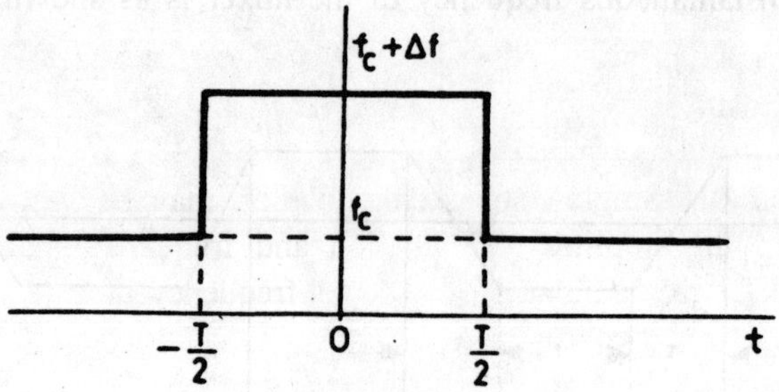

Fig. P. 2.19

We may thus express s (*t*) as follows

$$s(t) = \begin{cases} \cos(2\pi f_c t), & t < -\frac{T}{2}, \\ \cos\left[2\pi(f_c + \Delta f)t\right], & -\frac{T}{2} \le t \le \frac{T}{2}, \\ \cos\left[2\pi f_c t\right], & \frac{T}{2} < t, \end{cases}$$

The Fourier transform of $s(t)$ is therefore

$$s(f) = \int_{-\infty}^{-T/2} \cos(2\pi f_c t) \cdot \exp(-j2\pi f t)\, dt + \int_{-T/2}^{T/2} \cos\,[2\pi(f_c + \Delta f)\, t] \cdot$$

$$\exp(-j2\pi f t)\, dt + \int_{T/2}^{\infty} \cos(2\pi f_c t) \cdot \exp(-j2\pi f t)\, dt$$

$$= \int_{-\infty}^{\infty} \cos(2\pi f_c t) \cdot \exp(-j2\pi f t)\, dt + \int_{-T/2}^{T/2} \{\cos\,[2\pi(f_c + \Delta f)\, t -$$

$$\cos(2\pi f_c t)\}\, \exp(-j2\pi f t)\, dt \qquad ...(1)$$

The second term of Eq. (1) is recognized as the difference between the Fourier transforms of two RF pulses of unit amplitude, one having a frequency equal to $f_c + \Delta f$ and the other having a frequency equal to f_c. Hence assuming that $f_c T \gg 1$, we may express $S(f)$ as follows:

$$S(f) \approx \begin{cases} \frac{1}{2}\delta(f - f_c) + \frac{T}{2}\text{sin}\,c\,[T(f - f_c - \Delta f)] - \frac{T}{2}\text{sin}\,c\,[T(f - f_c)], & f > 0 \\ \frac{1}{2}\delta(f + f_c) + \frac{T}{2}\text{sin}\,c\,[T(f + f_c + \Delta f)] - \frac{T}{2}\text{sin}\,c\,[T(f + f_c)]. & f < 0 \end{cases}$$

Problem 2.20: Single-sideband modulation may be viewed as a hybrid form of amplitude modulation and frequency modulation. Evaluate the envelope and instantaneous frequency of an SSB wave for the following two cases:
(a) When only the upper sideband is transmitted.
(b) When only the lower sideband is transmitted.

Solution:

For SSB modulation, the modulated wave is

$$s(t) = \frac{A_c}{2}[m(t)\cos(2\pi f_c t) \pm \hat{m}(t)\sin(2\pi f_c t)],$$

the minus sign applying when transmitting the upper sideband and the plus sign applying when transmitting the lower one.

Regardless of the sign, the envelope is

$$a(t) = \frac{A_c}{2}\sqrt{m^2(t) + \hat{m}^2(t)}.$$

(a) For upper sideband transmission, the angle,

$$\theta_i(t) = 2\pi f_c t + \tan^{-1}\left(\frac{\hat{m}(t)}{m(t)}\right).$$

The instantaneous frequency is,

$$f_i(t) = \frac{1}{2\pi}\frac{d\theta_i(t)}{dt} = f_c + \frac{m(t)\,\hat{m}'(t) - \hat{m}(t)\,m'(t)}{2\pi(m^2(t) + \hat{m}^2(t))},$$

where $'$ denotes time derivative.

(b) For lower sideband transmission, we have

$$\theta_i(t) = 2\pi f_c t + \tan^{-1}\left(-\frac{\hat{m}(t)}{m(t)}\right).$$

$$f_i(t) = f_c + \frac{\hat{m}(t)\,m'(t) - m(t)\,\hat{m}'(t)}{2\pi(m^2(t) + \hat{m}^2(t))},$$

Problem 2.21: Consider a narrow-band FM signal approximately defined by

$$s(t) \simeq A_c \cos(2\pi f_c t) - \beta A_c \sin(2\pi f_c t)\sin(2\pi f_m t)$$

(a) Determine the envelope of this modulated signal. What is the ratio of the maximum to the minimum value of this envelope? Plot this ratio versus β, assuming that β is restricted to the interval $0 \le \beta \le 0.3$.

(b) Determine the average power of the narrow-band FM signal, expressed as a percentage of the average power of the unmodulated carrier wave. Plot this result versus β, assuming that β is restricted to the interval $0 \le \beta \le 0.3$.

(c) By expanding the angle $\theta_i(t)$ of the narrow-band FM signal $s(t)$ in the form of a power series, and restricting the modulation index β to a maximum value of 0.3 radians, show that

$$\theta_i(t) = 2\pi f_c t + \beta \sin(2\pi f_c t) - \frac{\beta^3}{3}\sin^3(2\pi f_m t)$$

What is the value of the harmonic distortion for $\beta = 0.3$?

Solution:

(a) The envelope of the FM wave $s(t)$ is

$$a(t) = Ac\sqrt{1 + \beta^2 \sin^2(2\pi f_m t)}$$

The maximum value of the envelope is

$$a_{\max} = Ac\sqrt{1 + \beta^2}$$

and its minimum value is

$$a_{\min} = A_c.$$

Therefore,

$$\frac{a_{\max}}{a_{\min}} = \sqrt{1 + \beta^2}$$

This ratio is shown plotted below for $0 < \beta < 0.3$:

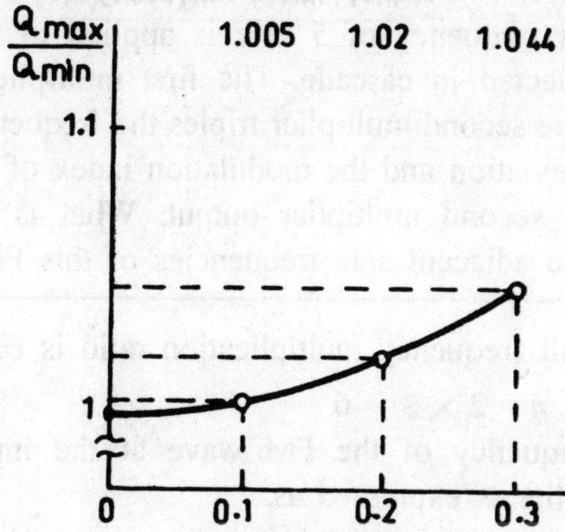

Fig. P. 2.21 (a)

(b) Expressing $s(t)$ in terms of its frequency components :

$$s(t) = A_c \cos(2\pi f_c t) + \frac{1}{2}\beta A_c \cos[f_c + f_m)t] - \frac{1}{2}\beta A_c \cos[f_c - f_m)t]$$

The mean power of s (t) is therefore

$$P_1 = \frac{A_c^2}{2} + \frac{\beta^2 A_c^2}{8} + \frac{\beta^2 A_c^2}{8} = \frac{A_c^2}{2}\left(1 + \frac{\beta^2}{2}\right)$$

The mean power of the unmodulated carrier is $P_c = \dfrac{A_c^2}{2}$

Therefore, $\dfrac{P_1}{P_c} = 1 + \dfrac{\beta^2}{2}$

which is shown plotted below for $0 \le \beta \le 0.3$.

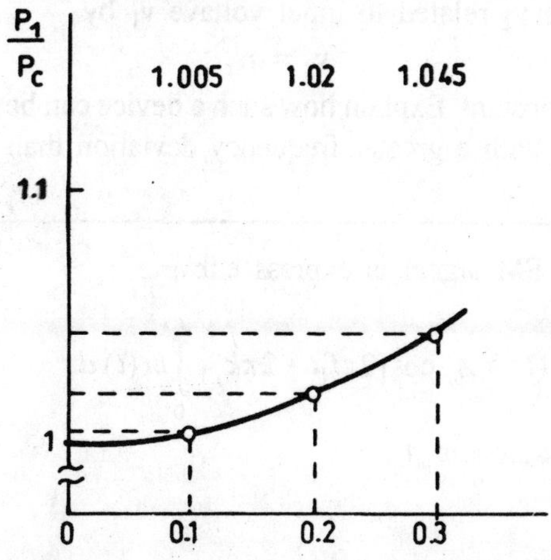

Problem 2.22: An FM signal with a frequency deviation of 10 kHz at a modulation frequency of 5 kHz is applied to two frequency multipliers connected in cascade. The first multiplier doubles the frequency and the second multiplier triples the frequency. Determine the frequency deviation and the modulation index of the FM signal obtained at the second multiplier output. What is the frequency separation of the adjacent side frequencies of this FM signal?

Solution: Overall frequency multiplication ratio is equal to

$$n = 2 \times 3 = 6$$

Instantaneous frequency of the FM wave at the input of the first frequency multiplier is expressed as,

$$f_{i1}(t) = f_c + \Delta f \cos(2\pi f_m t)$$

Now, the instantaneous frequency of the resulting FM wave at the output of the second frequency multiplier is given by,

$$f_{i2}(t) = nf_c + n\Delta f \cos(2\pi f_m t)$$

Hence, the frequency deviation of this FM wave is equal to,

$$= n\Delta f = 6 \times 10 = 60 \text{ kHz}$$

$$\therefore \text{ therefore, Modulation index} = \frac{n\Delta f}{f_m} = \frac{60}{5} = 12$$

Also, the frequency separation of the adjacent side-frequencies of this FM wave would be unchanged at f_m = 5 kHz.

Problem 2.23: An FM signal is applied to a square-law device with output voltage v_2 related to input voltave v_1 by

$$v_2 = av_1^2$$

where a is a constant. Explain how such a device can be used to obtain an FM signal with a greater frequency deviation than that available at the input.

Solution: An FM signal is express edby,

$$v_1(t) = A_c \cos[2\pi f_1 t + 2\pi k_{f1} \int_0^t m(t)\, dt$$

where $m(t) = a_m \cos\omega_m t$.

Therefore, the resulting output at the square-law device is given by,

$$v_2(t) = av_1^2(t)$$

$$\text{or,} \quad v_2(t) = a\,A_c^2 \cos^2\left[2\pi f_1 t + 2\pi k_{f1}\int_0^t m(t)\,dt\right]$$

$$\text{or,} \quad v_2(t) = \frac{1}{2}a\,A_c^2 \cos^2\left\{1 + \cos\left[4\pi f_1 t + 4\pi k_{f1}\int_0^t m(t)\,dt\right]\right\}$$

Passing $v_2(t)$ through a band-pass filter centered at $2f_1$ and with a bandwidth just large enough to pass the FM wave, component of $v_2(t)$, gives output as

$$v_0(t) = \frac{1}{2}a\,A_c^2 \cos\left[2\pi f_2 t + 2\pi k_{f2}\int_0^t m(t)\,dt\right],$$

where $f_2 = 2f_1$ and $k_{f2} = 2k_{f1}$

We know $k_{f1} = \dfrac{\Delta f}{f_m}$,

where a_m is the amplitude of message signal.

$$k_{f2} = \frac{2\Delta f}{f_m}.$$

Hence, it can be seen that, obtained FM wave has twice the frequency deviation as that of input FM wave.

Problem 2.24: A Carrier signal of 1 Volt amplitude and sinusoidal modulating signal of 0.5 V, put in series, are applied to a square law modulation of characteristics,

$$i_0 = (10 + kV_i + k'V_i^2)\,mA,$$

where V_i is input in volts, $k = 2\text{mA/V}$ and $k' = \dfrac{0.2\text{ mA}}{V^2}$.

Considering only the frequency components of the AM signal corresponding to the carrier frequency, find the depth of modulation in the resulting AM signal.

Solution: Given, input signal, $V_i(t) = \cos\omega_c t + 0.5\cos\omega_m t$

Then, output of square wave modulator, is given by

$$i_0 = 10 + 2 \times 10^{-3} [\cos(\omega_c t) + 0.5 \cos(\omega_m t)] + 0.2 \times 10^{-3} [\cos(\omega_c t) + 0.5 \times \cos(\omega_m t)]^2$$

Consider only terms corresponding to carrier terms, we get

$$i_0 = 2 \times 10^{-3} \cos(\omega_c t) + 0.2 \times 10^{-3} \times 0.5 \times 2 \times \cos(\omega_m t) \cos(\omega_m t)$$

or, $$i_0 = 2 \times 10^{-3} \cos \omega_c t \left[1 + \frac{0.2 \times 10^{-3} \times 1}{2 \times 10^{-3}} \cos \omega_m t\right] \cdot \cos \omega_c t$$

comparing with standard AM wave equation,

$$i_0 = A_m \cos \omega_c t \, [1 + \mu \cos \omega_m t]$$

we get

$$\mu = \frac{0.2 \times 10^{-3} \times 1}{2 \times 10^{-3}} = 0.1$$

Modulation depth = 0.1

Problem 2.25: An SSB signal is demodulated by using a synchronous demodulator. However, the locally arranged carrier has a phase error θ. Determine the effect of the error on demodulation. What will be the effect of this error if the input is DSB-SC in place of SSB?

Solution: An SSB signal is expressed by the equation,

$$x_{SSB}(t) = m(t) \cdot \cos(\omega_c t) \mp \hat{m}(t) \cdot \sin(\omega_c t)$$

where $\hat{m}(t)$ is Hilbert transform of message signal $m(t)$.

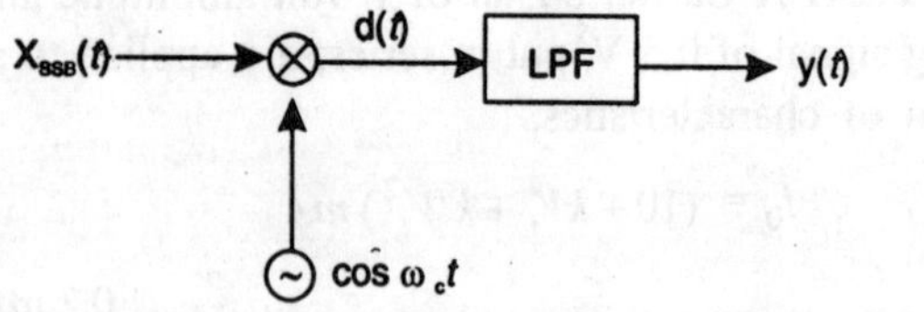

Fig. P. 2.25 (a)

then, $$d(t) = [m(t) \cdot \cos(\omega_c t) \mp \hat{m}(t) \cdot \sin(\omega_c t)] \cos[\omega_c t + \theta]$$

$$= \frac{m(t)}{2} [\cos(2\omega_c t + \theta) + \cos\theta] \mp \hat{m}(t) \cdot [\sin(2\omega_c t + \theta - \sin\theta]$$

after low-pass filtering, we get

Output, $y(t) = \dfrac{m(t)}{2} \cdot \cos\theta \mp \hat{m}(t) \cdot \sin\theta$

There is no attenuation but only phase distortion by angle θ in the output consider the next case,

When the input is DSB-SC.

then, $x_{dsB} = m(t) \cdot \cos(\omega_c t + \theta)$

and, $d(t) = [m(t) \cdot \cos(\omega_c t)] \cdot \cos[\omega_c t + \theta]$

$$= \frac{1}{2} m(t) [\cos\theta + \cos(2\omega_c t + \theta)]$$

after low-pass filtering, we obtain

$$y(t) = \frac{1}{2} m(t) \cdot \cos\theta$$

Hence, output is proportional to $m(t)$, when θ is constant. But if θ varies randomly with time, then output will vary also which is undersirable.

Problem 2.26: Obtain an expression for the signal $v_3(t)$ in Figure P. 2.26 for $v_1(t) = 10 \cos(2000\ \pi t) + 4 \sin(200\ \pi t)$. Assume that $v_2(t) = v_1(t) + 0.1\, v_1^2$ and that the BPF is an ideal unity gain filter with pass band from 800 Hz to 1200 Hz.

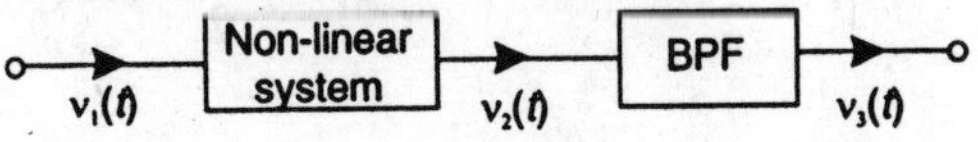

Fig. P. 2.26

Solution: From the given figure and the expression given, we have the Output at non-Linear system, given as,

$$v_2(t) = v_1(t) + 0.1\, v_1^2(t)$$

$$= [10 \cos(200\ \pi t) + 4 \sin(200\ \pi t)] + [10 \cos(2000\ \pi t) + 4 \sin(200\ \pi\tau)]^2 \times 0.1$$

$$= 10 \cos(2000\ \pi t) + 4 \sin(200\ \pi t) + 0.1 \times [100 \cos^2(200\ \pi t) + 16 \sin^2(200\ \pi t) + 80 \cos(2000\ \pi t) \sin(200\ \pi t)$$

$$= 10\cos(2000\,\pi t) + 4\sin(200\,\pi t) +$$

$$\left[100\left(\frac{1+\cos(4000\,\pi t)}{2}\right) + \frac{16\,[1-\cos|900\,\pi t|}{2}\right]\times 0.1$$

$$+\,40\,[\sin(2200\,\pi t) - \sin(1800\,\pi t)\times 0.1$$

$$= 10\cos(2000\,\pi t) + 0.5\cos(4000\,\pi t) - 0.8\cos(400\,\pi t)$$

$$+\,4\sin(200\,\pi t) + 4\sin(200\,\pi t) - 4\sin(1800\,\pi t) + 5.8$$

Since, BPF has a pass-band from 800 Hz-1200 Hz, we have the output after filtering,

$$V_3(t) = 10\cos(2000\,\pi t) + 4\sin(2200\,\pi t) - 4\sin(1800\,\pi t)$$

Problem 2.27: A given AM broadcast station transmits a total power of 5 kW when the carrier is modulated by a sinusoidal signal with a modulation index of 0.7071. Calculate

(*i*) the carrier power

(*ii*) the transmission efficiency, and

(*iii*) the peak amplitude of the carrier assuming the antenna to be represented by *a* $(50 + j0)\ \Omega$ load.

Solution: (*i*) An amplitude modulaed signal is given by

$$x_{AM}(t) = A\cos\omega_c t + \mu A\cos\omega_m t\cos\omega_c t$$

$$x_{AM}(t) = A\cos\omega_c t + \frac{1}{2}\mu A\cos(\omega_c - \omega_m)t + \frac{\mu A}{2}\cdot\cos(\omega_c + \omega_m)\,t \quad ...(1)$$

Hence,

$$P_C = \text{(carrier power)} = \frac{A^2}{2}$$

$$P_S = \text{(sideband power)} = \frac{1}{2}\left[\left(\frac{1}{2}\mu A\right)^2 + \left(\frac{\mu A}{2}\right)^2\right] = \frac{\mu^2 A^2}{4} \quad ...(2)$$

then, total power $P_t = \dfrac{A^2}{2}\left(1+\dfrac{\mu^2}{2}\right)$

or, $P_t = P_C\left(1+\dfrac{\mu^2}{2}\right)$

As given, $P_t = 50 \times 10^3$ watt,

We have, $$P_C = \frac{P_t}{1+\frac{\mu^2}{2}} = \frac{50 \times 10^3}{1.25} = 40 \text{ kW}.$$

(*ii*) Now, Transmission efficiency,

$$\eta = \frac{P_s}{P_t} \times 100\%$$

or, $$\eta = \frac{\frac{1}{4}\mu^2 A^2}{\left(\frac{1}{2}+\frac{\mu^2}{4}\right)A^2} \times 100\% = \frac{\mu^2}{2+\mu^2} \times 100\%$$

or, $$\eta = \frac{0.50}{2+0.50} \times 100\% = 20\%$$

(*iii*) And, Power delivered to the load $= \dfrac{A_c^2}{2R} = 40 \times 10^3$

Then, $A_c = \sqrt{2 \times 40 \times 10^3 \times 50} = 2 \text{ kW}$

Problem 2.28: A baseband signal $m(t)$ modulates a carrier to produce the angle modulated signal, $A_c \cos[2\pi \times 10^8 t + k_p m(t)]$, where $m(t)$ is shown in Fig. P. 2.28. Determine the value of k_p so that the peak-to-peak frequency deviation of the carrier is 100 kHz.

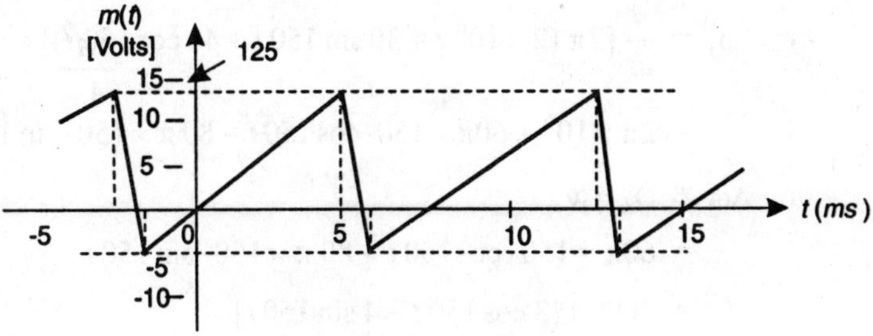

Fig. P. 2.28

Solution: For, PM signal instantaneous frequency is,

$$\omega_i = \omega_c + k_p \frac{dm(t)}{dt}$$

and, maximum frequency deviation, $|\omega_i - \omega_c|_{max} = k_p \left|\frac{dm(t)}{dt}\right|_{max}$

$$\text{or} \quad 100 \times 2\pi = k_p \left|\frac{dm(t)}{dt}\right|_{max} \qquad ...(1)$$

Here, $\left|\frac{dm(t)}{dt}\right|_{max} = \frac{17.5}{7} = 2.5$ [From the Fig. P. 2.28]

Using equation (1), we get, $k_p = \frac{100 \times 2\pi}{2.5} = 80\,\pi.$

Problem 2.29: An angle modulated signal with carrier frequency $\omega_c = 2 \times 10^6$ rad/sec. is given as

$$s(t) = \cos 2\pi\,(2 \times 10^6 t + 30 \sin 150\,t + 40 \cos/50\,t)$$

then,

(*i*) Find the maximum frequency deviation

(*ii*) maximum phase deviation and

(*iii*) the bandwidth of $s(t)$.

Solution: Instantaneous frequency is expressed by:

(*i*) $$\omega_i = \frac{d}{dt}\theta(t)$$

$$\text{or} \quad \omega_i = \frac{d}{dt}[2\pi\,(2 \times 10^6\, t + 30 \sin 150\,t + 40 \cos 150\,t)]$$

$$= 2\pi \times 10^6 + 60\pi \times 150 \cdot \cos 150\,t - 80\,\pi \times 150 \cdot \sin 150\,t$$

$$\text{or} \quad \Delta\omega = \omega_i - \omega_c$$

$$= 60\pi \times 150 \cdot \cos 150\,t - 80\,\pi \times 150 \cdot \sin 150\,t$$

$$= 3000\pi\,[3 \cos 150\,t - 4 \sin 150\,t]$$

$$\text{or} \quad = 15000\,\pi \cdot \cos(150\,t + \alpha).$$

where, $\alpha = \tan^{-1}\frac{4}{3}$.

Maximum frequency deviation is given by,

$$\Delta f = \frac{|\Delta\omega|_{max}}{2\pi} = \frac{15000\,\pi}{2\pi} = 7.5\text{ kHz}$$

(*ii*) Here, $\theta(t) = 2\pi[2\times10^6\, t + 30\sin 150\, t + 40\cos 150\, t]$

then, $\phi(t) = 2\pi(30\sin 150\, t + 40\cos 150\, t)$

$$= 100\,\pi\left(\frac{3}{5}\sin 150\, t + \frac{4}{5}\cos 150\, t\right)$$

$$= 100\,\pi\cdot\sin(150\, t + \alpha')$$

where, $\alpha' = \tan^{-1}\frac{4}{5}$

Hence, maximum phase deviation $|\phi(t)|_{max} = 100\,\pi$ radian

(*iii*) Here, $\beta = \frac{\Delta\omega}{\omega_m} = \frac{15000\,\pi}{150} = 100\,\pi$

and, Band width, $W_B = 2(\beta + 1)\,\omega_m$

As, $\beta >> 1$, $W_B \approx 2\,\beta\cdot\omega_m = 2\times100\,\pi\times150$

or, $f_\beta = 15$ kHz.

Problem 2.30: Explain the Quadrature null effect in a coherent detector for DSB-SC signals.

Solution:

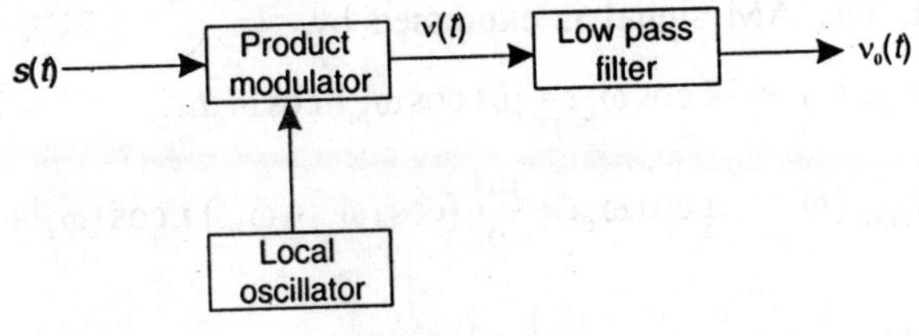

Fig. P. 2.30

The coherent detector in depicted line and an input signal $s(t)$ is being applied to the product modulator. Then, expressing local oscillator signal as, $A_c' \cos(2\pi f_c + \phi)$, the product modulator output can be expressed as,

$$v_0(t) = A_c' \cos(2\pi f_c t + \phi) \cdot s(t)$$

$$\text{or,} \quad v_0(t) = A_c' A_c \cos(2\pi f_c t + \phi) \cdot \cos(2\pi f_c t)\, m(t)$$

$$\left[\because A_c \cos 2\pi = \frac{1}{2}\right] \quad [\text{Here } s(t) = m(t) = m(t) \cdot A_c \cos 2\pi f_c t]$$

$$\text{or,} \quad v_0(t) = \frac{1}{2} A_c A_c' (\cos 4\pi f_c t + \phi(t)\, m(t) + \frac{1}{2} A_c\, A_c' \cos\phi\, m(t)$$

The first term is removed by low-pass filtering having cut-off frequency of this filter is greater than W but less than $2f_c$ - W.

Hence, filter output $v_0(t) = \frac{1}{2} A_c A_c' \cos\phi\, m(t)$

The demodulated signal $v_0(t)$ is therefore proportional to $m(t)$ if ϕ will be constant.

Here, the amplitude of the filter output goes maximum for $\phi = 0$, and minimum for $\phi = \pm\frac{\pi}{2}$. The zero demodulated signal occuring at $\phi = \pm\frac{\pi}{2}$ represents the **quadratue null effect** of synchronous demodulator or **coherent detector.**

Problem 2.31: In an AM system, the modulating signal is sinusoidal with frequency f_m Hz. If 80% modulation is used, then determine the ratio of total side-band power in the modulation signal, to the total power.

Solution: The AM signal is expressed by,

$$x_{AM}(t) = A \cos\omega_c t + \mu A \cos\omega_m t \cos\omega_c t$$

$$\text{or,} \quad x_{AM}(t) = A \cos\omega_c t + \frac{\mu A}{2}[\cos(\omega_c - \omega_m) t \cos(\omega_c + \omega_m) t]$$

$$\text{Here, } P_c \text{ (carrier power)} = \frac{1}{2} A^2$$

and, P_s (sideband power) $= \frac{1}{2}\left[\left(\frac{1}{2}\mu A\right)^2 + \left(\frac{1}{2}\mu A\right)^2\right] = \frac{1}{4}\mu^2 A^2$

then, Total power, $P_t = P_c + P_s = \frac{1}{2}\left(1 + \frac{\mu^2}{2}\right)A^2$

Hence, ratio $= \dfrac{\text{Side band power}}{\text{Total power}}$

$$= \frac{\frac{1}{4}\mu^2 A^2}{\frac{1}{4}(2+\mu^2)A^2} = \frac{\mu^2}{2+\mu^2} = \frac{0.80^2}{2+0.80^2} = \frac{0.64}{2.64} = 0.242$$

Problem 2.32: In an envelope detector the input is an AM signal expressed as

$$x_{AM}(t) = A(1 + \mu \cos \omega_m t) \cdot \cos \omega_c t$$

where μ is a constant, $0 < \mu < 1$, and $\omega_c >> \omega_m$. Then prove that

(*i*) At any time to, $\dfrac{1}{RC} \geq \omega_m \left(\dfrac{\mu \sin \omega_m t_0}{1 + \mu \cos \omega_m t_0}\right)$ and

(*ii*) $\dfrac{1}{RC} \geq \dfrac{\mu\omega_m}{\sqrt{1-\mu^2}}$

Solution: Envelope detector and envelope of $x_{AM}(t)$ are given in Fig. P. 2.32 (a) and (b) respectively.

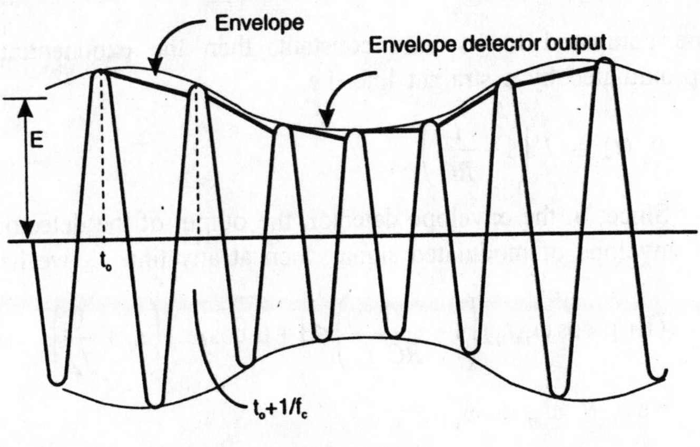

Fig. P. 2.32 (a)

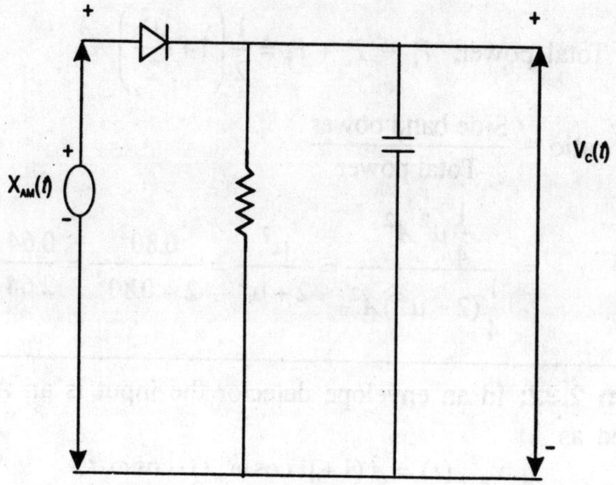

Fig. P. 2.32 (b)

Voltage across capacitor C is given by

$$v_c(t) = E_0 e^{-t/RC}$$

and interval between two peaks $= \frac{1}{f_c} = \frac{2\pi}{\omega_c}$

Now, as $RC >> \frac{1}{\omega_c}$, then $v_c(t)$ discharges exponentially for a short time compared to its time constant, then the exponential can be approximated by a straight line, i.e.,

$$v_c(t) \cong E\left(1 - \frac{t}{RC}\right)$$

Since, in the envelope detector, the output of the detector follows the envelope of modulated signal, then at any time t_o, we have,

$$(1 + \mu \cos \omega_m t_0)\left(1 - \frac{1}{RC\, f_c}\right) \le 1 + \mu \cos \omega_m \left(t_0 + \frac{1}{f_c}\right)$$

Now, If $\omega_m << \omega_c$,

then, $1+\mu\cos\omega_m\left(t_0+\frac{1}{f_c}\right)=1+\mu\cos\left(\omega_m t_0+\frac{\omega_m}{f_c}\right)$

$$\cong +\mu\cos\omega_m t_0-\frac{\mu\omega_m}{f_c}\sin\omega_m t_0$$

or, $(1+\mu\cos\omega_m t_0)\left(\frac{1}{RCf_c}\right)\geq\frac{\mu\omega_m}{f_c}\sin\omega_m t_0$

or $$\frac{1}{RC}\geq\omega_m\left(\frac{\mu\sin\omega_m t_0}{1+\mu\cos\omega_m t_0}\right) \quad ...(1)$$

Using equation (1), we have,

$$\frac{1}{RC}+\frac{\mu}{RC}\cos\omega_m t_0 \geq \mu\,\omega_m\sin\omega_m t_0$$

or, $$\mu\left(\omega_m\sin\omega_m t_0-\frac{1}{RC}\cos\omega_m t_0\right)\leq\frac{1}{RC}$$

or, $$\mu\sqrt{\omega_m^2+\frac{1}{(RC)^2}}\cdot\sin\left(\omega_m t_0-\tan^{-1}\frac{1}{\omega_m RC}\right)\leq\frac{1}{RC}$$

Since $\sin\theta\leq 1$, then,

$$\frac{1}{RC}\geq\mu\sqrt{\omega_m^2+\left(\frac{1}{RC}\right)^2}$$

or, $$\mu^2\left[\omega_m^2+\left(\frac{1}{RC}\right)^2\right]\leq\left(\frac{1}{RC}\right)^2$$

or, $$RC\leq\frac{1}{\omega_m}\frac{\sqrt{1-\mu^2}}{\mu}$$

Problem 2.33: An angle-modulated signal is given as,

$$s(t)=20\cos(\omega_c t+4\sin\omega_m t)$$

assuming as a PM signal and f_m = 2 kHz, calculate the modulation index and bandwidth when (a) f_m is increased two times (b) f_m is decreased by half.

Solution: A PM singal is expressed by,

$$s(t) = A_m \cos[\omega_c t + k_p m(t)] \quad (1)$$

where $m(t) = a_m \sin \omega_m t$

or, $$s(t) = 20 \cos[\omega_c t + 4 \sin \omega_m t] \quad (2)$$

Comparing equations (1) and (2), we obtain,

$$\beta = k_p a_m = 4$$

Hence, bandwidth, $f_B = 2(\beta + 1) f_m = 2(4 + 1) \cdot 2 = 20$ kHz

(*i*) When, $f_m = 2f_m = 4$ kHz.

$$f_B = 2(4 + 1) \cdot 4 = 40 \text{ kHz}$$

(*ii*) When, $f_{m_2} = \dfrac{f_m}{2} = 1\,\text{kHz}$

$$f_B = 2(b + 1) \cdot f_{m_2}$$

$$f_B = 2(4 + 1) \cdot 1 = 10 \text{ kHz}$$

Chapter 3

Random Processes

Problem 3.1: Consider the sinusoidal process

$$X(t) = A\cos(2\pi f_c t)$$

where the frequency f_c is constant and the amplitude A is uniformly distributed:

$$f_A(a) = \begin{cases} 1, & 0 \le a \le 1 \\ 0, & \text{otherwise} \end{cases}$$

Determine whether or not this process is stationary in the strict sense.

Solution:

$$x(t) = A\cos(2\pi f_c t)$$

Then, $\quad X_i = A\cos(2\pi f_c t_i)$

Since the amplitude A is uniformly distributed, then

$$f_{X_i}(x_i) = \begin{cases} \dfrac{1}{\cos(2\pi f_c t_i)}, & 0 \le x_i \le \cos(2\pi f_c t_i) \\ 0, & \text{otherwise} \end{cases}$$

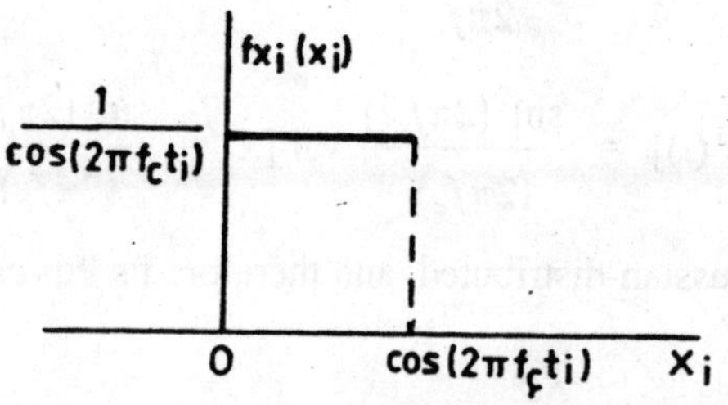

Fig. P. 3.1 (a)

Now, in a similar way,

$$X_i + \tau = A \cos [2\pi f_c (t_i + \tau)]$$

and

$$f_{X_{i+\tau}}(x_i) = \begin{cases} \dfrac{1}{\cos [2\pi f_c (t_i + \tau)]}, & 0 \le x_i \le \cos\left[2\pi f_c\left(t_i + \tau\right)\right] \\ 0 & \text{otherwise} \end{cases}$$

Hence, it can be seen that,

$$f_{X_i}(x_i) \neq f_{X_{i-\tau}}(x_2) \text{ and therefore } X(t) \text{ is non-stationary.}$$

> **Problem 3.2:** A random process $X(t)$ is defined by
>
> $$X(t) = A \cos (2\pi f_c t)$$
>
> where A is a Gaussian-distributed ramdon variable of zero mean and variance $\sigma^2{}_A$. This random process is applied to an ideal integrator, producing the output.
>
> $$Y(t) = \int_0^t X(\tau)\, d\tau$$
>
> (*a*) Determine the probability density function of the output $Y(t)$ at a particular time t_k.
> (*b*) Determine whether or not $Y(t)$ is stationary.
> (*c*) Determine whether or not $Y(t)$ is ergodic.

Solution: (*a*) The integration output at time t is

$$Y(t) = \int_0^t X(\tau)\, d\tau = A \int_0^t \cos (2\pi f_c \tau)\, d\tau = \frac{A}{2\pi fc} \sin (2\pi f_c t)$$

Then,

$$E[Y(t)] = \frac{\sin (2\pi f_c t)}{2\pi f_c} E(A) = 0$$

$$\text{Var}[Y(t)] = \frac{\sin^2 (2\pi f_c t)}{(2\pi f_c)^2} \text{Var}[A] = \frac{\sin^2 (2\pi f_c t)}{(2\pi f_c)^2} \sigma_A^2 \quad \ldots(1)$$

$Y(t)$ is Gaussian-distributed, and therefore its Pdf can be expressed as,

$$f_{Y(t)}(y) = \frac{\sqrt{2\pi}f_c}{\sigma_A \sin(2\pi f_c t)} \exp\left[-\frac{2\pi^2 f_c^2}{\sin^2(2\pi f_c t)\,\sigma_A^2} y^2\right]$$

(*b*) Eqn (1) tells that, as variance of $Y(t)$ depends on line, $y(t)$ therefore is not stationary.

(*c*) For a random process to be ergodic it has to be stationary. Since $Y(t)$ is nonstationary, it can't be ergodic.

Problem 3.3: The square wave $x(t)$ of Fig. P 3.3 of constant amplitude A, period T_0, and delay t_d, represents the sample function of a random process $X(t)$. The delay is random, described by the probability density function.

$$f_{T_d}(t_d) = \begin{cases} \frac{1}{T_0}, & -\frac{1}{2}T_0 \le t_d \le \frac{1}{2}T_0 \\ 0, & \text{otherwise} \end{cases}$$

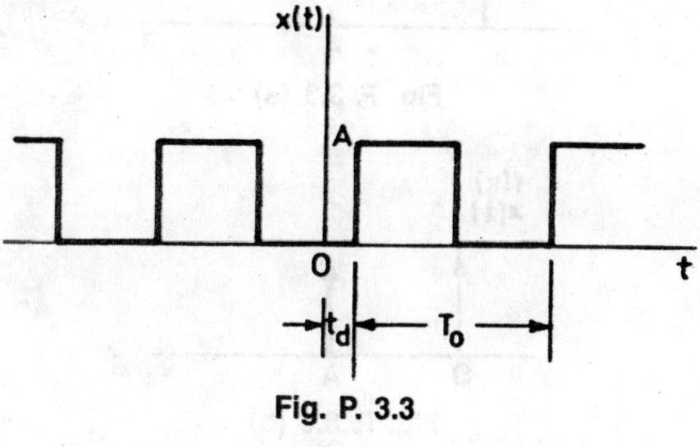

Fig. P. 3.3

(*a*) Determine the probability density function of the random variable $X(t_k)$ obtained by observing the random process $X(t)$ at time t_k.

(*b*) Determine the mean and autocorrelation function of $X(t)$ using ensemble-averaging.

(*c*) Determine the mean and autocorrelation function of $X(t)$ using time-averaging.

(*d*) Establish whether or not $X(t)$ is wide-sense stationary. In what sense is it ergodic?

Solution: The distribution function of $X(t)$ is,

$$F_{X(t)}(x) = \begin{cases} 0, & x < 0 \\ \frac{1}{2}, & 0 \le x \le A \\ 1, & A < x \end{cases}$$

and, the corresponding Pdf is,

$$f_{X(t)}(x) = \frac{1}{2}\delta(x) + \frac{1}{2}\delta(x - A)$$

which are depicted as,

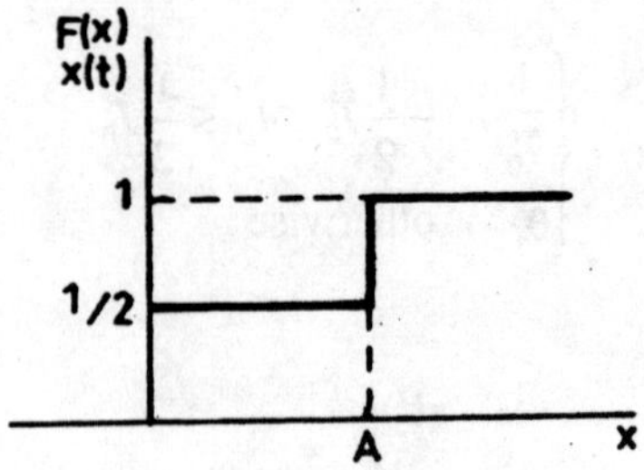

Fig. P. 3.3 (a)

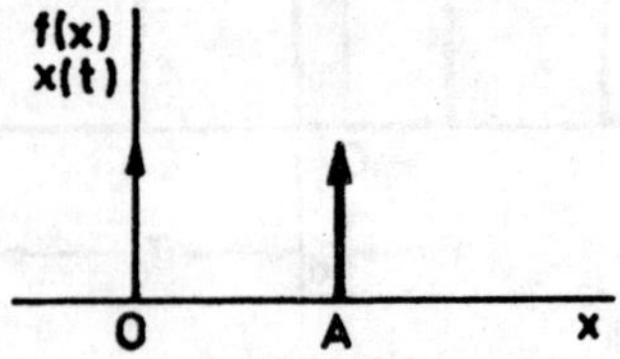

Fig. P. 3.3 (b)

(*b*) By ensemble-averaging, we have

$$E[X(t)] = \int_{-\infty}^{\infty} x\, f_{X(t)}(x)\, dx = \int_{-\infty}^{\infty} x\left[\frac{1}{2}\delta(x) + \frac{1}{2}\delta(x - A)\right] dx = \frac{A}{2}$$

The autocorrelation function of $X(t)$ is,

$$R_X(\tau) = E[X(t + \tau)\, X(t)]$$

Defining the square function $S_{q_{T_0}}(t)$ as the square-wave shown below,

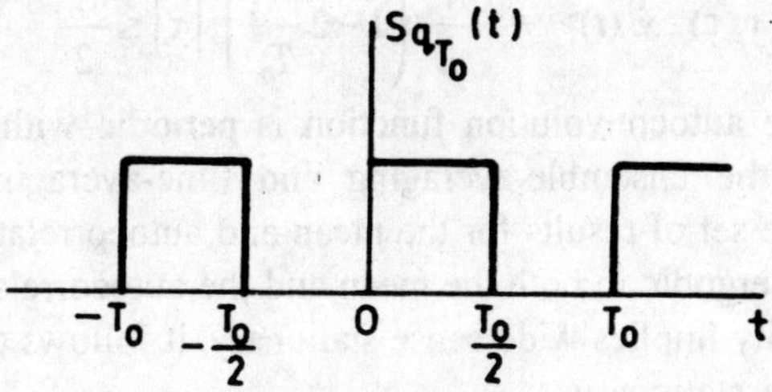

Fig. P. 3.3 (c)

Then,

$$R_X(\tau) = E\left[AS_{q_{T_o}}(t - t_d + \tau)\cdot AS_{q_{T_o}}(t - t_d)\right]$$

$$= A^2 \int_{-\infty}^{\infty} S_{q_{T_o}}(t - t_d + \tau)\cdot S_{q_{T_o}}(t - t_d)\; f_{T_d}(t_d)\cdot dt_d$$

$$= A^2 \int_{-T_o/2}^{T_o/2} S_{q_{T_o}}(t - t_d + \tau)\, S_{q_{T_o}}(t - t_d)\frac{1}{T_o}\, dt_d$$

$$= \frac{A^2}{2}\left(1 - \frac{2|\tau|}{T_o}\right)\cdot |\tau| \le \frac{T_o}{2}$$

Since the wave is periodic with period T_o, $R_X(\tau)$ must also be periodic with period T_o.

(c) On a time-averaging basis, from Fig. P. 3.3, it can inferred that, the mean is,

$$\langle X(t)\rangle = \frac{A}{2}$$

Next, the autocorrelation function,

$$\langle X(t+\tau)\, X(t)\rangle = \frac{1}{T_o}\int_{-T_o/2}^{T_o/2} x(t+\tau)\, x(t)\, dt$$

has its maximum value of $\frac{A^2}{2}$ at $\tau = 0$, and decreases linearly to zero at $\tau = \frac{T_o}{2}$.

Then,

$$<x(t+\tau)\cdot x(t)> = \frac{A^2}{2}\left(1-2\frac{|\tau|}{T_o}\right), |\tau| \le \frac{T_o}{2}$$

Here, the autoconvolution function is periodic with period T_o.

(*d*) Since, the ensemble-averaging and time-averaging procedures yield the same set of results for the mean and autocorrelation functions. Then, $X(t)$ is ergodic in both the mean and the autocorrelation function. Since ergodicity implies wide-sense stationary, it follows that $X(t)$ must be wide-sense stationary.

Problem 3.4: A binary wave consists of a random sequence of symbols 1 and 0, with one basic difference: symbol 1 is now represented by a pulse of amplitude A volts and symbol 0 is represented by zero volts. Show that for this new random binary wave $X(t)$:

(*a*) The autocorrelation function is

$$R_X(\tau) = \begin{cases} \frac{A^2}{4} + \frac{A^2}{4}\left(1-\frac{|\tau|}{T}\right), & |\tau| < T \\ \frac{A^2}{4}, & |\tau| \ge T \end{cases}$$

(*b*) The power spectral density is

$$S_X(f) = \frac{A^2}{4}\delta(f) + \frac{A^2 T}{4}\operatorname{sinc}^2(fT)$$

What is the percentage power contained in the dc component of the binary?

Solution: (*a*)

For $|\tau| > T$, since the random variables $X(t)$ and $X(t+\tau)$ occur in different pulse intervals, therefore $X(t)$ and $X(t+\tau)$ are independent. Then,

$$E[X(t)\,X(t+\tau)] = E[X(t)]\,E[X(t+\tau)],\ |\tau| > T.$$

Since both amplitudes are equally likely, then

$$E[X(t)] = E[x(t+\tau)] = \frac{A}{2}.$$

Therefore, for $|\tau| > T$,

$$R_X(\tau) = E[X(t)]\,E[X(t+\tau)] = \frac{A^2}{4}$$

For the interval

$$|\tau| \le T,$$

the random variables occur in the same pulse interval if $t_d < T - |\tau|$. They do occur in the same pulse interval, then If

$$R_X(\tau) = E[X(t)]\,X(t+\tau) = \frac{A^2}{2} + \frac{1}{2}0^2 = \frac{A^2}{2}$$

Thus we have a conditional expectation

$$E[X(t)\,X(t+\tau)] = \begin{cases} \dfrac{A^2}{2}, & t_d < T - |z| \\ \dfrac{A^2}{4}, & \text{otherwise} \end{cases}$$

Now, Averaging over t_d, we get

$$R_X(\tau) = \int_0^{T-|\tau|} \frac{A^2}{2T} dt_d + \int_{T-|\tau|}^{T} \frac{A^2}{4T} dt_d$$

$$= \left[\frac{A^2}{2T} \cdot t_d \Big|_0^{T-|\tau|}\right] + \left[\frac{A^2}{4T} \cdot t_d \Big|_{T-|\tau|}^{T}\right]$$

$$= \frac{A^2}{4}\left(1 - \frac{|\tau|}{T}\right) + \frac{A^2}{4}, \quad |\tau| \le T$$

(*b*) As we know that the power spectral density is the Fourier transform of the autocorrelation function.

Then, the Fourier transform if,

$$g(\tau) = 1 - \frac{|\tau|}{T}, \quad |\tau| \le T$$

$$= 0, \text{ otherwise}$$

is exprssed as,

$$G(f) = f[g(t)] = T \operatorname{sinc}^2(fT)$$

hence,

$$S_X(f) = \frac{A^2}{4}\delta(f) + \frac{A^2 T}{4}\operatorname{sinc}^2(fT)$$

Now, it should be noted further that,

$$\frac{A^2}{4}\int_{-\infty}^{\infty}\delta(f)\,df = \frac{A^2}{4},$$

$$\frac{A^2}{4}\int_{-\infty}^{\infty}T\,\text{sinc}^2(fT)\,df = \frac{A^2}{4},\quad \int_{-\infty}^{\infty}S_X(f)\,df = R_X(0) = \frac{A^2}{2}.$$

Hence, it can be inferred that half the power is in the dc component.

Problem 3.5: A random process $Y(t)$ consists of a dc component of $\sqrt{\frac{3}{2}}$ volts, a periodic component $g(t)$, and a random component $X(t)$. The correlation function of $Y(t)$ is shown in Fig. P. 3.5.

(*a*) What is the average power of the periodic component $g(t)$?

(*b*) What is the average power of the random component $X(t)$?

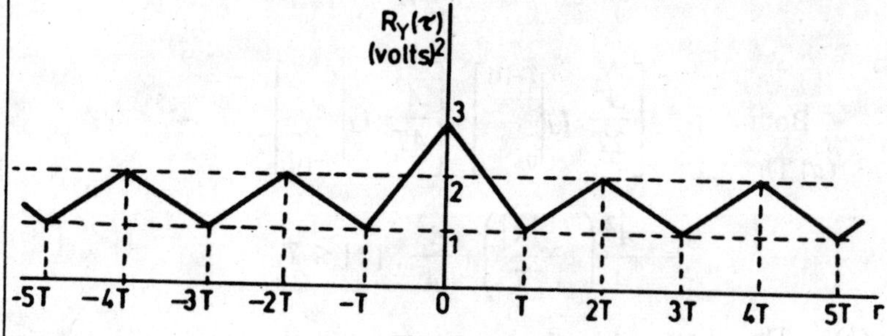

Fig. P. 3.5

Solution: As, $Y(t) = g_p(t) + X(t) + \sqrt{\frac{3}{2}}$

and $g_p(t)$ and $X(t)$ are uncorrelated

$$C_Y(\tau) = C_{g_p}(\tau) + C_X(\tau)$$

where $C_{gp}(\tau)$ is the autocovariance of the periodic component and $C_X(\tau)$ is the autocovariance of the random component. $C_Y(\tau)$ is the plot in Fig. P. 3.5 shifted down by $\frac{3}{2}$, removing the dc component. $C_{gp}(\tau)$ and $C_X(\tau)$ are depicted below,

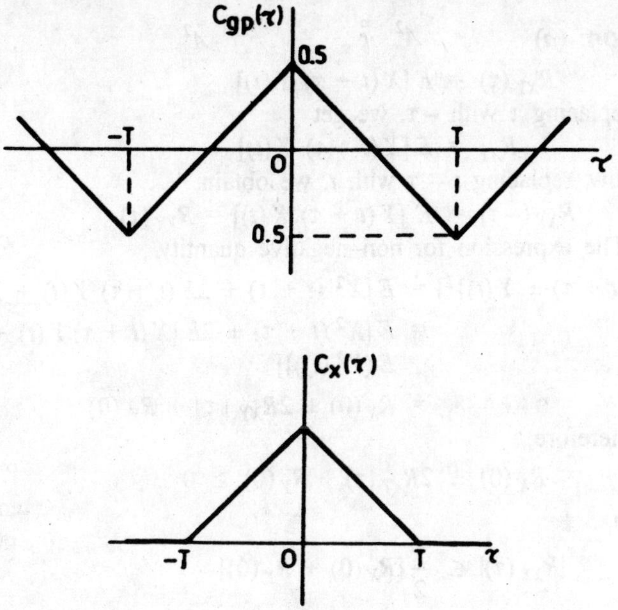

Fig. P. 3.5 (a)

Both $g_p(t)$ and $X(t)$ have zero mean.

(*a*) The average power of the periodic component $g_p(t)$ is,

$$\frac{1}{T_o}\int_{-T_o/2}^{T_o/2} g_p^2(t)\cdot dt = R_{g_p}(0) = \frac{1}{2}$$

(*b*) The average power of the random component $X(t)$ is,

$$E[X^2(t)] = R_X(0) = 1$$

Problem 3.6: Consider a pair of wide-sense stationary random processers $X(t)$ and $Y(t)$. Then, show that the cross-correlation $R_{XY}(\tau)$, and $R_{YX}(\tau)$ of these procesers have the following properties,

(*a*) $R_{XY}(\tau) = R_{YX}(-\tau)$

(*b*) $|R_{YX}(\tau)| \le \frac{1}{2}[R_X(0) + R_Y(0)]$

Where $R_X(\tau)$ and $R_Y(\tau)$ are the autocorrelation function of $X(t)$ and $Y(t)$ respectively.

Solution: (*a*)

$$R_{XY}(\tau) = E[X(t+\tau)\, Y(t)]$$

Replacing τ with $-\tau$, we get

$$R_{XY} = E[X(t-\tau)\, Y(t)]$$

Now, replacing $t - \tau$ with t, we obtain,

$$R_{XY}(-\tau) = E[Y(t+\tau)\, X(t)] = R_{YX}(\tau)$$

(*b*) The expression for non–negative quantity,

$$E[\{X(t+\tau) \pm Y(t)\}^2] = E[X^2(t+\tau) \pm 2X(t+\tau)\, Y(t) + Y^2(t)]$$

$$= E[X^2(t+\tau) \pm 2E[X(t+\tau)\, Y(t) + E(Y^2(t))]]$$

$$= R_X(0) \pm 2R_{XY}|\tau| + R_Y(0)$$

Therefore,

$$R_X(0) \pm 2R_{XY}(\tau) + R_Y(0) \geq 0$$

or,

$$|R_{XY}(\tau)| \leq \frac{1}{2}[R_X(0) + R_Y(0)]$$

Problem 3.7: A wide-sense stationary random process $X(t)$ is applied to a linear time-invariant filter of impulse response $h(t)$, producing an output $Y(t)$.

(a) Show that the corss-correlation function $R_{YX}(\tau)$ of the output $Y(t)$ and the input $X(t)$ is equal to the impulse response $h(\tau)$ convolved with the auto-correlation function $R_X(\tau)$ of hte input, as shown by

$$R_{YX}(\tau) = \int_{-\infty}^{\infty} h(u)\, R_X(\tau - u)\, du$$

Show that the second cross-correlation function $R_{XY}(\tau)$ equals

$$R_{XY}(\tau) = \int_{-\infty}^{\infty} h(-u)\, R_X(\tau - u)\, du$$

(*b*) Find the cross-spectral densities $S_{YX}(f)$ and $S_{XY}(f)$.

(*c*) Assuming that $X(t)$ is a white noise process with zero mean and power spectral density $\frac{N_0}{2}$, show that

$$R_{YX}(\tau) = \frac{N_0}{2} h(\tau)$$

Comment on the practical significance of this result.

Solution: (*a*) The cross-correlation function $R_{YX}(\tau)$ is given as,

$$R_{YX}(\tau) = E[Y(t+\tau)\,X(t)]$$

The $Y(t)$ and $X(t)$ are related by the equation

$$Y(t) = \int_{-\infty}^{\infty} X(u)\,h(t-u)\,du$$

Then, cross-correlation function $R_{XY}(\tau)$ is given by,

$$R_{XY}(\tau) = E\left[\int_{-\infty}^{\infty} X(u)X(t)\,h(t+\tau-u)\,du\right]$$

$$= \int_{-\infty}^{\infty} h(t+\tau-u)\,E[X(u)\,X(t)]\,du$$

Replacing $t + \tau - u$ by u,
We have, $R_{XY}(\tau)$ can be interpreted as,

$$R_{YX}(\tau) = \int_{-\infty}^{\infty} h(u)\,R_X(\tau-u)\,du$$

(*b*) Since

$$R_{XY}(\tau) = R_{YX}(-\tau),$$

then we have

$$R_{XY}(\tau) = \int_{-\infty}^{\infty} h(u)\,R_X(-\tau-u)\,du$$

Since $R_X(\tau)$ is an even function of τ, then

$$R_{XY}(\tau) = \int_{-\infty}^{\infty} h(u)\,R_X(\tau+u)\,du$$

Replacing u by $-u$, we get

$$R_{XY}(\tau) = \int_{-\infty}^{\infty} h(-u)\,R_X(\tau-u)\,du$$

(*c*) If $X(t)$ is a white noise process with zero mean and power spectral density $\frac{N_0}{2}$. then, $R_X(\tau)$ can be expressed as,

$$R_X(\tau) = \frac{N_0}{2}\delta(\tau)$$

Then, cross-correlation function $R_{YX}(\tau)$ is given by,

$$R_{YX}(\tau) = \frac{N_0}{2}\int_{-\infty}^{\infty} h(u)\,\delta(\tau - u)\,du$$

Using the shifting property of the delta function, we get

$$R_{YX}(\tau) = \int_{-\infty}^{\infty} h(\tau)$$

i.e., $$h(\tau) = \frac{2}{N_0}R_{YX}(\tau)$$

It implies that we can measure the impulse response of the filter by applying a white noise of power spectral density $\frac{N_0}{2}$ to the filter intput, cross-correlating the filter output with the input, and then multiplying the result by $\frac{2}{N_0}$.

Problem 3.8: The power spectral density of a random process $X(t)$ is shown in Fig. P. 3.8.

(*a*) Determine and sketch the autocorrelation function $R_X(\tau)$ of $X(t)$.

(*b*) What is the dc power contained in $X(t)$?

(*c*) What is the ac power contained in $X(t)$?

(*d*) What sampling rates will give uncorrelated samples of $X(t)$? Are the samples statistically independent?

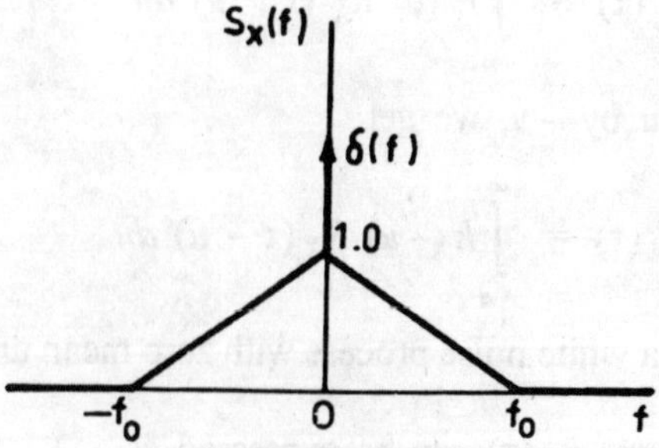

Fig. P. 3.8

Solution: (*a*) $S_X(f)$ has two components,

One $\delta(f)$ and another a triangular component of unit amplitude and width $2f_0$, centered at the origin, whose inverse Fourier transform is $f_0 \operatorname{sinc}^2(f_0\tau)$.

Hence, $R_X(\tau) = 1 + f_o \operatorname{sinc}^2(f_0\tau)$ depicted below,

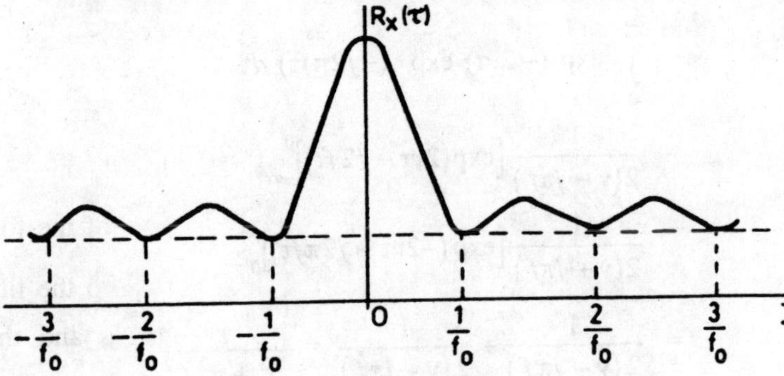

Fig. P. 3.8 (a)

(*b*) Since $R_X(\tau)$ contains a constant component of amplutude 1, it follows that the dc power contained in $X(t)$ is 1.

(*c*) The mean-square value of $X(t)$ is,

$$E[X^2(t)] = R_X(0) = 1 + f_0$$

The ac power contained in $X(f)$ is equal to f_0.

(*d*) If the sampling rate is $\frac{f_0}{n}$, where n is an integer, the samples are uncorrelated. They are not, however, statistically independent. They would be statistically independent if $X(t)$ were a Gaussian process.

Problem 3.9: A *random telegraph singal* $X(t)$, characterized by the autocorrelation function

$$R_X(\tau) = \exp(-2v|\tau|)$$

where v is a constant, is applied to the low-pass RC filter of Fig. P. 3.9. Determine the power spectral density and autocorrelation function of the random process at the filter output.

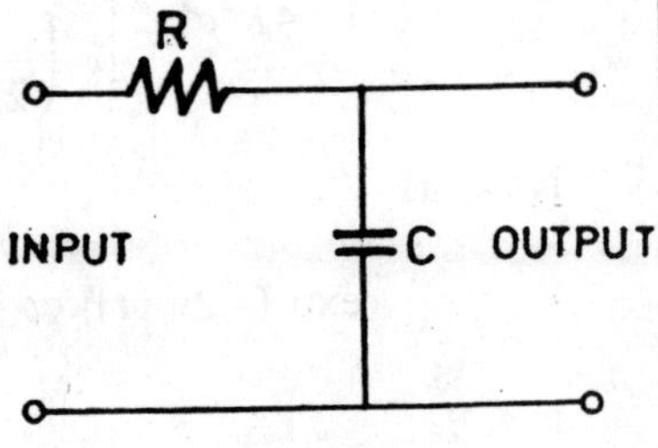

Fig. P. 3.9

Solution: Power spectral density of the $R_X(\tau)$ is given as,

$$S_X(f) = \int_{-\infty}^{\infty} R_X(\tau) \cdot \exp[-j2\pi f\tau]\, d\tau$$

$$= \int_{-\infty}^{\infty} \exp(+2v\tau) \exp(-j2\pi f\tau)\, d\tau + \int_{0}^{\infty} \exp(-2v\tau) \exp(-j2\pi f\tau)\, d\tau$$

$$= \frac{1}{2(v - j\pi f)} \left[\exp(2v\tau - j2f\tau)\right]_{-\infty}^{0} - \frac{1}{2(v + j\pi f)} \left[\exp(-2v\tau - j2\pi f\tau)\right]_{0}^{\infty}$$

$$= \frac{1}{2(v - j\pi f)} + \frac{1}{2(v + j\pi f)} = \frac{v}{v^2 + \pi^2 f^2}$$

The transfer function of the filter is,

$$H(f) = \frac{1}{1 + j2\pi f RC}$$

Then, Power spectral density at the output is,

$$S_Y(f) = [H(f)]^2 S_X(f)$$

$$= \frac{v}{[1 + (2\pi f RC)^2][v^2 + \pi^2 f^2]}$$

Expanding $S_y(f)$ in partial fraction, we have

$$S_X(f) = \frac{v}{1 - 4R^2c^2v^2} \left(-\frac{1}{\left(\frac{1}{2RC}\right)^2 + \pi^2 f^2} + \frac{1}{v^2 + \pi^2 f^2} \right)$$

Now, as

$$\exp(-2v\,|t|) \Leftrightarrow \frac{v}{v^2 + \pi^2 f^2}$$

and,

$$\exp\left(-\frac{|t|}{RC}\right) \Leftrightarrow \frac{\frac{1}{2}RC}{\left(\frac{1}{2RC}\right)^2 + \pi^2 f^2}$$

Hence,

$$R_Y(\tau) = \frac{\nu}{1 - 4R^2C^2\nu^2}\left[\frac{1}{\nu}\exp(-2\nu|\tau|) - 2RC\cdot\exp\left(-\frac{|\tau|}{RC}\right)\right]$$

Problem 3.10: The output of an oscillator is described by

$$X(t) = A\cos(2\pi ft + \Theta),$$

where A is a constant, and f and Θ are independent random variables. The probability density function of Θ is defined by

$$f_\Theta(\theta) = \begin{cases} \frac{1}{2\pi}, & 0 \le \theta \le 2\pi \\ 0, & \text{otherwise} \end{cases}$$

Find the power spectral density of $X(t)$ in terms of the probability density function of the frequency f. What happens to this power spectral density when the frequency f assumes a constant value?

Solution: $R_X(\tau) = E[X(t+\tau)X(t)]$

$$= A^2E[\cos(2\pi Ft + 2\pi f\tau - \Theta)\cos(2\pi Ft - \Theta)]$$

$$= \frac{A^2}{2}E[\cos(4\pi Ft + 2\pi F\tau - 2\Theta) + \cos(2\pi F\tau)]$$

Since $f_\Theta(\theta)$ is uniformly distributed over 2π radius, we have

$$R_X(\tau) = \frac{A^2}{2}E[\cos(2\pi F\tau)] = \frac{A^2}{2}\int_{-\infty}^{\infty} f_F(f)\cos(2\pi f\tau)\,df \quad \ldots(1)$$

As, $$R_X(\tau) = \int_{-\infty}^{\infty} S_X(f)\cos(2\pi f\tau)\,df \quad \ldots(2)$$

Comparing eqn (1) and eqn (2), we get

$$S_X(f) = \frac{A^2}{2}\cdot f_F(f)$$

When the frequency assumes a constant value, f_c, then

$$f_F(f) = \frac{1}{2}[\delta(f - f_c) + \frac{1}{2}\delta(f + f_c)]$$

then,

$$S_X(f) = \frac{A^2}{4}\delta(f - f_c) + \frac{A^2}{4}\delta(f + f_c)$$

Problem 3.11: A stationary Gaussian process $X(t)$ with mean μ_X and variance σ^2_X is passed through two linear filters with impulse responses $h_1(t)$ and $h_2(t)$, yielding processes $Y(t)$ and $Z(t)$, as shown in Fig. P. 3.11.

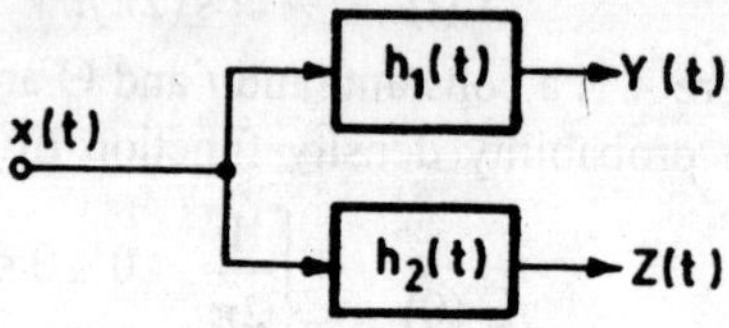

Fig. P. 3.11

(a) Determine the joint probability density function of the random variables $Y(t_1)$ and $Z(t_2)$

(b) What conditions are necessary and sufficient to ensure that $Y(t_1)$ and $Z(t_2)$ are statistically independent?

Solution: (a) The random variable $Y(t_1)$ is obtained by observing the filter output of impulse response $h_1(t)$, at time t_1 is expressed as,

$$Y(t_1) = \int_{-\infty}^{\infty} X(t_1 - \tau)\, h_1(\tau)\, d\tau$$

and the expected value of $y(t_1)$ is,

$$m_{Y_1} = E[y(t_1)] = H_1(0)\, m_X$$

where

$$H_1(0) = \int_{-\infty}^{\infty} h_1(\tau)\, d\tau$$

The ramdon variable $Z(t_2)$ is obtained by observing the filter output of impulse response $h_2(t)$, at time t_2, is expressed as,

$$Z(t_2) = \int_{-\infty}^{\infty} X(t_2 - u)\, h_2(u)\, du$$

The expected value of $z(t_2)$ is therefore,

$$m_{Z_2} = E[Z(t_2)] = H_2(0)\, m_X$$

where

$$H_2(0) = \int_{-\infty}^{\infty} h_2(u)\, du$$

Now, the covariance of $Y(t_1)$ and $Z(t_2)$ is

$$\begin{aligned}\text{cov}\,[Y(t_1)\, Z(t_2)] &= E[Y(t_1) - \mu_{Y_1})\,(Z(t_2) - \mu_{Z_2})] \\ &= E\,[\int_{-\infty}^{\infty}\int_{-\infty}^{\infty} (X(t_1 - \tau) - \mu_X)\,(X(t_2 - u) - \mu_X) \times \\ &\quad h_1(\tau)\, h_2(u)\, d\tau\, du] \\ &= \int_{-\infty}^{\infty}\int_{-\infty}^{\infty} E[(X(t_1 - \tau) - \mu_X)\,(X(t_2 - u) - \mu_X)] \times \\ &\quad h_1(\tau)\, h_2(u)\, d\tau\, du] \\ &= [\int_{-\infty}^{\infty}\int_{-\infty}^{\infty} C_X\,(t_1 - t_2 - \tau + u)\, h_1(\tau)\, h_2(u)\, d\tau\, du\end{aligned}$$

where $C_X(\tau)$ is the autocovariance function of $X(t)$. Next, note that the variance of $Y(t_1)$ is

$$\sigma_{Y_1}^2 = E\{[y(t_1) - \mu_{y_1}]^2\} = \int_{-\infty}^{\infty}\int_{-\infty}^{\infty} k_X(\tau - u)\, h_1(\tau)\, h_1(u)\, d\tau\, du$$

and the variance of $Z(t_2)$ is

$$\sigma_{Z_2}^2 = E\{[Z(t_2) - \mu_{Z_2}]^2\} = \int_{-\infty}^{\infty}\int_{-\infty}^{\infty} C_X(\tau - u)\, h_2(\tau)\, h_2(u)\, d\tau\, du$$

The correlation coefficient of $Y(t_1)$ and $Z(t_2)$ is

$$\rho = \frac{\text{cov}\left[Y(t_1)\, Z(t_2)\right]}{\sigma_{Y_1}\sigma_{Z_2}}$$

Since $X(t)$ is a Gaussian process, it follows that $Y(t_1)$ and $Z(t_2)$ are jointly Gaussian with a probability density function given by

$$f_{Y(t_1),\, Z(t_2)}(y_1, z_2) = k \exp[-Q(y_1, z_2)]$$

where $k = \dfrac{1}{2\pi\sigma_{Y_1}\sigma_{Z_2}\sqrt{1-\rho^2}}$

$Q(y_1, z_2) =$

$$\frac{1}{2(1-\rho^2)}\left[\left(\frac{y_1-\mu_{Y1}}{\sigma_{Y_1}}\right)^2 - 2\rho\left(\frac{y_1-\mu_{Y1}}{\sigma_{Y_1}}\right)\left(\frac{z_2-\mu_{Z2}}{\sigma_{Z_2}}\right) + \left(\frac{z_2-\mu_{Z2}}{\sigma_{Z_2}}\right)^2\right]$$

(*b*) The ramdon variables $Y(t_1)$ and $Z(t_2)$ are uncorrelated if and only if their covariance is zero. Since $Y(t)$ and $Z(t)$ are jointly Gaussian processes, it follows that $Y(t_1)$ and $Z(t_2)$ are statistically independent if Cov $[Y(t_1)\ Z(t_2)]$ is zero. Therefore, the necessary and sufficient condition for $Y(t_1)$ and $Z(t_2)$ to be statistically independent is that

$$\int_{-\infty}^{\infty}\int_{-\infty}^{\infty} k_X(t_1 - t_2 - \tau + u)\, h_1(\tau)\, h_2(u)\, d\tau\, du = 0$$

for choices of t_1 and t_2.

Problem 3.12: A stationary, Gaussian process $X(t)$ with zero mean and power spectral density $S_X(f)$ is applied to a linear filter whose impulse response $h(t)$ is shown in Fig. P. 3.12. A sample Y is taken of the random process at the filter output at time T.

(*a*) Determine the mean and variance of Y.

(*b*) What is the probability density function of Y?

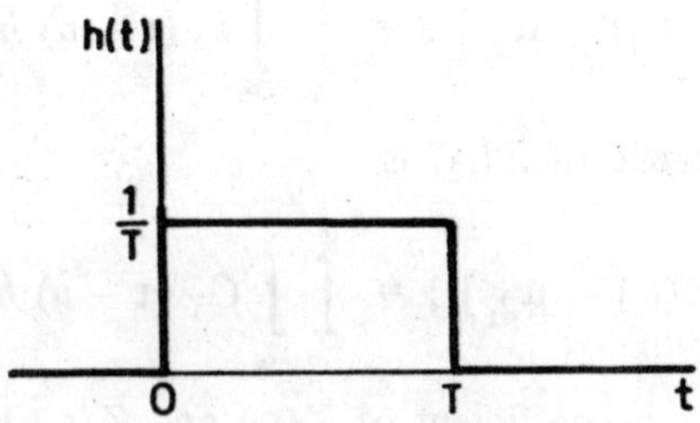

Fig. P. 3.12

Solution: (*a*) The filter output is,

$$Y(t) = \int_{-\infty}^{\infty} h(\tau)\, X(t-\tau)\, d\tau = \frac{1}{T}\int_{0}^{T} X(T-\tau)\, d\tau$$

putting $T - \tau = u$,

we have sample value of $Y(t)$ at $t = T$ equals,

$$Y = \frac{1}{T}\int_0^T X(u)\, du$$

The mean of Y is then,

$$E(Y) = E\left[\frac{1}{T}\int_0^T X(u)\, du\right] = \frac{1}{T}\int_0^T E[X(u)]\, du = 0$$

and, the variance,

$$\sigma^2_Y = E[Y^2] - \{E[Y]\}^2 = R_Y(0)$$

$$= \int_{-\infty}^{\infty} S_Y(f)\, df = \int_{-\infty}^{\infty} S_X(f)\, |H(f)|^2\, df$$

But, $H(f) = \int_{-\infty}^{\infty} h(t) \cdot \exp(-j2\pi ft)\, dt$

$$= \frac{1}{T}\int_0^T \exp(-j2\pi ft)\, dt = \frac{1}{T}\left[\frac{\exp(-j2\pi ft)}{-j2\pi f}\right]_0^T$$

$$= \frac{1}{j2\pi fT}\, 1 - \exp(-j2\pi fT)]$$

$$= \text{sinc}(fT)\, \exp(-j\pi T)$$

Hence,

$$\sigma^2_Y = \int_{-\infty}^{\infty} S_X \sin^2 c(fT)\, df$$

(*b*) Since, the filter input is Gaussian, it follows that Y is also Gaussian. Hence the pdf of Y is,

$$f_Y(y) = \frac{1}{\sqrt{2\pi}\,\sigma_Y} \exp\left(\frac{-y^2}{2\sigma_y^2}\right)$$

Where σ^2_Y is defined above.

Problem 3.13: Consider a white Gaussian noise process of zero mean and power spectral density $\frac{N_0}{2}$ that is applied to the input of the high-pass RL filter shown in Fig. P. 3.13.

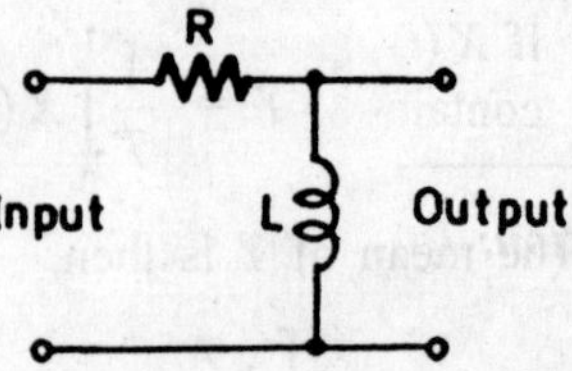

Fig. P. 3.13

(*a*) Find the autocorrelation function and power spectral density of the random process at the output of the filter.

(*b*) What are the mean and variance of this output?

Solution: (a) The power spectral density of the noise at the filter output is,

$$S_N(f) = \frac{N_0}{2}\left|\frac{j2\pi f L}{R + j2\pi f L}\right|^2 = \frac{N_0}{2}\frac{\left(2\pi f \frac{L}{R}\right)^2}{1+\left(2\pi f \frac{L}{R}\right)^2}$$

$$= \frac{N_0}{2}\left[1 - \frac{1}{1+\left(2\pi f \frac{L}{R}\right)^2}\right]$$

Then, autocorrelation function,

$$R_N(\tau) = \frac{N_0}{2}\left[\delta(\tau) - \frac{R}{2L}\exp\left(-\frac{R}{L}|\tau|\right)\right]$$

(*b*) The mean of the filter output is equal to $H(0)$ times the mean of the filter intput. The process at the filter input has zero mean. Here $H'(f) = 0$ at $f = 0$, which tells that the filter output has also zero mean. The mean-square value of the filter output is equal to $R_N(0)$.

Then the variance of the filter output $\sigma^2_N = R_N(0)$. As $R_N(\tau)$ contains a delta function $\delta(\tau)$ centered at $\tau = 0$, then σ^2_N will be infinitely large.

Problem 3.14: Prove the following two properties of the autocorrelation function $R_X(\tau)$ of a random process $X(t)$:

(*a*) **If $X(t)$ contains a dc component equal to A, then $R_X(\tau)$ will contain a constant component equal to A^2.**
(*b*) **If $X(t)$ contains a sinusodial component, then $R_X(\tau)$ will also contain a sinusoidal component of the same frequency.**

Solution: (*a*) let

$$X(t) = A + Y(t)$$

Where A is a constant and $Y(t)$ is a zero–mena random process. The autocorrelation function of $X(t)$ is,

$$\begin{aligned} R_X(\tau) &= E[X(t+\tau)\,X(t)] = E\{[A + Y(t+\tau)]\,[A + Y(t)]\} \\ &= E[A^2 + A\,Y(t+\tau) + A\,Y(t) + Y(t+\tau)\,Y(t)] \\ &= A^2 + R_Y(\tau)\ \{\because E[Y(t)] = 0, \text{ and } E[Y(t+\tau)] = 0\} \end{aligned}$$

(*b*) Let $\quad X(t) = A_c \cos(2\pi f_c t + \theta) + z(t)$

Where $A_c \cos(2\pi f_c t + \theta)$ represents the sinusoidal component of $X(t)$ and θ is a random process variable. Then, the autocorrelation function of $X(t)$ is,

$$\begin{aligned} R_X(\tau) &= E[X(t+\tau)\,X(t)] \\ &= E\{[A_c \cos(2\pi f_c t + 2\pi f_c \tau + \theta] + z(t+\tau)\} \\ &\qquad\qquad [A_c \cos(2\pi f_c t + \theta) + z(t)] \\ &= E[A_c^2 \cos(2\pi f_c t + 2\pi f_c \tau + \theta) \cdot \cos(2\pi f_c t + \theta)] + \\ &\quad E[Z(t+\tau)\,A_c \cos(2\pi f_c t + \theta)] + E[A_c \cos(2\pi f_c t + \\ &\quad 2\pi f_c \tau\, t + \theta)\,Z(t)] + E[2\,(t+\tau)\,Z(t)] \\ &= \left(\frac{A_c^2}{2}\right) \cos(2\pi f_c \tau) + R_Z(\tau) \end{aligned}$$

It can be inferred that $R_X(\tau)$ contains a sinusoidal component of the same frequency as $X(t)$.

Problem 3.15: Consider two linear filters connected in cascade as in Fig. P. 3.15. Let $X(t)$ be a wide–sense stationary process with autocorrelation function $R_X(\tau)$. The random process appearing at the first filter output is $V(t)$ and that at the second filter output is $Y(t)$.
(*a*) Find the autocorrelation function of $Y(t)$.
(*b*) Find the cross-correlation function $R_{VY}(\tau)$ of $V(t)$ and $Y(t)$.

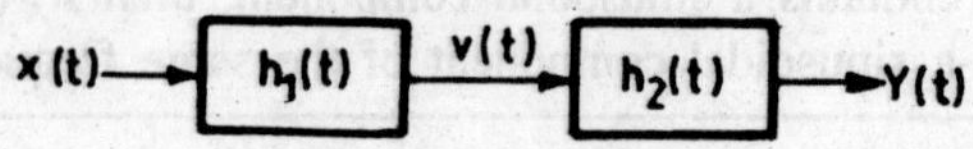

Fig. P. 3.15

Solution: (*a*) The cascade connection of the two filters is equivalent to a filter with impulse response

$$h(t) = \int_{-\infty}^{\infty} h_1(u)\, h_2(t-u) \cdot du$$

The autocorelation function of $Y(t)$ is expressed by,

$$R_Y(\tau) = \int_{-\infty}^{\infty}\int_{-\infty}^{\infty} h(\tau_1)\, h(\tau_2)\, R_X(\tau - \tau_1 + \tau_2)\, d\tau_1\, d\tau_2$$

(*b*) The cross-correlation function of $V(t)$ and $Y(t)$ is,

$$R_{VY}(\tau) = E[V(t+\tau)\, Y(t)]$$

The $Y(t)$ and $V(t+\tau)$ are related as,

$$Y(t) = \int_{-\infty}^{\infty} V(\lambda)\, h_2(t-\lambda)\, d\lambda$$

Then, $$R_{VY}(\tau) = E\left[V(t+\tau)\int_{-\infty}^{\infty} V(\lambda)\, h_2(t-\lambda)\, d\lambda\right]$$

$$= \int_{-\infty}^{\infty} h_2(t-\lambda)\, E[V(t+\tau)\, V(\lambda)]\, d\lambda$$

$$= \int_{-\infty}^{\infty} h_2(t-\lambda)\, R_V(t+\tau-\lambda)\, d\lambda$$

Putting λ by $t - \lambda$, we have

$$R_{VY}(\tau) = \int_{-\infty}^{\infty} h_2(\lambda)\, R_v(\tau+\lambda)\, d\lambda$$

hence, R_v is related to $R_X(\tau)$ as,

$$R_v = \int_{-\infty}^{\infty}\int_{-\infty}^{\infty} h_1(\tau_1)\, h_2(\tau_2)\, R_X(\tau - \tau_1 + \tau_2)\, d\tau_1\, d\tau_2.$$

Problem 3.16: A white noise $w(t)$ of power spectral density $\frac{N_0}{2}$ is applied to a *Butterworth* low-pass filter of order n, whose amplitude response is defined by

$$|H(f)| = \frac{1}{\left[1+\left(\frac{f}{f_0}\right)^{2n}\right]^{\frac{1}{2}}}$$

(*a*) Determine the noise equivalent bandwidth for this low-pass filter.

(*b*) What is the limiting value of the noise equivalent bandwidth as n approaches infinity?

Solution: (*a*) The noise-equivalent bandwidth is given by,

$$w_N = \frac{\frac{1}{2}\cdot\int_{-\infty}^{\infty}[H(f)]^2\,df}{H^2(0)} = \frac{1}{2}\int_{-\infty}^{\infty}\frac{df}{\left[1+\left(\frac{f}{f_o}\right)^{2n}\right]} \quad [\text{sinc } H(0) = 1]$$

$$= \frac{\pi f_0}{2n\sin\left(\frac{\pi}{2n}\right)} = \frac{f_0}{\operatorname{sinc}\left(\frac{1}{2n}\right)}$$

(*b*) When $n \to \infty$, then

$$w_N = f_0 \cdot \lim_{n\to\infty}\frac{1}{\operatorname{sinc}\left(\frac{1}{2n}\right)} = f_0$$

Problem 3.17: White Gaussian noise of zero mean and power spectral density $\frac{N_0}{2}$ is applied to the filtering scheme shown in Fig. P. 3.17. The noise at the lowpass filter output is denoted by $n(t)$.

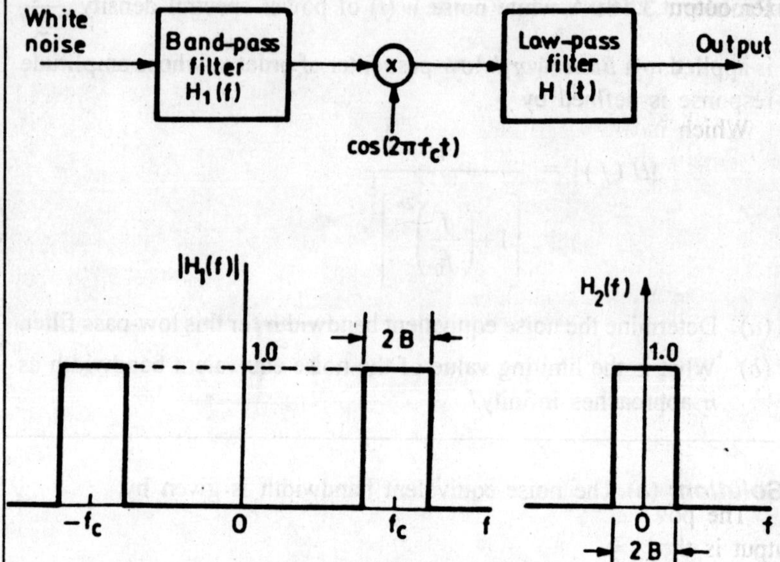

Fig. P. 3.17

(*a*) Find the power spectral density and the autocorrelation function of $n(t)$.

(*b*) Find the mean and variance of $n(t)$.

(*c*) What is the maximum rate at which $n(t)$ can be sampled so that the resulting samples are essentially uncorrelated?

Solution: (*a*) Let $S_1(f)$ denote the power spectral density of the noise at the first filter output. The dependence of $S_1(f)$ on frequency is illustrated below.

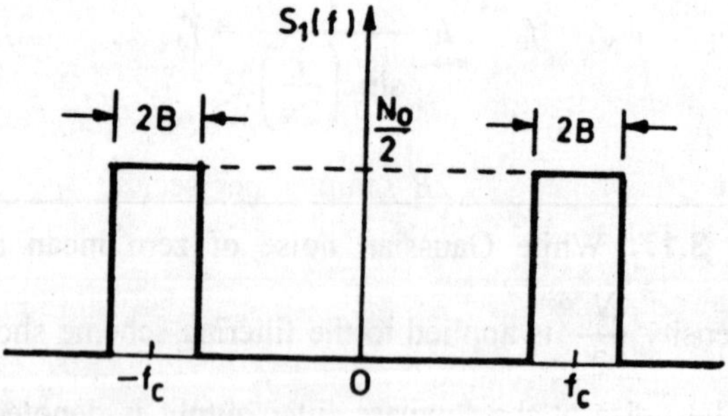

Fig. P. 3.17 (a)

Let $S_2(f)$ denote the power spectral density of the noise at the mixer output, then, we may write

$$S_2(f) = \frac{1}{4}[S_1(f+f_c) + S_1(f-f_c)]$$

Which is illustrated below.

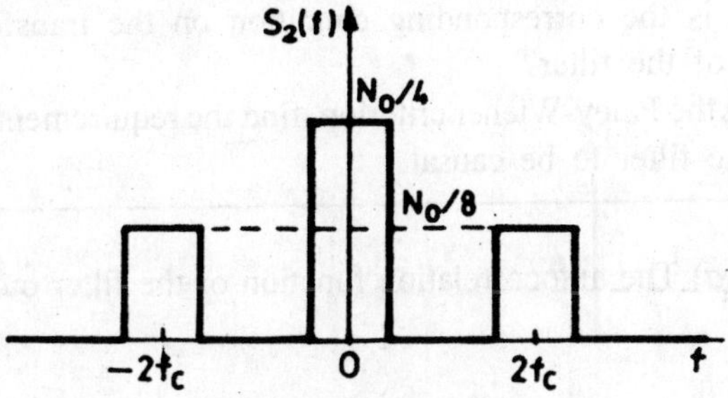

Fig. P. 3.17 (b)

The power spectral density of the noise $n(t)$ at the second filter output is therefore defined by

$$S_0(f) = \begin{cases} \frac{N_0}{4}, & -B < f < B \\ 0, & \text{otherwise} \end{cases}$$

The autocorrelation function of the noise $n(t)$ is

$$R_0(\tau) = \frac{N_0 B}{2} \sin c\,(2BC)$$

(*b*) The mean value of the noise at the system output is zero hence, the variance and mean-square value of this noise are the same. Now the total area under $S_0(f)$ is equal to $\left(\frac{N_0}{4}\right)(2B) = \frac{N_0 B}{2}$. The variance of the noise at the system output is therefore $\frac{N_0 B}{2}$.

(*c*) The maximum rate at which $n(t)$ can be sampled for the resulting samples to be uncorrelated is $2B$ samples per second.

Problem 3.18: Let $X(t)$ be a stationary process with zero mean, autocorrelation function $R_X(\tau)$, and power spectral density $S_X(f)$. We are required to find a linear filter with impulse resopnse $h(t)$, such that the filter output is $X(t)$ when the input is whit enoise of power spectral density $\frac{N_0}{2}$

(a) Determine the condition that the impulse response $h(t)$ must satisfy in order to achieve this requirement.

(b) What is the corresponding condition on the transfer function $H(f)$ of the filter?

(c) Using the Paley-Wiener criterion, find the requirement on $S_X(f)$ for the filter to be causal.

Solution: (a) The autocorrelation function of the filter output is given by

$$R_X(\tau) = \int_{-\infty}^{\infty}\int_{-\infty}^{\infty} h(\tau_1)\, h(\tau_2) R_W(\tau - \tau_1 + \tau_2)\, d\tau_1\, d\tau_2$$

Since

$R_W(\tau) = \frac{N_0}{2}\delta(\tau)$, then the impulse response $h(t)$ of the filter must satisfy following conditions

$$R_X(\tau) = \frac{N_0}{2}\int_{-\infty}^{\infty}\int_{-\infty}^{\infty} h(\tau_1)\, h(\tau_2)\, \delta(\tau - \tau_1 + \tau_2)\, d\tau_1\, d\tau_2$$

$$= \frac{N_0}{2}\int_{-\infty}^{\infty} h(\tau + \tau_2)\, h(\tau_2)\, d\tau_2$$

(b) For the filter output to have a power spectral density equal to $S_X(f)$, we have to choose the transfer function $H(f)$ of the filter such that

$$S_X(f) = \frac{N_0}{2}|H(f)|^2$$

or $$|H(f)| = \sqrt{\frac{2S_X(f)}{N_0}}$$

(c) For the filter to be causal, it should satisfy the Paley–Wiener criterion which is given as,

$$\int_{-\infty}^{\infty} \frac{|\ln [H(f)]|}{1+f^2} df < \infty$$

or equivalently
$$\int_{-\infty}^{\infty} \frac{|\ln S_X(f)|}{1+f^2} df < \infty$$

Problem 3.19: Consider a narrow-band noise $n(t)$ with its Hilbert transform denoted by $\hat{n}$.

(*a*) Show that the cross-correlation functions of $n(t)$ and $\hat{n}(t)$ are given by

$$R_{N\hat{N}}(\tau) = -\hat{R}_N(\tau)$$

and

$$R_{\hat{N}N}(\tau) = \hat{R}_N(\tau)$$

where $\hat{R}_N(\tau)$ is the Hilbert transform of the autocorrelation function $R_N(\tau)$ of $n(t)$. *Hint:* Use the formula

$$\hat{n}(t) = \frac{1}{\pi}\int_{-\infty}^{\infty} \frac{n(\lambda)}{t-\lambda} d\lambda$$

(*b*) Show that $R_{N\hat{N}}(0) = 0$

Solution: (*a*) The Hilbert transform of $n(t)$ is given by

$$\hat{n}(t) = \frac{1}{\pi}\int_{-\infty}^{\infty} \frac{n(\lambda)}{t-\lambda} d\lambda$$

Then, the cross-correlation function of $n(t)$ and $\hat{n}(t)$ can be expressed as

$$\hat{R}_{NN}(\tau) = E[n(t+\tau)\ \hat{n}(t)] = E\left[n(t+\tau) \cdot \frac{1}{\pi}\int_{-\infty}^{\infty} \frac{n(\lambda)}{t-\lambda} d\lambda\right]$$

$$= \frac{1}{\pi}\int_{-\infty}^{\infty} \frac{1}{t-\lambda} E[n(t+\tau)\, n(\lambda)]\, d\lambda$$

$$= \frac{1}{\pi}\int_{-\infty}^{\infty} \frac{R_N(t+\tau-\lambda)}{t-\lambda}\, d\lambda \qquad \text{...(1)}$$

where $R_N(\tau)$ is the autocorrelation function of $n(t)$.

Now, let $\quad u = t + \tau - \lambda.$

$\hat{R}_{NN}(\tau)$ can be written as

$$\hat{R}_{NN}(\tau) = \frac{1}{n}\int_{\infty}^{-\infty} \frac{R_N(u)}{u-\tau}(-du) = \frac{1}{n}\int_{-\infty}^{\infty} \frac{R_N(u)}{u-\tau}\, du \qquad \text{...(2)}$$

$$= -\hat{R}_N(t)$$

where $R_N(\tau)$ is the Hilbert transform of the autocorrelation function of $n(t)$ from the properties of correlation functions, we have

$$R_{NN}(\tau) = R_{NN}(-\tau)$$

or, $$R_{NN}(\tau) = \frac{1}{\pi}\int_{-\infty}^{\infty} \frac{R_N(u)}{u-\tau}\, du$$

or, $R_{NN}(\tau) = \hat{R}_{NN}(\tau)$ **Proved**

(*b*) Pulling $\tau = 0$, in eqn (2), we get

$$\hat{R}_{NN}(0) = \frac{1}{\pi}\int_{-\infty}^{\infty} \frac{R_N(u)}{u}\, du.$$

Since $R_N(u)$ is an even function of u, then it follows that the integrand $\frac{R_N(u)}{u}$ is an odd function of u. The integral from $-\infty$ to $+\infty$ of an odd function is zero. Hence,

$$\hat{R}_{NN}(0) = 0$$

Accordingly, $n(t)$ and $\hat{n}(t)$ are orthogonal.

Problem 3.20: A narrow-band noise $n(t)$ has zero mean and autocorrelation function $R_N(\tau)$. Its power spectral density $S_N(f)$ is centered about $\pm f_c$. The quadrature components $n_I(t)$ and $n_Q(t)$ of $n(t)$ are defined by the weighted sums

$$n_I(t) = n(t)\cos(2\pi f_c t) + \hat{n}(t)\sin(2\pi f_c t)$$

and

$$n_Q(t) = \hat{n}(t)\cos(2\pi f_c t) + n(t)\sin(2\pi f_c t)$$

show that $n_I(t)$ and $n_Q(t)$ have the correlation functions

$$R_{N_I}(\tau) = R_{N_Q}(\tau) = R_N(\tau)\cos(2\pi f_c\tau) + \hat{R}_N(\tau)\sin(2\pi f_c\tau)$$

and

$$R_{N_I N_Q}(\tau) = R_{N_Q N_I}(\tau) = R_N(\tau)\sin(2\pi f_c\tau) - \hat{R}_N(\tau)\cos(2\pi f_c\tau)$$

Solution: The autocorrelation of $n_I(t)$ is expressed by

$$\begin{aligned} R_N(\tau) &= E[n_I(t+\tau)\, n_I(t)] \\ &= E\{[n(t+\tau)\cos(2\pi f_c t + 2\pi f_c\tau) + \hat{n}(t+\tau) \\ &\quad \sin(2\pi f_c t + 2\pi f_c t)]\cdot[n(t)\cos(2\pi f_c t) + \hat{n}(t) \\ &\quad \sin(2\pi f_c t)]\} \\ &= E[n(t+\tau)\, n(t)]\cos(2\pi f_c t + 2\pi f_c\tau)\cos(2\pi f_c t) \\ &\quad + E[\hat{n}(t+\tau)\,\hat{n}(t)]\sin(2\pi f_c t + 2\pi f_c\tau)\sin(2\pi f_c t) \\ &\quad + E[n(t+\tau)\,\hat{n}(t)]\cos(2\pi f_c t + 2\pi f_c\tau)\sin(2\pi f_c t) \\ &\quad + E[\hat{n}(t+\tau)\, n(t)]\sin(2\pi f_c t + 2\pi f_c\tau)\sin(2\pi f_c t) \end{aligned}$$

Now, using the relations for the auto-correlation functions, we get

$$\begin{aligned} E[n(t+\tau)\, n(t)] &= R_N(\tau) \\ E[\hat{n}(t+\tau)\,\hat{n}(t)] &= R_{\hat{N}}(\tau) = R_N(\tau) \\ E[n(t+\tau)\,\hat{n}(t)] &= \hat{R}_{NN}(\tau) = -\hat{R}_N(\tau) \\ E[\hat{n}(t+\tau)\, n(t)] &= \hat{R}_{NN}(\tau) = \hat{R}_N(\tau) \end{aligned}$$

Now, it can be written as,

$$\begin{aligned} R_N(\tau) &= R_N(\tau)[\cos(2\pi f_c t + 2\pi f_c\tau)\cos(2\pi f_c t) + \sin(2\pi f_c t + 2\pi f_c\tau) \\ &\quad \sin(2\pi f_c t)] - \hat{R}_N(\tau)[\cos(2\pi f_c t + 2\pi f_c\tau)\sin(2\pi f_c t) - \\ &\quad \sin(2\pi f_c t + 2\pi f_c\tau)\cos(2\pi f_c t)] \\ &= R_N(\tau)\cos(2\pi f_c\tau) + \hat{R}_N(\tau)\sin(2\pi f_c\tau) \end{aligned}$$

Similarly, it can be shown that $R_{N_C}(\tau)$ also equals this result.

The cross-correlation function of $n_I(t)$ and $n_Q(t)$ is expressed by,

$$N_I N_Q(\tau) = E[n_I(t+\tau)\, n_Q(t)]$$

$$= E\{[n(t+\tau)\cos(2\pi f_c t + 2\pi f_c \tau) + \hat{n}(t+\tau)$$
$$\sin(2\pi f_c t + 2\pi f_c \tau)] \cdot [\hat{n}(t)\cos(2\pi f_c t) - n(t)$$
$$\sin(2\pi f_c t)]\}$$
$$= E[n(t+\tau)\,\hat{n}(t)]\cos(2\pi f_c t + 2\pi f_c \tau)$$
$$\cos(2\pi f_c t) - E[\hat{n}(t+\tau)\,n(t)]$$
$$\sin(2\pi f_c t + 2\pi f_c \tau)\sin(2\pi f_c t) - E[n(t+\tau)\,n(t)]$$
$$\cos(2\pi f_c t + 2\pi f_c \tau)\sin(2\pi f_c t) + E[\hat{n}(t+\tau)\,\hat{n}(t)]$$
$$\sin(2\pi f_c t + 2\pi f_c \tau)\cos(2\pi f_c t)$$
$$= -\hat{R}_N(\tau)[\cos(2\pi f_c t + 2\pi f_c \tau)\cos(2\pi f_c t) +$$
$$\sin(2\pi f_c t + 2\pi f_c \tau)\sin(2\pi f_c t) + R_N(\tau)$$
$$[-\cos(2\pi f_c t + 2\pi f_c \tau)\sin(2\pi f_c t) +$$
$$\sin(2\pi f_c t + 2\pi f_c \tau)\cos(2\pi f_c t)]$$
$$= R_N(\tau)\sin(2\pi f_c \tau) - \hat{R}_N(\tau)\cos(2\pi f_c t)$$

Similarly, it can be shown that

$$R_{N_Q N_I}(\tau) = -R_N(\tau)\sin(2\pi f_c \tau) + \hat{R}_N(\tau)\cos(2\pi f_c \tau).$$

Problem 3.21: The power spectral density of a narrow-band noise $n(t)$ is as shown in Fig. P. 3.21. The carrier frequency is 5 Hz.

(*a*) Find the power spectral densities of the in-phase and quadrature components of $n(t)$.

(*b*) Find their cross-spectral densities.

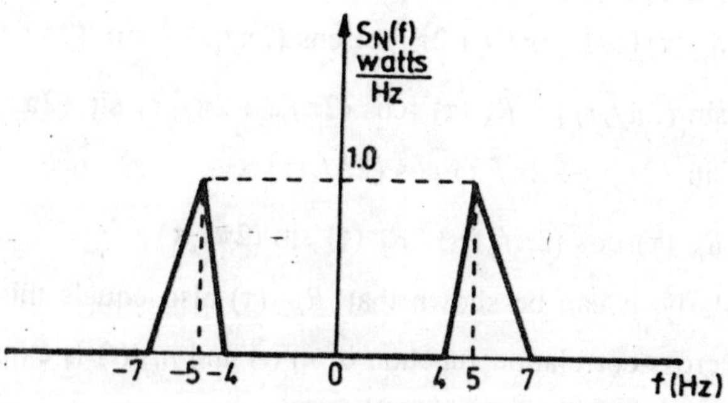

Fig. P. 3.21

Solution: (*a*) The power spectral density of the in-phase component or quadrature component is expressed as,

$$S_{N_I}(f) = S_{N_Q}(f) = \begin{cases} S_N(f+f_c) + S_N(f-f_c), & -B \le f \le B \\ 0, & \text{otherwise} \end{cases}$$

It can also be noted that,

for $-2 \le f \le 2$, the $S_N(f+5)$ and $S_N(f-5)$ are as shown below:

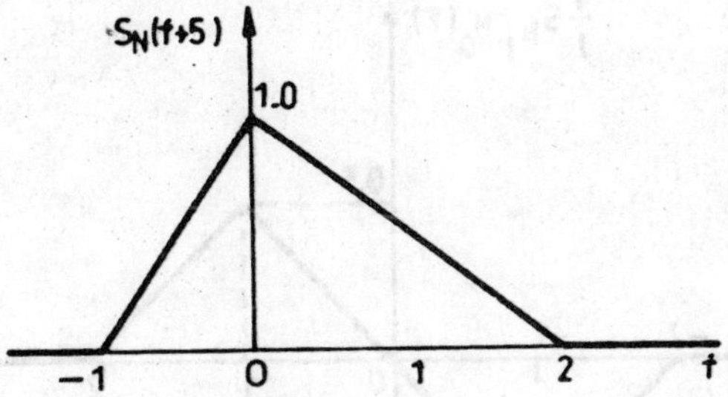

Fig. P. 3.21 (a)

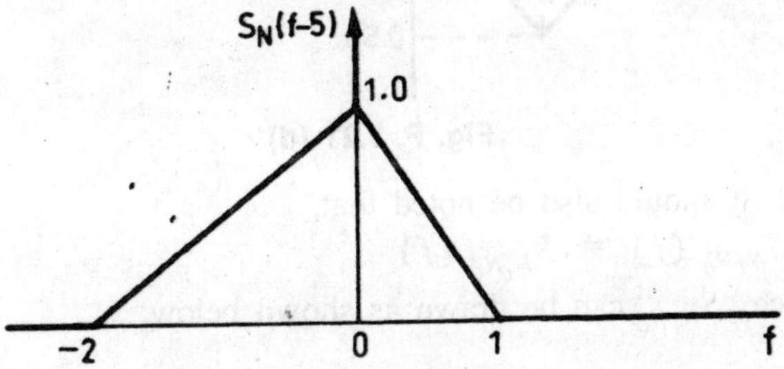

Fig. P. 3.21 (b)

Then, $S_{N_I}(f)$ or $S_{N_Q}(f)$ can be depicted as in figure given below

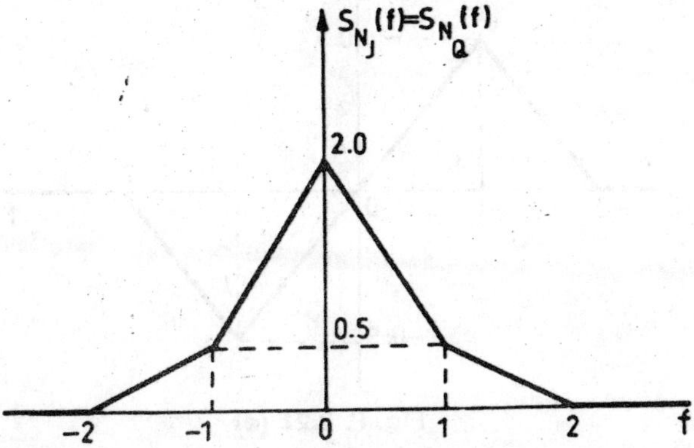

Fig. P. 3.21 (c)

(*b*) The cross-spectral density $S_{N_I N_Q}(f)$ is expressed by

$$S_{N_I N_Q}(f) = \begin{cases} j[S_N(f+f_c) - S_N(f-f_c)], & -B \le f \le B \\ 0, & \text{otherwise} \end{cases}$$

Thus, $S_{N_I} S_{N_Q} / j$ can be depicted in figure given below.

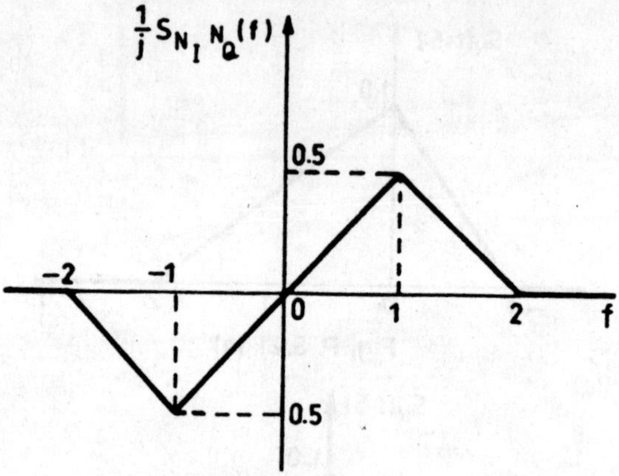

Fig. P. 3.21 (d)

Next, it should also be noted that,

$$S_{N_I N_Q}(f) = S_{N_I N_C}(f)$$

Hence, $S_{N_I N_Q}$ can be drawn as shown below.

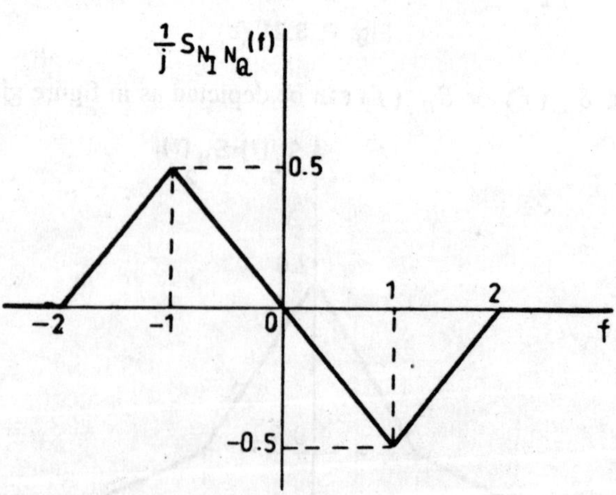

Fig. P. 3.21 (e)

Problem 3.22: Consider a Gaussian noise $n(t)$ with zero mean and the power spectral density $S_N(f)$ shown in Fig. P. 3.22.

(*a*) Find the probability density function of the envelope of $n(t)$.

(*b*) What are the mean and variance of this envelope?

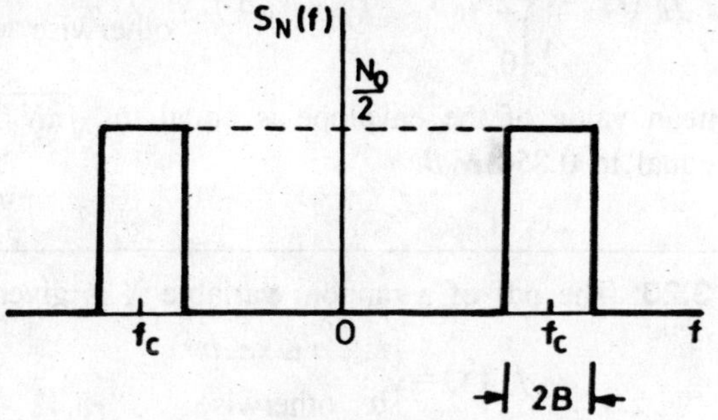

Fig. P. 3.22

Solution: (*a*) Noise $n(t)$ in terms of its in-phase and quadrature components can be expressed as,

$$n(t) = n_I(t)\cos(2\pi f_c t) - n_Q \sin(2\pi f_c t)$$

Now, the envelope of $n(t)$ is given by,

$$r(t) = \sqrt{n_I^2(t) + n_Q^2(t)}$$

Which is Rayleigh-distributed. That is

$$f_R(r) = \begin{cases} \dfrac{r}{\sigma^2}\exp\left(-\dfrac{r^2}{2\sigma^2}\right), & r \geq 0 \\ 0, & \text{otherwise} \end{cases}$$

To evaluate the variance σ^2 for this envelope, the Power Spectral Density of $n_I(t)$ or $n_Q(t)$ is first drawn which is shown next.

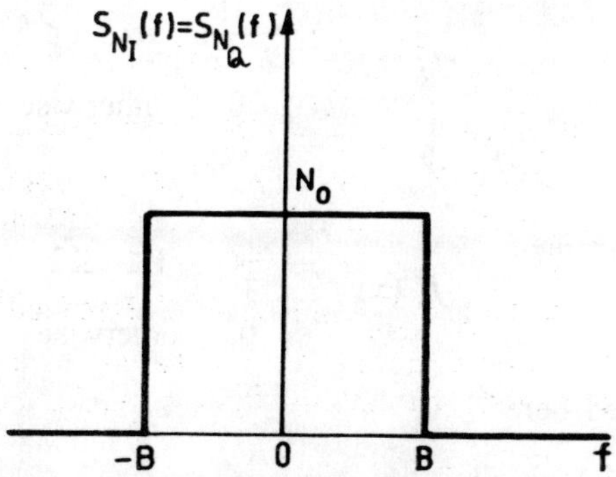

Fig. P. 3.22 (a)

Since the mean of $n(t)$ is zero, therefore

$$\sigma^2 = 2 N_0 B$$

Hence, $f_R(r)$ can be expressed as,

$$f_R(r) = \begin{cases} \dfrac{r}{2N_0B}\exp\left(-\dfrac{r^2}{4N_0B}\right), & r \le 0 \\ 0, & \text{otherwise} \end{cases}$$

(*b*) The mean value of the envelope is equal to $\sqrt{\pi N_0 B}$, and its variance is equal to 0.858 N_0B.

Problem 3.23: The pdf of a random variable X is given by,

$$f_x(x) = \begin{cases} k & a \le x \le b \\ 0 & \text{otherwise} \end{cases}$$

where k is a constant.

(*i*) Determine the value of k.

(*ii*) When $a = -1$ and $b = 2$, calculate $p(|x| \le c)$ for $c = \dfrac{1}{2}$.

Solution: (i) $f_x(x) \ge 0$ implies that k is a positive constant.

By definition, $$\int_{-\infty}^{\infty} f_x(x)\,dx = 1$$

then $$\int_a^b k\,dx = 1$$

or, $$k = \frac{1}{b-a}$$

Hence, $$f_x(x) = \begin{cases} \dfrac{1}{b-a} & +a \le x \le b \\ 0 & \text{otherwise} \end{cases}$$

(*ii*) When $a = 1$, $b = 2$,

$$f_x(x) = \begin{cases} \dfrac{1}{3}, & 1 \le x \le 2 \\ 0, & \text{otherwise} \end{cases}$$

as illustrated here

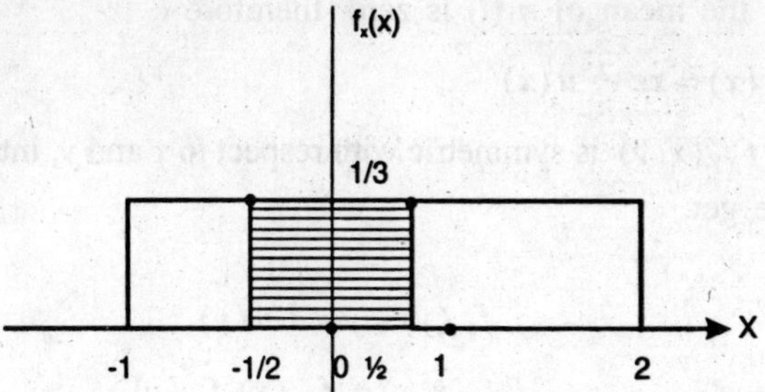

Fig. P. 3.23

Now, $p\left(|x| \le \frac{1}{2}\right) = p\left(-\frac{1}{2} \le x \le \frac{1}{2}\right)$

or, $$p\left(|x| \le \frac{1}{2}\right) = \int_{-1/2}^{1/2} f_x(x)\, dx = \frac{1}{3}\int_{-1/2}^{1/2} dx = \frac{1}{3}\left[x \Big|_{-1/2}^{1/2}\right] = \frac{1}{3}.$$

Problem 3.24: The joint pdf of x and y is given by

$$f_{XY}(x,y) = xy\, e^{-\frac{(x^2+y^2)}{2}} \cdot u(x)\, u(y)$$

(*i*) Find the marginal pdf's $f_x(x)$ and $f_y(y)$

(*ii*) Are x and y independent.

Solution:

(i) Marghinal pdf, $$f_X(x) = \int_{-\infty}^{\infty} f_{XY}(x,y)\, dy$$

$$= \int_{-\infty}^{\infty} xy \cdot e^{\frac{-(x^2+y^2)}{2}}\, u(x)\, u(y)\, dy$$

or, $$f_x(x) = xe^{\frac{-x^2}{2}}\, u(x) \int_0^{\infty} ye^{-\frac{y^2}{2}}\, dy$$

or, $f_x(x) = xe^{\frac{-x^2}{2}} u(x)$

Since $f_{XY}(x, y)$ is symmetric with respect to x and y, interchanging x and y, we get,

$$f_Y(y) = ye^{-\frac{y^2}{2}} u(y)$$

(*b*) Since, $f_{XY}(x, y) = f_X(x) f_Y(y)$

it can be inferred that X and Y are independent.

Problem 3.25: Let $Y = \sin X$, where X is uniformily distributed with

$$f_x(x) = \begin{cases} \frac{1}{2\pi}, & 0 \le x \le 2\pi \\ 0, & \text{otherwise} \end{cases}$$

(*i*) Find $f_Y(y)$ and $f_Y(y)$.

Solution: (*i*) For $|y| > 2$, $y = \sin x$ has no solutions. Hence, $f_Y(y) = 0$.

For $|y| < 1$, $y = \sin x$ has two solutions in the interval $0 \le x \le 2\pi$ as depicted have

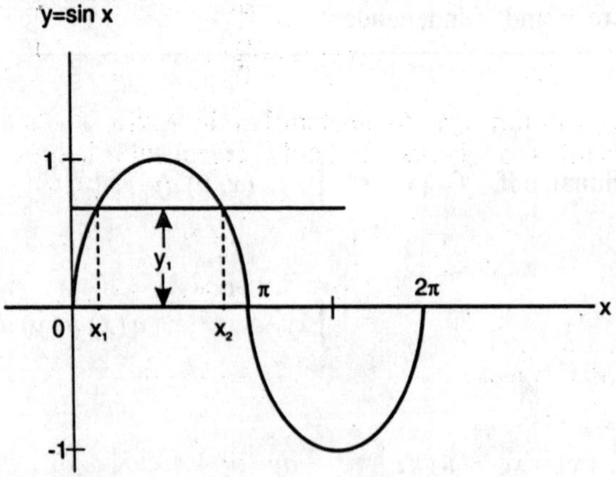

Fig. P. 3.25

$$\text{Now,} \quad y = \sin x_1$$
$$\text{or,} \quad x_1 = \sin^{-1} y$$
$$\text{and} \quad x_2 = \pi - x_1 = \pi - \sin^{-1} y$$
$$\text{Now,} \quad y(x_1) = \cos x_1 = \cos(\sin^{-1} y) = \sqrt{1-y^2}$$
$$\text{and} \quad y'(x_2) = \cos x_2 = \cos(\pi - x_1) = -\cos x_1 = -\sqrt{1-y^2}$$

$$\text{Since,} \quad f_Y(y) = \sum_k \frac{f_X |x_k|}{|g'(x_k)|},$$

$$\text{then,} \quad f_Y(y) = \frac{f_X |x_1|}{|g(x_1)|} + \frac{f_X |x_2|}{|g(x_2)|}$$

$$= \frac{1}{2\pi\sqrt{1-y^2}} + \frac{1}{2\pi\sqrt{1-y^2}} = \frac{1}{\pi\sqrt{1-y^2}}, |y| < 1$$

$$\text{Now, using } F_X(x) = \int_{-\infty}^{x} f_X(r)\, dr$$

$$\text{We have, } F_Y(y) = \begin{cases} 0, & y < -1 \\ \dfrac{1}{2} + \dfrac{\sin^{-1} y}{\pi}, & -1 \le y < 1 \\ 1, & 1 \le y \end{cases}$$

Problem 3.26: Let X and Y be defined by

$$X = \cos\Theta \text{ and } Y = \sin\Theta$$

where Θ is a random variable uniformly distributed over $[0, 2\pi]$.

(*i*) Show that X and Y are uncorrelated.

(*ii*) Show that X and Y are not independent.

Solution: (*i*) Since random variable Θ is uniformly distributed, then $f_\Theta(\theta)$ can be given by,

$$f_\Theta(\theta) = \begin{cases} \dfrac{1}{2}\pi & 0 \le \theta \le 2\pi \\ 0 & \text{otherwise} \end{cases}$$

$$\text{then mean of } X \quad \mu_X = E[X] = \int_{-\infty}^{\infty} x f_X(x)\, dx$$

or, $$\mu_X = \int_{-\infty}^{\infty} [\cos\theta] \cdot f_{\Theta}(\theta)\, d\theta$$

or, $$\mu_X = \frac{1}{2\pi}\int_0^{2\pi} \cos\theta\, d\theta = 0$$

Similarly, $$E[Y] = \int_{-\infty}^{\infty} y f_Y(y)\, dy$$

and, $$E[Y] = \int_0^{2\pi} \sin\theta\, d\theta = 0$$

and $$E[XY] = \frac{1}{2\pi}\int_0^{2\pi} \cos\theta \sin\theta\, d\theta$$

$$= \frac{1}{4\pi}\int_0^{2\pi} \sin 2\theta\, d\theta = 0 = E[X] \cdot E[Y]$$

Now, it can be inferred that X and Y are uncorrelated.

(b) $$E[X^2] = \frac{1}{2\pi}\int_0^{2\pi} \cos^2\theta\, d\theta = \frac{1}{2\pi}\int_0^{2\pi} \frac{1}{2}(1+\cos 2\theta)\, d\theta = \frac{1}{2}$$

$$E[Y^2] = \frac{1}{2\pi}\int_0^{2\pi} \sin^2\theta\, d\theta = \frac{1}{2\pi}\int_0^{2\pi} \frac{1}{2}(1-\cos 2\theta)\, d\theta = \frac{1}{2}$$

$$E[X^2Y^2] = \frac{1}{2\pi}\int_0^{2\pi} \cos^2\theta \sin^2\theta\, d\theta = \frac{1}{8\pi}\int_0^{2\pi} \frac{(1-\cos 4\theta)}{2}\, d\theta = \frac{1}{8}$$

Hence $E[X^2Y^2] = \frac{1}{8} \neq \frac{1}{4} = E(X^2)\,E(Y^2)$ and therefore X and Y are not independent.

Problem 3.27: The relation between the input $X(t)$ and the output $Y(t)$ of a diode expressed as

$$Y(t) = X^2(t)$$

Lt $X(t)$ be a zero-mean stationary Gaussian random process with autocorrelation.

$R_{XX}(\tau) = e^{-\lambda|\tau|} \quad \alpha > 0$

Find the output mean $\mu_Y(t)$, the output autocorrelation $R_{YY}(\tau)$, and the output power spectral density $S_{YY}(\omega)$.

Solution: Here,

$$\mu_Y(t) = E[Y(t)] = E[X^2(t)] = R_{XX}(0) = 1 \quad (1)$$

and, $$R_{YY}(t_1, t_2) = E[Y(t_1) \cdot Y(t_2)] = E[X^2(t_1) X^2(t_2)]$$

$$=$$

$$= E[X^2(t_1)] E[X^2(t_2) + 2\{E[X(t_1) \cdot X(t_2)]\}^2 \quad (2)$$

Now, as $X(t)$ is stationary, we have

$$E[X^2(t_1)] = E[X^2(t_2)] = R_{XX}(0)$$

and $$E[X(t_1) X(t_2)] = R_{XX}(t_2 - t_1) = R_{XX}(\tau)$$

then, equation (2) becomes

$$R_{YY}(t_1, t_2) = R_{YY}(\tau) = [R_{XX}(0)]^2 + 2[R_{XX}(\tau)]^2$$

Now, taking Fourier transform both sides and using

$$1 = 2\pi\,\delta(\omega) \text{ and } x,(t)\, x_2(t) = \frac{1}{2\pi} X_1(\omega) * X_2(\omega)$$

We get $s_{YY}(\omega) = \tau[R_{YY}(\tau)]$

or, $$s_{YY}(\omega) = 2\pi[R_{XX}(0)]^2 \cdot \delta(\omega) + \frac{1}{\pi} s_{XX}(\omega) * s_{XX}(\omega)$$

Now, as $\mu_y(t) = R_{XX}(0) = 1$ [from equation (1)]

$$R_{YY}(\tau) = 1 + 2 \cdot e^{-\lambda|\tau|}$$

Using $$e^{-a|t|} = \frac{2a}{\omega^2 + a^2}$$ for $a > 0$, we get

$$s_{YY}(\omega) = 2\pi\,\delta(\omega) + \frac{8\lambda}{\omega^2 + 4\alpha^2}$$

> **Problem 3.28:** Consider a random process $X(t) = A\sin(\omega t + \theta)$, where θ and ω are constants and A is a random variable. Determine whether $X(t)$ is WSS or not.

Solution: Mean of $X(t)$

$$\mu_X(t) = E[X(t)] = E[A\sin(\omega t + \theta)]$$

$$\mu_X(t) = \sin(\omega t + \theta) \cdot E[A]$$

Here, it can be inferred that, $\mu_X(t)$ is not constant unless

$$E[A] = 0.$$

Now, Autocorrelation of $X(t)$ is given as,

$$R_{XX}(t, t+\tau) = E[X(t) \cdot X(t+\tau)$$

$$= E[A^2 \cdot \sin(\omega t + \theta) \cdot \sin[\omega(t+\tau) + \theta)]$$

$$R_{XX}(t, t+\tau) = \frac{1}{2}[\cos(\omega\tau) - \cos(2\omega t + 2\theta + \omega\tau)] \cdot E[A^2]$$

as autocorrelation of $X(t)$ is not a function of the time difference τ only and mean is not constant. The process $X(t)$ is not WSS.

Chapter 4

Noise in CW Modulation Systems

Problem 4.1: The sample function

$$x(t) = A_c \cos(2\pi f_c t) + w(t)$$

is applied to the low-pass RC filter of Fig. P. 4.1. The amplitude A_c and frequency f_c of the sinusoidal component are constants, and $w(t)$ is a white Gaussian noise of zero mean and power spectral density $\frac{N_0}{2}$. Find an expresson for the output signal-to-noise ratio with the sinusoidal component of $x(t)$ regarded as the signal of interest.

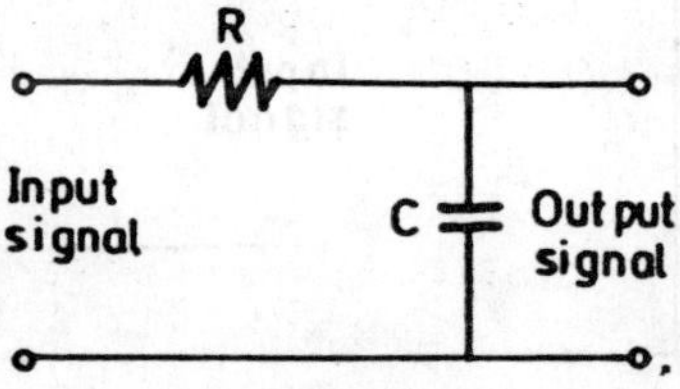

Fig. P. 4.1

Solution:

In the absence of noise, the input signal $x(t) = A_c \cos(2\pi f_c t)$. The corresponding value of the signal amplitude at the filter output is $\dfrac{A_c}{\left[1+(2\pi f_c CR)^2\right]^{\frac{1}{2}}}$. *The output signal power is therefore equal to*

$$\frac{A_c^2}{2}[1+(2\pi f_c t\, CR)^2].$$

In the absence of signal, the input $x(t) = w(t)$

Hence we find that the corresponding output noise power is $\frac{N_0}{4CR}$

The output signal to noise ratio of the filter is therefore

$$(\text{SNR})_0 = \frac{2A_c^2 CR}{N_0\left[1+(2\pi f_c CR)^2\right]}$$

Problem 4.2: Suppose the sample function $x(t)$ of Problem 4.1 is applied to the band-pass LCR filter of Fig. P. 4.2, which is tuned to the frequency f_c of the sinusoidal component. Assume that the Q-factor of the filter is high compared with unity. Find an expression for the output signal-to-noise ratio by treating the sinusoidal component of $x(t)$ as the signal of interest.

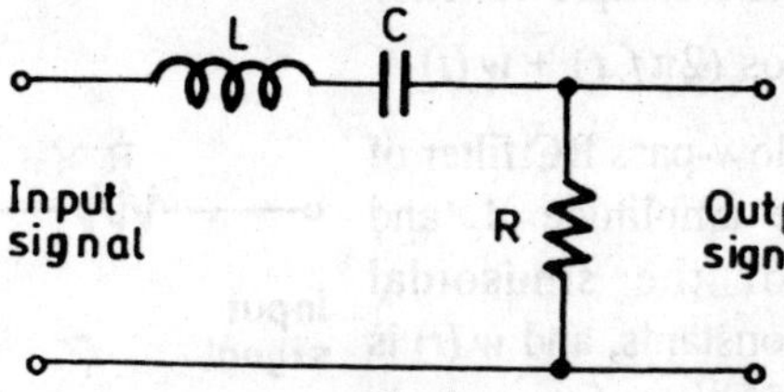

Fig. P. 4.2

Solution: The transfer function of the filter, assuming that the Q-factor is high compared with unity is given by

$$H(f)\begin{cases}\dfrac{1}{1+j2Q(f-f_c)/f_c}, & f>0\\[2ex] \dfrac{1}{1+j2Q(f+f_c)/f_c} & f<0\end{cases}$$

Where
$$f_c = \frac{1}{2\pi\sqrt{Lc}}$$

$$Q = \frac{2\pi f_c L}{R}$$

In the absence of noise, $x(t) = A_c \cos(2\pi f_c t)$.

Since $H(f_c) = 1$, it follows that the corresponding output is also equal to $A_c \cos(2\pi f_c t)$. Hence output signal power is $\frac{A_c^2}{2}$.

In the absence of the singal component $X(t) = w(t)$. Since the filter is narrow band, we may represent the resulting noise at the filter output as

$$n(t) = n_I(t)\cos(2\pi f_c t) - n_Q(t)\sin(2\pi f_c t)$$

The power of spêctral density of $n(t)$ is defined by

$$S_N(f) = \frac{N_0}{2}|H(f)|^2 = \begin{cases} \dfrac{\frac{N_0}{2}}{1+\frac{4Q^2(f-f_c)^2}{f_c^2}}, & f>0 \\ \dfrac{\frac{N_0}{2}}{1+\frac{4Q^2(f-f_c)^2}{f_c^2}}, & f<0 \end{cases}$$

Hence we may express the power of spectral density of the in-phase component $n_I(t)$ or the quadrature component $n_Q(t)$ as

$$S_{NI}(f) = S_{NQ}(f) = \frac{N_0}{1+\frac{4Q^2 f^2}{f_c^2}}$$

$$\text{Average output noise power} = \int_{-\infty}^{\infty} \frac{N_0}{1+\frac{4Q^2 f^2}{f_c^2}}\, df = \frac{\pi N_0 f_c}{2Q}$$

The output signal to noise ratio is therefore

$$(SNR)_0 = \frac{\frac{A_c^2}{2}}{\frac{\pi N_0 f_c}{2Q}}$$

Problem 4.3: A DSB-SC modulated signal is transmitted over a noisy channel, with the power spectral density of the noise being as shown in Fig. P. 4.3. The message bandwidth is 4 kHz and the carrier frequency is 200 kHz. Assuming that the average power of the modulated wave is 10 watts, determine the output signal–to–noise ratio of the receiver.

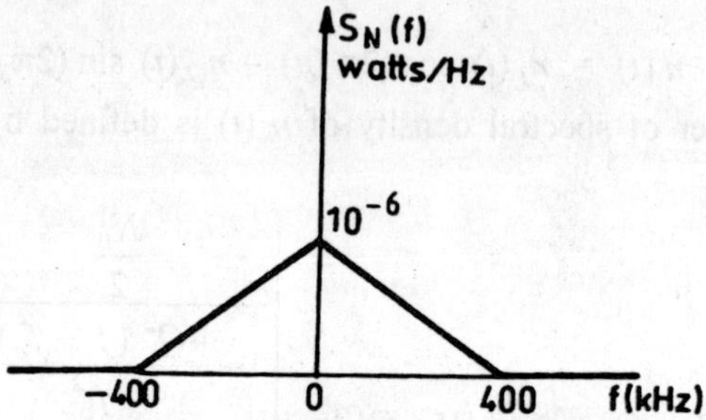

Fig. P. 4.3

Solution: The signal at the predetection fitter output is defined by

$$X(t) = s(t) + n(t)$$

$$= \frac{A_c}{2} m(t) \cos(2\pi f_c t) - \frac{A_c}{2} \hat{m}(t) \sin(2\pi f_c t)$$

$$+ n_I(t) \cos[\pi t(2f_c + W)] - n_Q t \sin[\pi t(2f_c + W)]$$

Where $\hat{m}(t)$ is the Hilbert transform of the message signal, $m(t)$, $n_I(t)$ and $n_Q(t)$ are the in-phase and quadrature components of the narrow band noise $n(t)$.

The coherent detector output is therefore

$$y(t) = \frac{A_c}{4} m(t) + \frac{1}{2} n_I(t) \cos(\pi wt) - \frac{1}{2} n_Q(t) \sin(\pi wt)$$

Problem 4.4: Evaluate the autocorrelation functions and cross-correlation functions of the in-phase and quadrature components of the narrow-band noise at the coherent detector input for

(*a*) the DSB-SC system,

(*b*) an SSB system using the lower sideband, and

(*c*) an SSB system using the upper sideband.

Solution: As we note that the quadrature components of a narrow-band noise have autocorrelations

$$R_{N_I}(\tau) = R_{N_Q}(\tau) = R_N(\tau)\cos(2\pi f_c\tau) + \hat{R}_N(\tau)\sin(2\pi f_c\tau)$$

Where $R_N(\tau)$ is the autocorrelation of the narrow band noise, $R_N(\tau)$ is the Hilbert transform of $R_N(\tau)$ and f_c is the band center.

The cross-correlations of the quadrature components are

$$R_{N_iN_Q}(\tau) = -R_{N_iN_Q}(\tau) = R_N(\tau)\sin(2\pi f_c t) - \hat{R}_N(\tau)\cos(2\pi f_c\tau)$$

(*a*) For a DSBSC system

$$R_{N_I}(\tau) = R_{N_Q}(\tau) = R_N(\tau)\cos(2\pi f_c t) + \hat{R}_N\tau\sin(2\pi f_c t)$$

$$R_{N_IN_Q}(\tau) = -R_{N_QN_I}(\tau) = R_N(\tau)\sin(2\pi f_c t) - \hat{R}_N\tau\cos(2\pi f_c t)$$

Where f_c is the carrier frequency, and $R_N(\tau)$ is the autocorrelation function of the narrow-band noise on the interval

$$f_c - W \le f \le f_c + W.$$

(*b*) For an SSB system using the lower siδand

$$R_{N_I}(\tau) = R_{N_Q}(\tau)$$

$$= R_N(\tau)\cos\left[2\pi\left(f_c - \frac{W}{2}\right)\tau\right] + \hat{R}_N(\tau)\left[\sin 2\pi\left(f_c - \frac{W}{2}\right)\tau\right]$$

$$R_{N_IN_Q}(\tau) = -R_{N_QN_I}(\tau) = \hat{R}_N(\tau)\cos 2\pi\left[\sin\left(2\pi f_c - \frac{W}{2}\right)\tau\right]$$

$$- \hat{R}_N(\tau)\cos 2\pi\left(f_c - \frac{W}{2}\right)\tau$$

Where in this case, $R_N(\tau)$ is the autocorrelation of the narrow band noise on the interval $f_c - W < f < f_c$.

(*c*) For an SSB system with only the upperside lean transmitted, the correlations are similar to (*b*) above except that $\left(f_c - \frac{W}{2}\right)$ is replaced by $\left(f_c + \frac{W}{2}\right)$ and the narrow-band noise is on the interval $f_c \le f \le f_c + W$.

Problem 4.5: In a receiver using coherent detection, the sinusodial wave generated by the local oscillator suffers from a phase error $\theta(t)$ with respect to the carrier wave $\cos(2\pi f_c t)$. Assuming that

$\theta(t)$ is a sample function of a zero-mean Gaussian process of variance σ_θ^2, and that most of the time the maximum value of $\theta(t)$ is small compared with unity, find the mean-square error of the receiver output of
(*a*) DSB-SC modulation and
(*b*) SSB modulation. The mean-square error is defined as the expected value of the squared difference between the receiver output and the message signal component of the receiver output.

Solution:

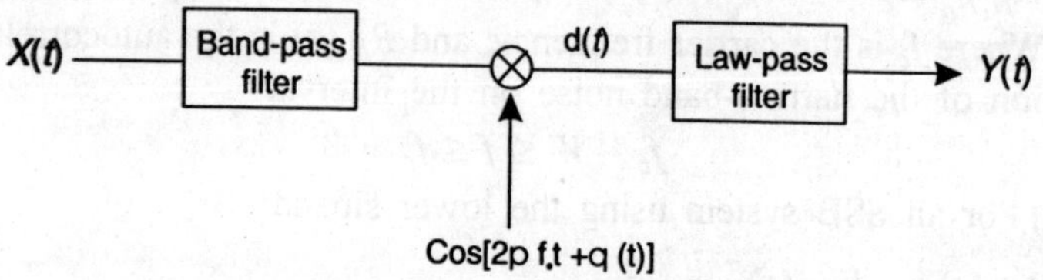

Fig. P. 4.5

The signal at the mixer input is equal to $s(t) + n(t)$ where $s(t)$ is the modulated wave and $n(t)$ is defined by

$$n(t) = n_I(t)\cos(2\pi f_c t) - n_Q(t)\sin(2\pi f_c t)$$

with

$$E[n_I^2(t)] = E[n_Q^2(t)] = N_0 B_T$$

The $s(t)$ is defined by

$$s(t) = A_c[m_1(t)\cos(2\pi f_c t) - m_2(t)\sin(2\pi f_c t)]$$

In case of a DSBSC modulated wave, $m(t) = m(t)$ and $m_2(t) = 0$. Whereas in the case of an SSB modulated wave with only the upper sideband transmitted. $m_1(t) = \frac{1}{2}m(t)$ and $m_2 = \frac{1}{2}\hat{m}(t)$, where $m(t)$ is the modulating wave and $\hat{m}(t)$ is the Helbert transform of $m(t)$

The mixer output

$$v(t) - [s(t) + n(t)\cos 2\pi f_c t + \theta(t)]$$

$$= \{[A_c m_1(t) + n_c(t)\cos(2\pi f_c t) - A_c m_2(t) + n_s(t)]\}$$
$$\cos 2\pi f_c t + \theta(t)]$$

$$= \frac{1}{2}[A_c m_1(t) + n_c(t)]\{\cos[\theta(t)]\} + \cos 4\pi f_c t + \theta(t)] +$$

$$\frac{1}{2}[A_c m_2(t) + n_s(t)]\{\sin[\theta(t)] - \sin[4\pi f_c t + \theta(t)]$$

The post-detection low-pass filter removes the high frequency component of $v(t)$ producing the output

$$y(t) = \frac{1}{2}[A_c m_1(t) + n_c(t)]\cos[\theta(t)] +$$

$$\frac{1}{2}[A_c m_2(t) + n_s(t)]\sin[\theta(t)] \qquad \text{...(1)}$$

When the phase error $\theta(t)$ is zero, we find that the message signal component of the receiver output is $\frac{1}{2}A_c m_1(t)$. The error at the receiver output is therefore

$$e(t) = y(t) - \frac{A_c}{2}m_1(t)$$

The mean square value of this error is

$$\varepsilon = [Ee^2(t)] = E[(y(t) - \frac{A_c}{2}m_1(t))^2] \qquad \text{...(2)}$$

Substituting eq. (1) into (2), expanding hte expectation and noting that the process $m_1(t)$, $m_2(t)$, $\theta(t)$, $n_I(t)$ and $n_Q(t)$ are all independent of one another, we get

$$\varepsilon = \frac{A_c^2}{4}E[m_1^2(t)]E[\cos^2\theta(t)] + \frac{1}{4}E[n_c^2(t)] + E[\cos^2\theta(t)] +$$

$$\frac{A_c^2}{4}E[m_2^2(t)]E[\sin^2\theta(t)] + \frac{1}{4}E[n_S^2(t)] + E[\sin^2\theta(t)]$$

$$+\frac{A_c^2}{4}E[m^2{}_1(t)] - \frac{A_c^2}{2}E[m_1^2(t)]E[\cos\theta(t)]$$

We note that

$$E[n_I^2(t)] = E[n_Q^2(t)] = \sigma_N^2$$

$$E[n_I^2(t)]\ E[\cos^2\theta(t)] + E[n_Q^2(t)]\ E[\sin^2\theta(t)] = \sigma_N^2$$

Therefore

$$\varepsilon = \frac{A_c^2}{4} E[m_1^2(t)]\, E\{[1 - \cos\theta(t)]^2\}$$

$$+ \frac{A_c^2}{4} E[m_2^2(t)]\, E \sin^2\theta(t) + \frac{\sigma_N^2}{4} \quad \ldots(3)$$

(*a*) DSBSC system

For thes case we have

$$m_1(t) = m(t) \qquad E[m_1^2(t)] = P$$
$$m_2(t) = 0$$

Hence eqn (3) reduces to

$$\varepsilon = \frac{A_c^2}{4} E\{[1 - \cos\theta\,(t)^2]\} + \frac{\sigma_N^2}{4}$$

The small value of $\theta(t)$, we may use the approximation

$$1 - \cos\theta(t) = \frac{\theta^2(t)}{2}$$

Hence

$$\varepsilon = \frac{A_c^2 P}{16} E[\theta^4(t)] + \frac{\sigma_N^2}{4}$$

Since $\theta_{(t)}$ is Gausian distributed with zero, mean and variance σ_Q^2, we have

$$E[\theta^4(t)] = 3\sigma_\theta^4$$

The mean square error for the case of a DSBSC system is therefore

$$\varepsilon = \frac{3A_c^2 P\sigma_\theta^4}{16} + \frac{\sigma_N^2}{4}$$

(*b*) SSB system

For this case, we have

$$m_1(t) = \frac{1}{2} m(t) \qquad m_2(t) = \frac{1}{2}\hat{m}(t)$$

$$E[m_1^2(t)] = E[m_2^2(t)] = \frac{1}{4} P$$

Hence eqn (3) gives

$$\varepsilon = \frac{A_c^2 P}{16} E[(1 - \cos\theta\,(t)^2 + \sin^2\theta\,(t))] + \frac{\sigma_N^2}{4}$$

$$= \frac{A_c^2 P}{8} E[1 - \cos\theta\, t] + \frac{\sigma_N^2}{4}$$

For small value of θ (*t*), we may approximate ε as follows

$$\varepsilon = \frac{A_c^2 P}{16} E[\theta^2(t)] + \frac{\sigma_N^2}{4} = \frac{A_c^2 P \sigma_\theta^2}{16} + \frac{\sigma_N^2}{4}$$

Problem 4.6: Let a message signal *m* (*t*) be transmitted using single–sideband modulation. The power spectral density of *m* (*t*) is

$$S_M(f) = \begin{cases} a\dfrac{|f|}{W}, & |f| \leq W \\ 0, & \text{otherwise} \end{cases}$$

Where *a* and *W* are constants. White Gaussian noise of zero mean and power spectral density $\frac{N_0}{2}$ is added to the SSB modulated wave at the receiver input. Find an expression for the output signal-to-noise ratio of the receiver.

Solution: The power density of the message signal *m* (*t*) is as follows

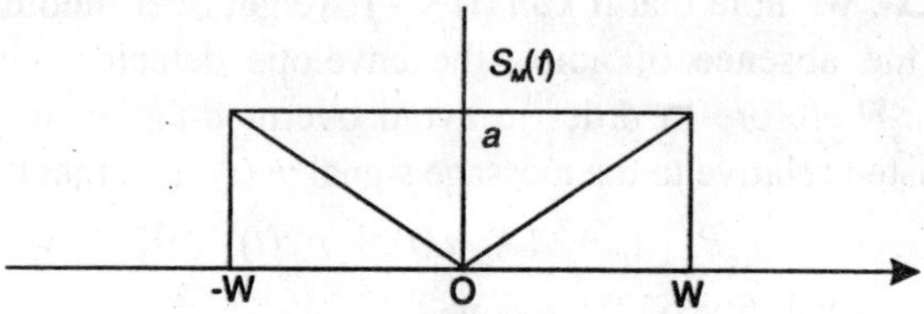

Fig. P. 4.6

The average signal power is therefore

$$P = \int_{-\infty}^{\infty} S_M(f)\,df = 2\int_0^W a\frac{f}{W}\,df = aW$$

Problem 4.7: Consider the output of an envelope detector defined by Eq. which is reproduced here for convenience

$$y(t) = \{[A_c + A_c k_a m(t) + n_I(t)^2 + n_Q^2(t)]\}^{1/2}$$

(*a*) Assume that the probability of the event

$$|n_Q(t)| > \varepsilon A_c |1 + k_a m(t)|$$

is equal to or less than δ_1, where $\varepsilon \ll 1$. What is the probability that the effect of the quadrature component $n_Q(t)$ is negligible?

(*b*) Suppose that k_a is adjusted relative to the message signal $m(t)$ such that the probability of the event

$$A_c[1 + k_a m(t)] + n_I(t) < 0$$

is equal to δ_2. What is the probablity that the approximation

$$y(t) \cong A_c[1 + k_a m(t)] + n_I(t)$$

is valid?

(*c*) Comment on the significance of the result in part (*b*) for the case when δ_1 and δ_2 are both small compared with unity.

Solution: (*a*) If the probability

$$P\{|n_S(t)|\}\ \varepsilon\ A_c\ |1 + k_a m(t)| \leq \delta_1,$$

then with the probability greater than $1 - \delta_1$ we may say that

$$y(t) \cong \{[A_c + A_c k_a m(t) + n_c(t)]^2\}^{1/2}$$

This is, the probability that the quadrature component $n_S(t)$ is negligibly small is greater than $1 - \delta_1$.

(*b*) Next, we note that if $k_a m(t) < -1$ we get over modulation, so that even in the absence of noise, the envelope detector output is badly distorted. Therefore in order to avoid overmodulation we assume that k_a is adjusted relative to the message signal $m(t)$ such that the probability

$$P\{A_c + A_c k_a m(t) + n_c(t) < 0\} = \delta_2$$

The probability of the event

$$y(t) = A_c[1 + k_a m(t)] + n_c(t)$$

For any value of t is greater than $(1 - \delta_1)(1 - \delta_2)$

(*c*) When δ_1 and δ_2 are both small compared with unity that the probability of the event

$$y(t) \cong A_c[1 + k_a m(t) + n_c(t)]$$

For any value of t is very close to unity. Then the output of the envelope detector is approximately the same as the corresponding output detector.

Problem 4.8: Evaluate the output signal-to-noise ratio of a vestigial sideband system, the receiver of which uses coherent detection. The additive noise at the detector input is narrow band.

Solution: The received signal is

$$X(t) = s(t) + n(t) \quad \text{...(1)}$$

Where $s(t)$ is the VSB modulated wave and $n(t)$ is the narrow–band noise at the coherent detector input. The $s(t)$ is defined by

$$s(t) = \frac{1}{2}A_c m(t)\cos(2\pi f_c t) - \frac{1}{2}A_c \cdot m_s(t)\sin(2\pi f_c t) \quad \text{...(2)}$$

The power spectral density of the noise $n(t)$ is as follows:

$$S_{N_I'}(f) = S_{N_Q'}(f)$$

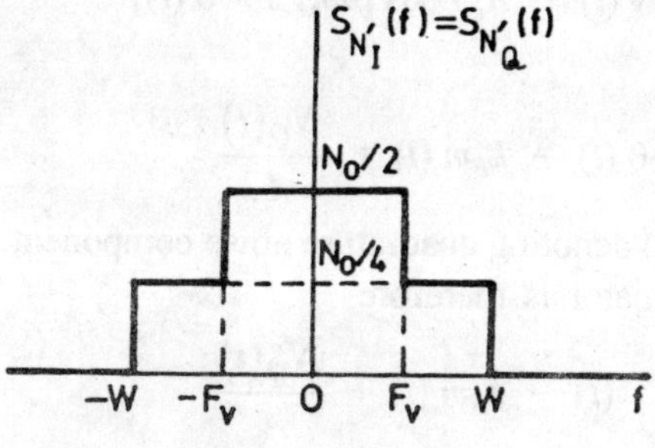

Fig. P. 4.8

From eqn (4) we see that the noise component of the coherent detector output $y(t)$ is $\frac{1}{2}[n_c'(t) - n_s'(t)]$.

The average output noise power is therefore

$$N_0 = 2 \times \frac{1}{4}\left[2W \times \frac{N_0}{4} + 2f_v \times \frac{N_0}{4}\right] = \frac{N_0}{4}(W + f_v)$$

We thus find that the output signal-to-noise ratio of a VSB system using coherent detection is

$$(SNR)_0 = \frac{A_c^2 \frac{P}{16}}{\frac{N_0(f_v + W)}{4}} = \frac{A_c^2 P}{4N_0(f_v + W)}$$

Problem 4.9: Consider a phase modulation (PM) system, with the modulated wave defined by

$$s(t) = A_c \cos[2\pi f_c t + k_P m(t)]$$

Where k_P is a constant and $m(t)$ is the message signal. The additive noise $n(t)$ at the phase detector input is

$$n(t) = n_I(t)\cos(2\pi f_c t) - n_Q(t)\sin(2\pi f_c t)$$

Assuming that the carrier-to-noise ratio at the detector input is high compared with unity, determine

(*a*) The output signal-to-noise ratio and

(*b*) The figure of merit of the system. Compare your results with the FM system for the case of sinusoidal modulation.

Solution: (*a*) The following procedure, similar to that described for the case of an FM system, we find that the input of the phase detector is

$$v(t) = A_c \cdot \cos[2\pi f_c t + \theta(t)]$$

where

$$\theta(t) = k_P m(t) + \frac{N_Q(t)}{A_c}$$

With $n_Q(t)$ denoting quadrature noise component. The output of the phase descriminator is therefore

$$y(t) = k_P m(t) + \frac{N_Q(t)}{A_c}$$

The message signal component of $y(t)$ is equal to $k_P m(t)$. Hence, the average output signal power is $k_P^2 P$ where P is message signal power with the past detection low-pass filter following the phase detector restricted to the message bandwidth, W, we find that the average output noise power is $2W\frac{N_0}{A_c^2}$.

Hence, the output signal-to-noise ratio of the PM system is

$$(\text{SNR})_0 = \frac{k_P^2 P A_c^2}{2WN_0}$$

Problem 4.10: An FDM system uses single-sideband modulation to combine 12 independent voice signals and then uses frequency modulation to transmit the composite baseband signal. Each voice signal has an average power P and occurs the frequency band 0.3–3.4 kHz; the system allocates it a bandwidth of 4 kHz. For each voice signal, only the lower sideband is transmitted. The subcarrier waves used for the first stage of modulation are defined by

$$c_k(t) = A_k \cos(2\pi k f_0 t), \; 0 \le k \le 11$$

The received signal consists of the transmitted FM signal plus white Gaussian noise of zero mean and power spectral density $\dfrac{N_0}{2}$.

(*a*) Sketch the power spectral density of the signal produced at the frequency discriminator output, showing both the signal and noise components.

(*b*) Find the relationship between the subcarrier amplitudes A_k, so that the modulated voice signals have equal signal-to-noise ratios.

Solution: (*a*) The power spectral densities of the original message signal, and the signal and noise components at the frequency discriminator output (for positive frequencies) are illustrated in Fig. P. 4.10 (a).

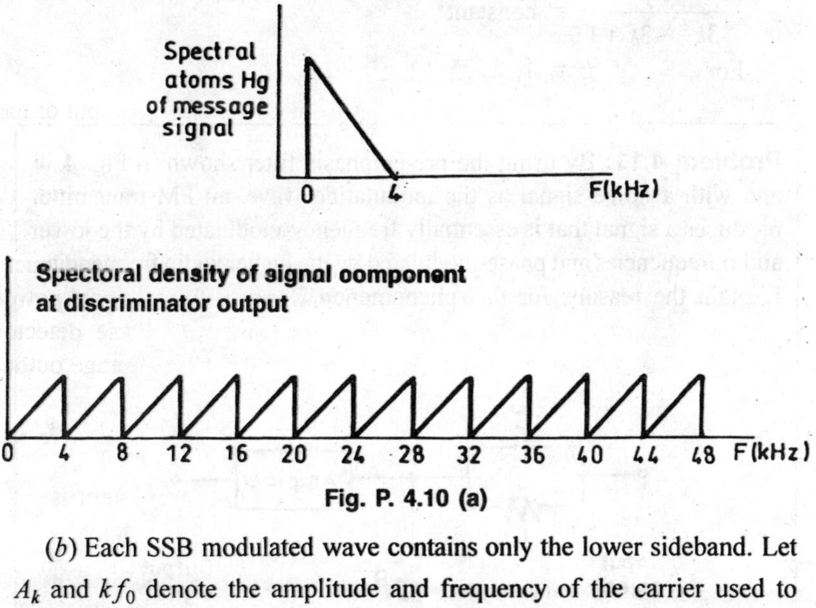

Fig. P. 4.10 (a)

(*b*) Each SSB modulated wave contains only the lower sideband. Let A_k and kf_0 denote the amplitude and frequency of the carrier used to generate the *k*th modulated wave where f_0 = 4 kHz and k = 1, 2, … 12. Then we find that the *k*th wave occupied the frequency interval $(k-1) f_0 \le |f| \le kf_0$. We may define this modulated wave by

$$S_k(t) = \frac{A_k}{2} m(t) \cos(2\pi k f_0) + \frac{A_k}{2} \hat{m}(t) \sin(2\pi k f_0 t)$$

Where $m(t)$ is the original message signal and $\hat{m}(t)$ is its Hilbert transform. Therefore the average power of $S_k(t)$ is $\frac{A_k P}{4}$ where P is the mean power of $m(t)$.

Thus, we may express the output signal-to-noise ratio.

For the *k*th SSB modulated wave as follows

$$(\text{SNR})_0 = \frac{3A_c^2 k_f^2 A_k^2 \frac{P}{4}}{2N_0\left[k^3 f_0^3 - (k-1)^3 f_0^3\right]} = \frac{3\, A_c^2 A_k^2 k_f^2 P}{3\, N_0 f_0^3 (3k^2 - 3k + 1)}$$

Where A_c is the carrier amplitude of the FM wave. For equal signal-to-noise ratios, we must therefore choose the *ak* so as to satisfy the condition

$$\frac{A_k^2}{3k^2 - 3k + 1} = \text{constant}$$

For $k = 1, 2, \ldots 12$

Problem 4.11: By using the pre-emphasis filter shown in Fig. 4.11 and with a noice signal as the modulating wave, an FM transmitter produces a signal that is essentially frequency-modulated by the lower audio frequencies and phase-modulated by the higher audio frequencies. Explain the reasons for this phenomenon.

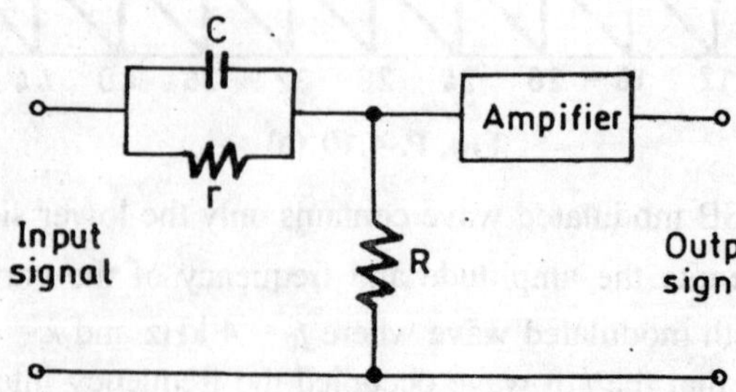

Fig. P. 4.11

Solution:

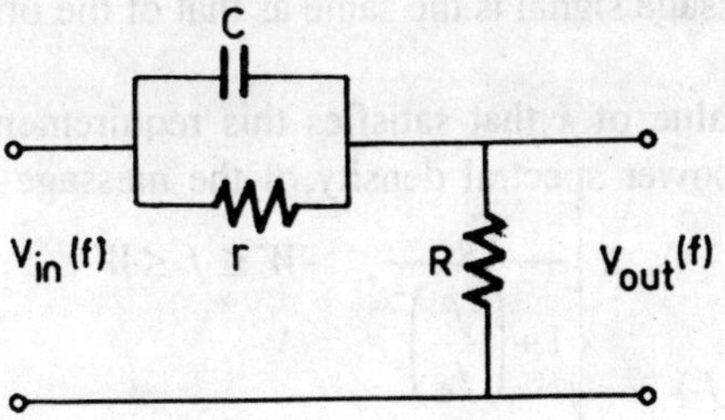

Fig. P. 4.11 (a)

Let $H(f)$ be $V_{out}(f)/V_{in}(f)$ or the transfer function of the filter. At low frequencies the capacitor behaves as an open circuit. Then

$$H(f) \cong \frac{R}{r+R} \cong \frac{R}{r}$$

Thus the low frequencies of the input are frequencies modulated. At high frequencies, the capacitor behaves as a short circuit in relation to resistor. Then

$$H(f) \cong \frac{R}{R+\dfrac{1}{j2\pi f_c}} \cong j2\pi fcR$$

and output

$$V_{out}(t) \cong RC\frac{d}{dt}V_{in}(t)$$

frequency modulating the derivative of a wave form is equivalent to phase modulating the waveform. Thus, the high frequency of the input are phase modulated.

Problem 4.12: Suppose that the transfer functions of the pre-emphasis and de-emphasis filters of an FM system are scaled as follows:

$$H_{pe}(f) = k\left(1+\frac{jf}{f_0}\right)$$

and

$$H_{de}(f) = \frac{1}{k}\left(\frac{1}{1+\dfrac{jf}{f_0}}\right)$$

The scaling factor k is to be chosen so that the average power of the emphasized message signal is the same as that of the original message signal $m(t)$.

(*a*) Find the value of k that satisfies this requirement for the case when the power spectral density of the message signal $m(t)$ is

$$S_M(f) = \begin{cases} \dfrac{S_0}{1+\left(\dfrac{f}{f_0}\right)^2}, & -W \le f \le W \\ 0, & \text{elsewhere} \end{cases}$$

(*b*) What is the corresponding value of the improvement factor I produced by using this pair of pre-emphasis and de-emphasis filters?

Solution: (*a*) For the average power of the emphasized signal to be the same as the average power of the original message signal, we must choose the transfer function $H_{pe}(f)$ of the preemphasize filter so as the satisfy the relation

$$\int_{-\infty}^{\infty} S_M(f)\,df = \int_{-\infty}^{\infty} |H_{pe}|^2 S_M(f)\,df$$

with

$$S_M(f) = \begin{cases} \dfrac{S_0}{1+\left(\dfrac{f}{f_0}\right)^2} & -W \le f \le W \\ 0, & \text{elsewhere} \end{cases}$$

$$H_{pe}(f) = k\left(1+\frac{jf}{f_0}\right)$$

We have

$$\int_{-W}^{W} \frac{df}{1+\left(\dfrac{f}{f_o}\right)^2} = k^2 \int_{-W}^{W} df$$

Then, solving for k we get

$$k = \left[\frac{f_0}{W}\tan^{-1}\left(\frac{W}{f_0}\right)\right]^{\frac{1}{2}} \qquad \text{...(1)}$$

(*b*) The component in output signal-to-noise ratio obtained by using pre-emphasis in the transmitter and de-emphasis in the defined by ratio

$$D = \frac{2W^3}{3\int_{-W}^{W} f^2 |H_{de}(f)|^2 df} = \frac{2W^3}{3\int_{-W}^{W} \frac{f^2}{k^2} \cdot \frac{df}{1+\left(\frac{f}{f_0}\right)^2}}$$

$$= \frac{k^2 (W f_0)^3}{3\left[\left(\frac{W}{f_0}\right) - \tan^{-1}\left(\frac{W}{f_0}\right)\right]} \quad \text{...(2)}$$

Substituting eqn (1) and (2), we get

$$D = \frac{\left(\frac{W}{f_0}\right)^2 \tan^{-1}\left(\frac{W}{f_0}\right)}{3\left[\left(\frac{W}{f_0}\right) - \tan^{-1}\left(\frac{W}{f_0}\right)\right]} \quad \text{...(3)}$$

This result applies to the ease when the rms bandwidth of the FM system is maintained the same with or without pre-emphasis. When, however, there is no such constraint, we can express it as

$$D = \frac{\left(\frac{W}{f_0}\right)^3}{3\left[\left(\frac{W}{f_0}\right) - \tan^{-1}\left(\frac{W}{f_0}\right)\right]} \quad \text{...(4)}$$

In the diagram below, we have plotted the improvement D (expressed in decibels) versus the ratio $\frac{W}{f_0}$ for the two cases when there is a transmission bandwidth constraint and when there is no such constraint

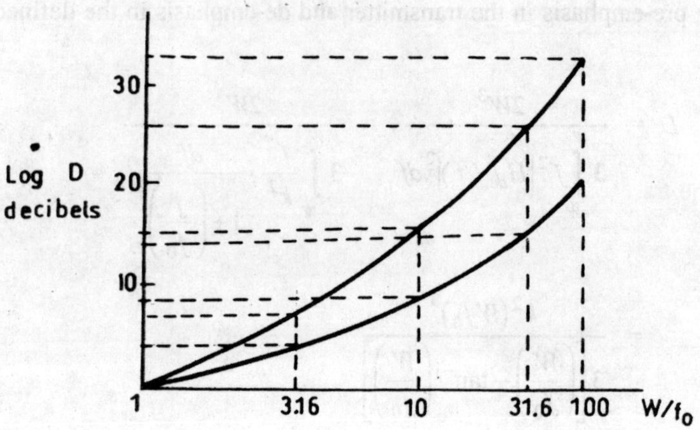

Fig. P. 4.13

Problem 4.14: A phase modulation (PM) system uses a pair of pre-emphasis and de-emphasis filters defined by the transfer functions

$$H_{pe}(f) = 1 + \frac{jf}{f_0} \text{ and } H_{de}(f) = \frac{1}{1+\left(\frac{jf}{f_0}\right)}$$

Show that the improvement in output signal-to-noise ratio produced by using this pair of filters is

$$I = \frac{\frac{W}{f_0}}{\tan^{-1}\left(\frac{W}{f_0}\right)}$$

where W is the message bandwidth. Evaluate this improvement for the case when $W = 15$ kHz and $f_0 = 2.2$ kHz, and compare your result with the corresponding value for an FM system.

Solution:

In a PM system, the power spectra density of the noise at the phase discriminator output (in the absence of pre-emphasis and de-emphasis) is approximately constant. Therefore the improvement in output signal-to-noise ratio obtained by using pre-emphasis in the transmitter and de-emphasis in the receiver of a PM system is given by

$$D = \frac{\int_0^W df}{\int_0^W \left|H_{de}(f)\right|^2 df}$$

with the transfer function $H_{de}(f)$ of the de–emphasis filter defined by

$$H_{de}(f) = \frac{1}{1+\left(\frac{jf}{f_0}\right)}$$

we find that the corresponding value of D is

$$D = \frac{W}{\int_0^W \frac{df}{1+\left(\frac{f}{f_0}\right)^2}} = \frac{\frac{W}{f_0}}{\tan^{-1}\left(\frac{W}{f_0}\right)}$$

For the case when W = 15 kHz, f_0 = 2.1 kHz, we find that D = 5, or 7 dB. The corresponding value of the improvement ratio D for an FM system is equal to 13 dB (see example 4 of chapter 5). Therefore, the improvement obtained by using pre-emphasis and de-emphasis in a PM system is smaller by an amount equal to 6 dB.

Problem 4.15: Compare the average transmitter power and channel bandwidth requirements of DSB, SSB and AM schemes for transmitting on audio signal with a bandwidth of 10 KHz with a destination signal-to-noise ratio of 50 dB. Assume that the channel introduces a 50 dB power loss and that the noise power spectral density at a receiver input is 10^{-12} W/Hz. Assume the ratio of total sideband power to the carrier power (i.e. m^2 S) for AM as 0.5. IES-95

Solution:

From the spectrum of DSB, SSB and AM signals depicted above, we have

Bandwidth of DSB = Bandwidth of AM = $2f_m$ = 20 kHz

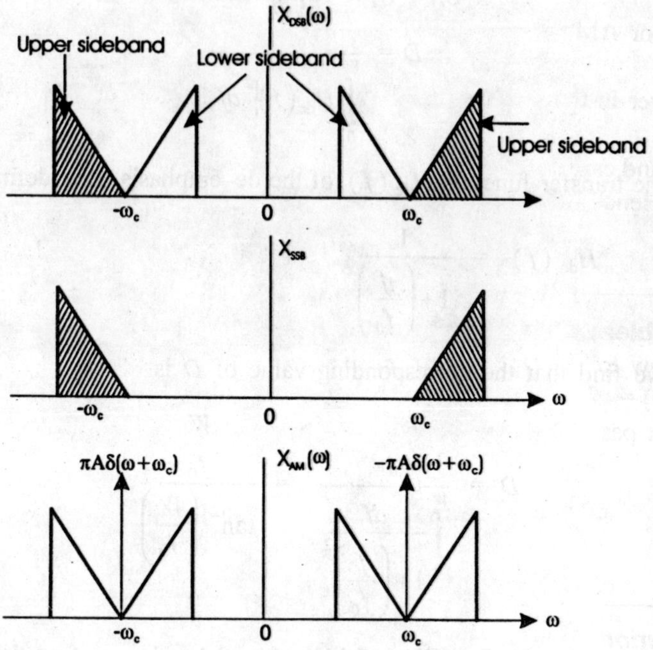

Fig. P. 4.14

and Bandwidth for SSB = 10 kHz

Now, $$\left(\frac{S}{N}\right)_{0,dB} = \left(\frac{S}{N}\right)_{i,dB} + (\text{loss})_{\text{in, }dB}$$

or, $$\left(\frac{S}{N}\right)_{i,dB} = \left(\frac{S}{N}\right)_{0,dB} + (\text{loss})_{\text{in,}dB} = 50 + 50 = 100 \text{ dB}$$

or, $$\left(\frac{S}{N}\right)_{i} = 10^{10}$$

(*i*) For DSB, $$N_i = \text{BW} \times (10^{-12} \text{ W/Hz})$$
$$= 10^{-12} \times 20 \times 10^3 = 2 \times 10^{-8} \text{ watt}$$

then, $$S_i = 2 \times 10^{-8} \times 10^{10} = 200 \text{ watt}$$

(*ii*) For SSB, $$N_i = \text{BW} \times (10^{-12} \text{ W / Hz})$$
$$= 10^4 \times 10^{-12} \text{ watt} = 10^{-8} \text{ watt}$$

As, $$\left(\frac{S}{N}\right)_{i} = 10^{10}$$

$$S_i = N_i \times 10^{10} = 100 \text{ watt}$$

(*iii*) For AM

Power in the sidebands, $P_s = (\text{BW} \times 10^{-12} \text{ W/Hz}) \times \left(\frac{S}{N}\right)_i = 200$ watt

and,carrier power, $P_c = 2P_s = 400$ watt
Hence, total power at the receiver input,

$$P_t = P_L + P_s = 400 + 200 = 600 \text{ watt.}$$

Problem 4.16: Obtain an expression for the signal v_3 (*t*) in the figure below for v_1 (*t*) =- 10 cos (2000 πt) + 4 sin (200 πt). Assume that v_2 (t) = v_1 (t) + 0.1 v_1^2 (*t*) and that the BPF is an ideal unity gain filter with pass band from 800 Hz to 1200 Hz.

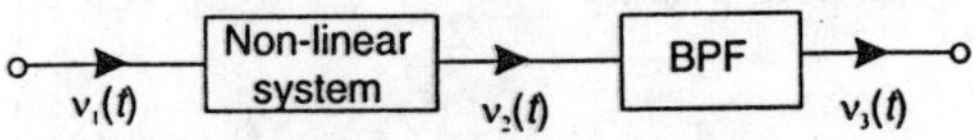

Solution: Output of non-Linear system, is given by,

$$v_2(t) = v_1(t) + 0.1\, v_1^2(t)$$

or, $$v_2(t) = [10\cos(2000\,\pi t) + 4\sin(200\pi + 1)] + [10\cos(2000\,\pi t) + 4\sin(200\,\pi t)]^2 \times 0.1$$

or, $$v_2(t) = 10\cos(2000\,\pi t) + 4\sin(200\pi t) + 0.1 \times [100\cos^2(200\,\pi t) + 16\sin^2(200\,\pi t) + 80\cos(2000\,\pi t)\sin(200\pi t)]$$

or, $$v_2(t) = 10\cos(2000\,\pi t) + 4\sin(200\,\pi t) + \left[100\left(\frac{1+\cos(4000\,\pi t)}{2}\right) + \frac{16}{2}\,\frac{[1-\cos 400\,\pi t]}{2}\right] \times 0.1$$

$$+ 40[\sin(2200\,\pi t) - \sin(1800\,\pi t)] \times 0.1$$

or, $$v_2(t) = 10\cos(2000\,\pi t) + 0.5\cos(4000\,\pi t) - 0.8\cos(400\,\pi t) + 4\sin(200\,\pi t) + 4\sin(2200\,\pi t) - 4\sin(1800\,\pi t) + 5.8$$

Since, BPF has a pas-band from 800 HZ - 1200 HZ.

$$V_3(t) = 10\cos(2000\,\pi t) + 4\sin(2200\,\pi t) - 4\sin(1800\,\pi t)$$

Problem 4.17: A given AM broadcast station transmits a total power of 5 kW when the carrier is modulated by a sinusoidal signal with a modulation index of 0.7071. Calculate:

(*i*) the carrier power

(*ii*) the transmission efficiency, and

(*iii*) the peak amplitude of the carrier assuming the antenna to be represented by a $(500 + j\omega)\ \Omega$ load.

Solution: (i) An amplitude modulated signal is expressed as

$$x_{AM}(t) = A\cos\omega_c t + \mu A\cos\omega_m t\cos\omega_c t$$

or, $$x_{AM}(t) = A\cos\omega_c t + \frac{1}{2}\mu A\cos(\omega_c - \omega_m)t + \frac{\mu A}{2}\cdot\cos(\omega_c + \omega_m)t$$

Now, P_C (carrier power) $= \dfrac{A^2}{2}$.

and, P_S (sideband power) $= \dfrac{1}{2}\left[\left(\dfrac{1}{2}\mu A\right)^2 + \left(\dfrac{\mu A}{2}\right)^2\right] = \dfrac{\mu^2 A^2}{4}$

Hence, total power, $P_t = \dfrac{A^2}{2}\left(1 + \dfrac{\mu^2}{2}\right)$

or, $$P_t = P_C\left(1 + \frac{\mu^2}{2}\right)$$

As, given, $P_t = 50 \times 10^3$ watt,

Then, $$P_C = \frac{P_t}{1 + \frac{\mu^2}{2}} = \frac{50 \times 10^3}{1.25} = 40\ \text{kW}$$

(*ii*) Transmission efficiency, $\eta = \dfrac{P_s}{P_t} \times 100\%$

or, $$\eta = \frac{\frac{1}{4}\mu^2 A^2}{\left(\frac{1}{2} + \frac{\mu^2}{4}\right)A^2} \times 100\% = \frac{\mu^2}{2 + \mu^2} \times 100\%$$

$$\text{or, } \eta = \frac{0.50}{2+0.50} \times 100\% = 20\%$$

(*iii*) Power delivered to the load $= \dfrac{A_c^2}{2R} = 40 \times 10^3$

then, $A_c = \sqrt{2 \times 40 \times 10^3 \times 50} = 2\text{ kW}$

Problem 4.18: The sample function $x(t) = A_c \cos(2\pi f_c t) + \omega(t)$ is applied to the low-pass RC filter shown in the figure below. The amplitude Ac and frequency f_c of the sinusoidal component are constants, and $\omega(t)$ is a white Gaussian noise of zero mean and power spectral density $\dfrac{N_0}{2}$. Find an expression for the output signal-to-noise ratio with the sinusoidal component of $x(t)$ regarded as the signal of interest.

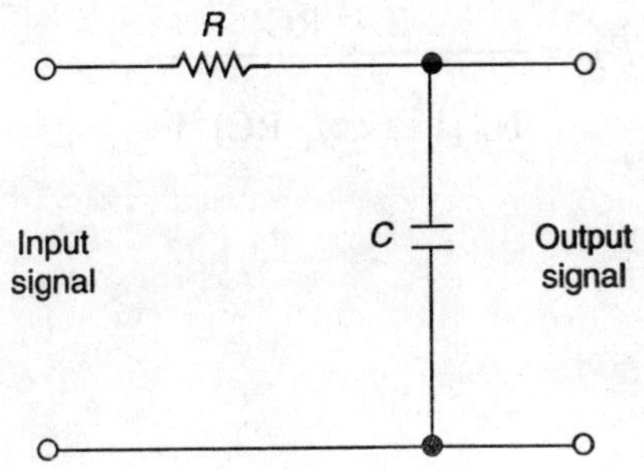

Fig. P. 4.18

Solution: Frequency response $H(\omega)$ of the given RC low-pass filter is expressed as,

$$H(\omega) = \frac{1}{j\omega RC + 1}$$

and, output noise power, $N_0 = E(\eta_0^2(t))$

or, $$N_0 = \frac{1}{2\pi}\int_{-\infty}^{\infty} S_{xx}(\omega)\cdot|H(\omega)|^2\, d\omega$$

or, $$N_0 = \frac{1}{2\pi}\int_{-\infty}^{\infty} \frac{\eta}{2}\,\frac{d\omega}{(\omega\, \text{Rc})^2+1} \quad \left[\text{Given, } S_{xx}(\omega)=\frac{\eta}{2}\right].$$

or, $$N_0 = \frac{1}{2\pi}\left(\frac{\eta}{2}\right)\frac{1}{\text{RC}}\left[\tan^{-1}\omega\, \text{RC}\big|_{-\infty}^{\infty}\right]$$

or, $$N_0 = \frac{\eta}{4\,\text{RC}}$$

Here, input $x(t) = A_c \cos(2\pi f_c t)$.

then, corresponding value of the signal amplitude at the filter output

$$= \frac{A_C}{\left[1+(2\pi f_c\, \text{RC})^2\right]^{\frac{1}{2}}}$$

Hence, $$(SNR)_0 = \frac{2A_c^2\, \text{RC}}{\text{N}_0\,[1+(2\pi f_c\, \text{RC})^2]^{\frac{1}{2}}}$$

Chapter 5

Pulse Modulation

Problem 5.1: In natural sampling an analog signal $g(t)$ is multiplied by a periodic train of rectangular pulses $c(t)$. Given that the pulse repetition frequency of this periodic train is f_s and the duration of each rectangular pulse is T (with $f_s T \gg 1$), do the following:
(*a*) Find the spectrum of the signal $s(t)$ that results from the use of natural sampling; you may assume that time $t = 0$ corresponds to the midpoint of a rectangular pulse in $c(t)$.
(*b*) Show that the original signal $m(t)$ may be recovered exactly from its naturally sampled version, provided that the conditions embodied in the sampling theorem are satisfied.

Solution:

(*a*) Let a periodic train $c(f)$ of rectangular pulses, each of duration T, and the Fourier series expansion of $c(t)$ (assuming that a pulse of the train is centered on the origin) is expressed as,

$$c(t) = \sum_{n=-\infty}^{\infty} f_s \operatorname{sinc}(nf_sT) \exp(j2\pi nf_s t)$$

where f_s is the repetition frequency, and the amplitude of a rectangular pulse is assumed to be $\frac{1}{T}$ (i.e., each pulse has unit area). The assumption that $f_sT \gg 1$ means that the spectral lines (i.e., harmonics) of the periodic pulse train $c(t)$ are well separated from each other.

Multiplying a message signal $g(t)$ by $c(t)$ gives,

$$s(t) = c(t)\, g(t)$$

$$= \sum_{n=-\infty} f_s \operatorname{sinc}(nf_sT)\, g(t) \exp[j2\pi nf_s(t)] \quad \ldots(1)$$

Taking the Fourier transform of both sides of Eq. (1) and using the frequency-shifting property of the Fourier transform; we have,

$$S(f) = \sum_{n=-\infty} f_s \operatorname{sinc}(nf_sT)\, G(f - nf_s) \qquad ...(2)$$

where $G(f) = F[g(t)$. Thus, the spectrum $S(f)$ consists of frequency-shifted replicas of the original spectrum $G(f)$, with the nth replica being scaled in amplitude by the factor $f_s \operatorname{sinc}(nf_sT)$

(*b*) In accordance with the sampling theorem, it can be assumed that,

The signal $g(t)$ is band-limited with

$G(f) = 0$ for $-W < f < W$

and, the sampling frequency f_s is defined as,

$f_s > 2W$

Then, the different frequency-shifted replicas of $G(f)$ involved in the construction of $S(f)$ will not overlap. Under the conditions, the original spectrum $G(f)$, and therefore the signal $g(t)$, can be recovered exactly (except for a trivial amplitude scaling) by passing $s(t)$ through a low-pass filter of bandwidth W.

Problem 5.2: (*a*) Plot the spectrum of a PAM wave produced by the modulating signal

$$m(t) = A_m \cos(2\pi f_m t)$$

assuming a modulation frequency $f_m = 0.25$ Hz, sampling period $T_s = 1$ *s*, and pulse duration $T = 0.45$ *s*.

(*b*) Using an ideal reconstruction filter, plot the spectrum of the filter output. Compare this result with the output that would be obtained if there were no aperture effect.

Solution: (*a*) The PAM wave is expressed as,

$$s(t) = \sum_{n=-\infty}^{\infty} [1 + \mu m'(nT_S)]\, g(t - nT_S),$$

where $g(t)$ is the pulse shape, and $m'(t) = m(t)/A_M = \cos(2\pi f_m t)$. The PAM wave is equivalent to the convolution of the instantenously sampled $[1 + \mu m'(t)]$ and the pulse shape $g(t)$:

$$s(t) = \{\sum_{n=-\infty}^{\infty} [1 + \mu m'(nT_S)]\ \delta(t - nT_S)\} * g(t)$$

$$= \{[1 + \mu m'(t)] \sum_{n=-\infty}^{\infty} \delta(t - nT_S)\} * g(t)$$

Then the spectrum of the PAM wave is,

$$S(f) = \{[\delta(t) + \mu M'(f)] * \frac{1}{T} \sum_{m=-\infty}^{\infty} \delta\left(f - \frac{m}{T_S}\right)\} G(f)$$

$$= \frac{1}{T_S} G(f) \sum_{m=-\infty}^{\infty} \left[\delta\left(f - \frac{m}{T_S}\right) + \mu M'\left(f - \frac{m}{T_S}\right)\right]$$

For a rectangular pulse $g(t)$ of duration $T = 0.45$s, and with AT = 1, we have then

$$G(f) = AT\,\text{sinc}(fT) = \text{sinc}(0.45f)$$

For $m'(t) = \cos(2\pi f_m t)$,

and with $f_m = 0.25$ Hz, we have:

$$M'(f) = \frac{1}{2}[\delta(f - 0.25) + \delta(f + 0.25)]$$

For $T_S = 1$s, the ideally sampled spectrum is

$$S_\delta(f) = \sum_{m=-\infty}^{\infty} [\delta(f - m) + \mu M'(f - m)]$$

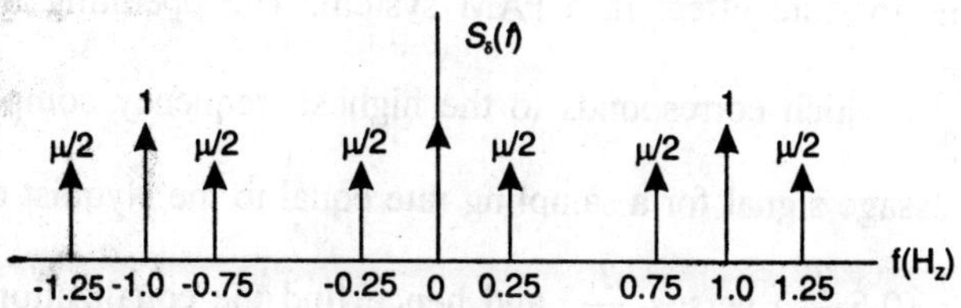

Fig. P. 5.2 (a)

The actual sampled spectrum is

$$\delta(f) = \sum_{m=-\infty}^{\infty} \text{sin}\,c\,(0.45\,f)\,[\delta\,(f-m) + \mu M'\,(f-m)]$$

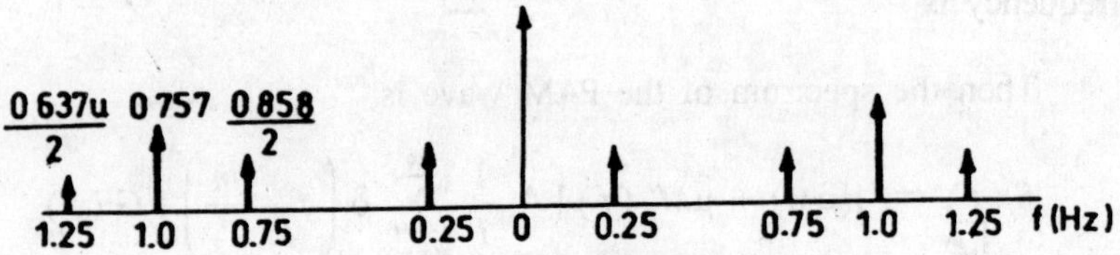

Fig. P. 5.2 (b)

(*b*) The ideal reconstruction filter would retain the centre 3 delta functions of $S(f)$ or:

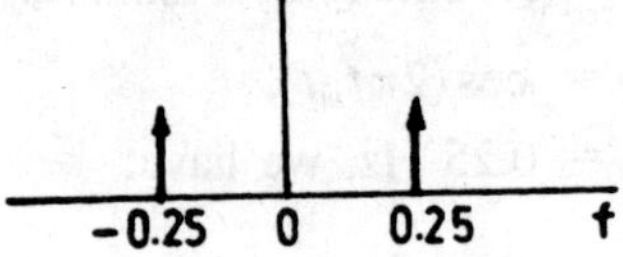

Fig. P. 5.2 (c)

With no aperture effect, the two outer delta functions would have amplitude $\frac{\mu}{2}$. Aperature effect distorts the reconstructed signal by attenuating the high frequency portion of the message signal.

Problem 5.3: In this problem we evaluate the equalization needed for the aperture effect in a PAM system. The operating frequency $f = \frac{f_s}{2}$, which corresponds to the highest frequency component of the message signal for a sampling rate equal to the Nyquist rate. Plot $1/\text{sin}\,c\,(0.5\frac{T}{T_s})$ versus $\frac{T}{T_s}$, and hence find the equalization needed when $\frac{T}{T_s} = 0.1$.

Solution: At $f = \dfrac{1}{2T_s}$ which corresponds to the highest frequency component of the message signal for a sampling rate equal to the Nyquist rate. The amplitude response of the equalizer normalized to that at zero frequency is equal to

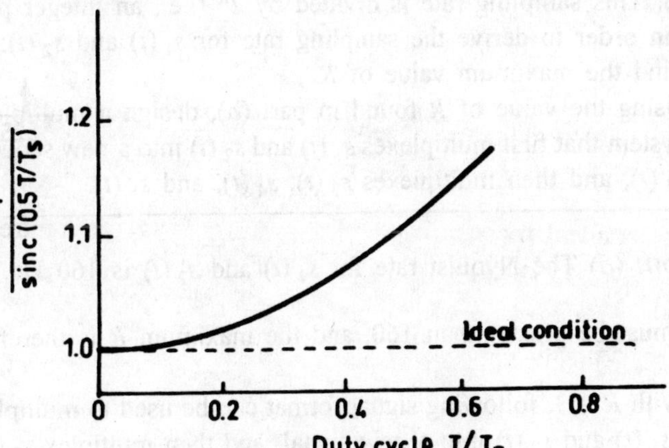

Fig. P. 5.3

$$\frac{1}{\text{sinc}\left(0.5\dfrac{T}{T_s}\right)} = \frac{\left(\dfrac{\pi}{2}\right)\left(\dfrac{T}{T_s}\right)}{\sin\left[\left(\dfrac{\pi}{2}\right)\left(\dfrac{T}{T_s}\right)\right]}$$

where the ratio $\dfrac{T}{T_s}$ is equal to the duty cycle of the sampling pulses.

In Fig. 2, this result is plotted as a function of $\dfrac{T}{T_s}$. Ideally, it should be equal to one for all values of $\dfrac{T}{T_s}$. For a duty cycle of 10 percent, it is equal to 1.0041. It follows therefore that for duty cycles of less than 10 percent, the aperature effect becomes negligible and the need for equalization can be omitted altogether.

Problem 5.4: A PAM *telemetry* system involves the multiplexing of four input signals: $s_i(t)$, $i = 1, 2, 3, 4$. Two of the signals $s_1(t)$ and $s_2(t)$ have bandwidths of 80 Hz each, whereas the remaining two signals $s_3(t)$ and $s_4(t)$ have bandwidths of 1 kHz each. The signals $s_3(t)$ and $s_4(t)$ are each sampled at the rate of 2400 samples per second. This sampling rate is divided by 2^R (i.e., an integer power of 2) in order to derive the sampling rate for $s_1(t)$ and $s_2(t)$.

(*a*) Find the maximum value of *R*.

(*b*) Using the value of *R* found in part (*a*), design a multiplexing system that first multiplexes $s_1(t)$ and $s_2(t)$ into a new sequence, $s_5(t)$, and then multiplexes $s_3(t)$, $s_4(t)$, and $s_5(t)$.

Solution: (*a*) The Nyquist rate for $s_1(t)$ and $s_2(t)$ is 160 Hz. Then, $\dfrac{2400}{2^R}$ must be greater than 160, and the maximum *R* is therefore 3.

(*b*) With $R = 3$, following signal format can be used to multiplex the signals $s_1(t)$ and $s_2(t)$ into a new signal, and then multiplex $s_3(t)$ and $s_4(t)$ and $s_5(t)$ including markers for synchronization:

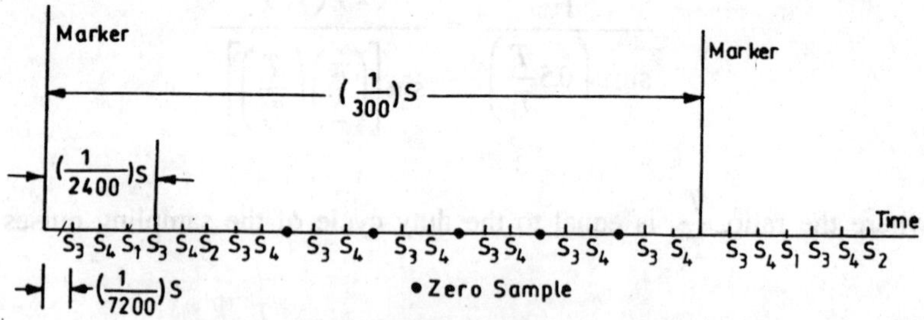

Fig. P. 5.4 (a)

Based on this signal format, following multiplexing system can be developed as,

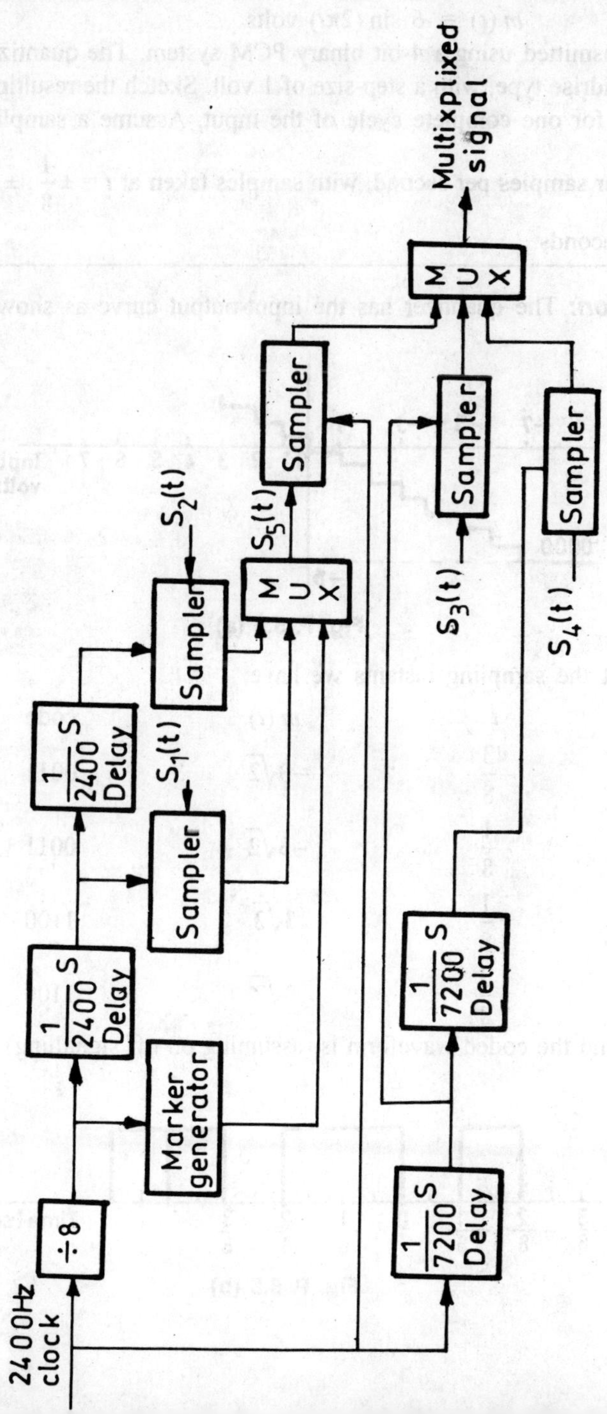
2400Hz clock
÷8
Marker generator
1/2400 S Delay
1/2400 S Delay
Sampler
Sampler
$S_1(t)$
$S_2(t)$
MUX
$S_5(t)$
Sampler
1/7200 S Delay
1/7200 S Delay
Sampler
Sampler
$S_3(t)$
$S_4(t)$
MUX
Multixplixed signal

Fig. P. 5.4 (b)

Problem 5.5: The signal

$$m(t) = 6\sin(2\pi t) \text{ volts}$$

is transmitted using a 4-bit binary PCM system. The quantizer is of the midrise type, with a step-size of 1 volt. Sketch the resulting PCM wave for one complete cycle of the input. Assume a sampling rate of four samples per second, with samples taken at $t = \pm\frac{1}{8}, \pm\frac{3}{8}, \pm\frac{5}{8}$, ..., seconds.

Solution: The quantizer has the input-output curve as shown below,

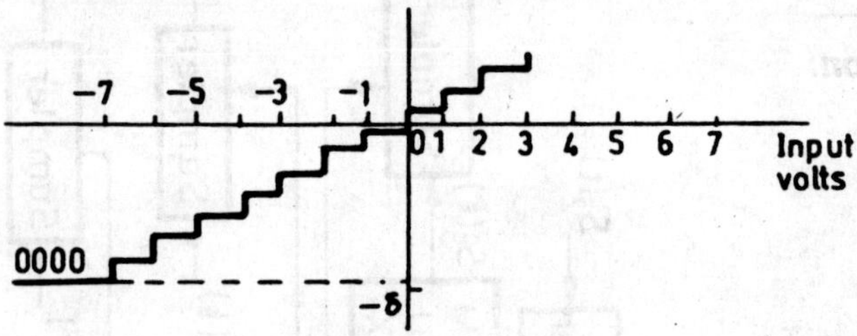

Fig. P. 5.5 (a)

At the sampling instants we have:

t	$m(t)$	code
$-\frac{3}{8}$	$-3\sqrt{2}$	0011
$-\frac{1}{8}$	$-3\sqrt{2}$	0011
$+\frac{1}{8}$	$3\sqrt{2}$	1100
$+\frac{3}{8}$	$3\sqrt{2}$	1100

And the coded waveform is (assuming on-off signalling) as shown below

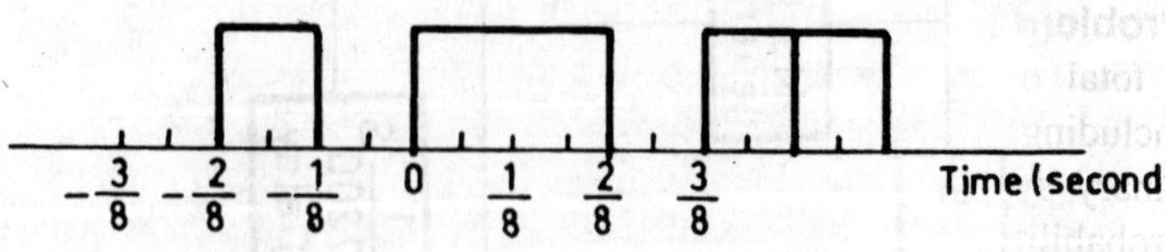

Fig. P. 5.5 (b)

Problem 5.6: Figure P. 5.6 shows a PCM signal in which the amplitude levels of +1 volt and –1 volt are used to represent binary symbols 1 and 0, respectively. The code word used consists of three bits. Find the sampled version of an analog signal from which this PCM signal is derived.

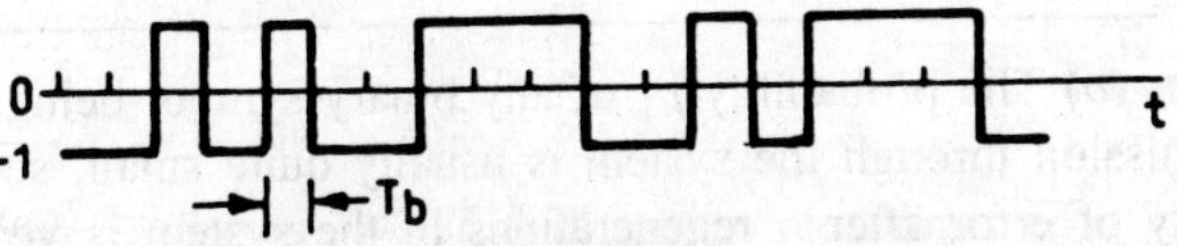

Fig. P. 5.6

Solution: The transmitted code words are given as,

t/Tb	*code*
1	001
2	010
3	011
4	100
5	101
6	110

The sampled analog signal is depicted next.

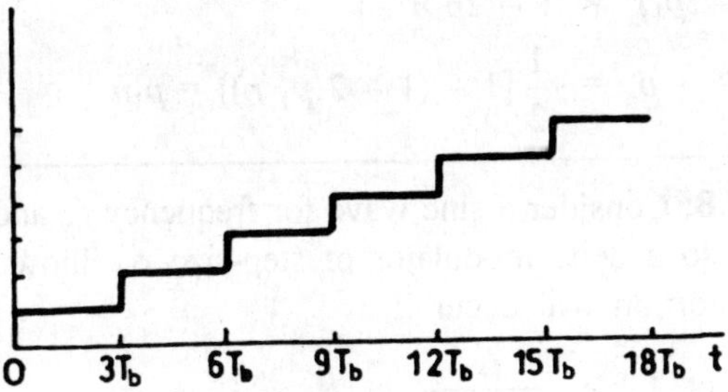

Fig. P. 5.6 (a)

Problem 5.7: Consider a chain of $(n-1)$ regenerative repeaters, with a total of n sequential decisions made on a binary PCM wave, including the final decision made at the receiver. Assume that any binary symbol transmitted through the system has an independent probability p_1 of being inverted by any repeater. Let p_n represent the probability that a binary symbol is in error after transmission through the complete system.

(*a*) Show that $p_n = \frac{1}{2}[1 - (1 - 2p_1)^n]$

(*b*) If p_1 is very small and n is not too large, what is the corresponding value of p_n?

Solution: (*a*) The probability p_1 of any binary symbol being inverted by transmission through the system is usually quite small, so that the probability of error after n regenerations in the system is very nearly equal to np_1. For very large n, the probability of more than one inversion must be taken into account. Let p_n denote the probability that a binary symbol is in error after transmission through the complete system. Then, p_n is also the probability of an odd number of errors, since an even number of errors restores the original value. Counting zero as an even number, the probability of an even number of errors is $1 - p_n$. Hence

$$p_n + 1 = p_n(1 - p_1) + (1 - p_n)\,p_1 = (1 - 2p_1)\,p_n + p_1$$

This is a linear difference equation of the first order. Its solution is

$$p_n = \frac{1}{2}[1 - (1 - 2p_1)^n]$$

(*b*) If p_1 is very small and n is not too large, then

$$(1 - 2p_1)^n = 1 - 2p_1 n$$

and

$$p_n = \frac{1}{2}[1 - (1 - 2\,p_1\,n)] = p_1 n$$

Problem 5.8: Consider a sine wave for frequency f_m and amplitude A_m, applied to a delta modulator of step-size Δ. Show that slope-overload distortion will occur if

$$A_m > \frac{\Delta}{2\pi f_m T_s}$$

where T_s is the sampling period. What is the maximum power that may be transmitted without slope-overload distortion?

Solution: The modulating wave is

$$m(t) = A_m \cos(2\pi f_m t)$$

then the slope of $m(t)$ is

$$\frac{dm(t)}{dt} = -2\pi f_m A_m \sin(2\pi f_m t)$$

and, the maximum slope of $m(t)$ is $2\pi f_m A_m$.

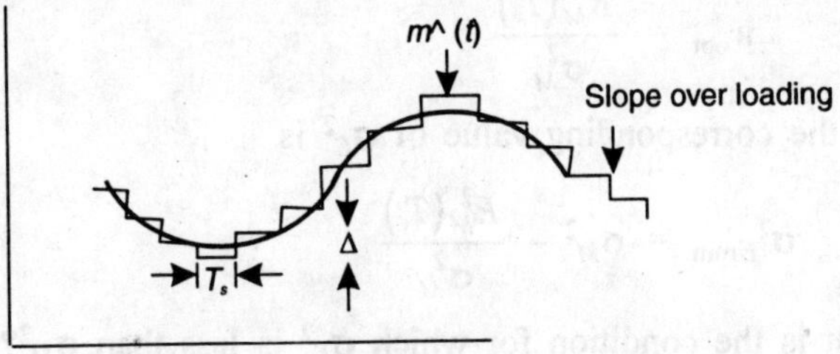

Fig. P. 5.8

The maximum average slope of the approximating signal $m_a(t)$ produced by the delta modulator is $\frac{\delta}{T_s}$, where δ is the step size and T_s is the sampling period. The limiting value of A_m is therefore given by

$$2\pi f_m A_m > \frac{\delta}{T_s}$$

or

$$A_m > \frac{\delta}{2\pi f_m T_s}$$

Assuming a load of 1 ohm, the transmitted powe is $\frac{A_m^2}{2}$. Therefore, the maximum power that may be transmitted without slope-overload distortion is equal to $\frac{\delta^2}{8\pi f_m^2 T_s^2}$.

Problem 5.9: Consider the first-order prediction defined by

$$\hat{m}(nT_s) = wm(nT_s - T_s)$$

where $m(nT_s)$ is the sample of a stationary signal of zero mean, T_s is the sampling period, and w is a constant.

(*a*) Show that the prediction error

$$e(nT_s) = m(nT_s) - \hat{m}(nT_s)$$

has variance

$$\sigma_E^2 = \sigma_M^2\left[1 + w^2 - \frac{2wR_M(T_s)}{\sigma_M^2}\right]$$

where σ_M^2 is the variance of the input signal, and $R_M(T_s)$ is its autocorrelation function for a lag of T_s.

(*b*) Show that the variance of the prediction error is minimized for

$$w_{\text{opt}} = \frac{R_M(T_s)}{\sigma_M^2}$$

and that the corresponding value of σ_E^2 is

$$\sigma^2_{E\min} = \sigma_M^2 - \frac{R_M^2(T_s)}{\sigma_M^2}$$

(*c*) What is the condition for which σ_E^2 is less than σ_M^2?

Solution: (*a*)

$$e(nT_s) = m(nT_s) - wm(nT_s - T_s)$$

$$E[e(nT_s)] = E[m(nT_s)] - wE[m(nT_s - T_s)]$$

$$= 0, \text{ because } m(nT_s) \text{ has zero mean.}$$

$$\sigma_E^2 = E[e^2(nT_s)] = \{[m(nT_s) - wm(nT_s - T_s)]^2\}$$

$$= E[m^2(nT_s) + w^2m^2(nT_s - T_s) - 2wm(nT_s)\, m(nT_s - T_s)]$$

$$= R_M(0) + w^2R_M(0) - 2wR_M(T_s)$$

$$= \sigma_M^2\left[1 + w^2 - \frac{2w\, R_M(T_s)}{\sigma_M^2}\right]$$

(*b*) For minimum prediction error variance,

$$\frac{d\sigma_E^2}{\partial w} = 0$$

$$\frac{\partial\sigma_E^2}{\partial w} = \sigma_M^2\left[2w - \frac{2R_M(T_s)}{\sigma_M^2}\right]$$

$$0 = 2w_{\text{opt}} - \frac{2R_M(T_s)}{\sigma_M^2}$$

$$w_{\text{opt}} = \frac{R_M(T_s)}{\sigma_M^2}$$

$$\sigma^2_{E,\min} = \sigma_M^2\left[1 + \frac{R_M^2(T_s)}{\sigma_M^4} - \frac{2R_M^2(T_s)}{\sigma_M^4}\right] = \sigma_M^2 - \frac{R_M^2(T_s)}{\sigma_M^2}$$

(c) For σ_E^2 to be less than σ_M^2 we must have

$$\sigma_M^2\left[1+w^2-\frac{2wR_M(T_s)}{\sigma_M^2}\right]\le\sigma_M^2$$

Equivalently, we must have $w \ge \dfrac{2R_M(T_s)}{\sigma_M^2}$

Problem 5.10: If $m(t)$ is a band-limited signal, show that

$$\int_{-\infty}^{\infty} m(t)\,\phi_n(t)\,dt = T_s m(nT_s)$$

where $\phi_n(t)$ is the function defined as $\phi_n(t) = \dfrac{\sin\omega_M(t-nT_s)}{\omega_M(t-nT_s)}$

Solution: Since $m(t)$ is a real-valued band-limiting signal, therefore $m(t)$ can be uniquely determined from its values $m(nT_s)$ sampled at uniform intervals $T_s\left[\le\dfrac{1}{(2f_M)}\right]$, and it is expressed as,

$$m(t) = \sum_{n=-\infty}^{\infty} m(nT_s)\frac{\sin\omega_M(t-nT_s)}{\omega_M(t-nT_s)}$$

or $$m(t) = \sum_{n=-\infty}^{\infty} m(nT_s)\cdot\phi_n(t)$$

Now, $$\int_{-\infty}^{\infty} m(t)\,\phi_n(t)\,dt = \int_{-\infty}^{\infty}\left[\sum_{n=-\infty}^{\infty} m(nT_s)\cdot\phi_n(t)\right]\cdot\phi_n(t)\,dt$$

or, $$\int_{-\infty}^{\infty} m(t)\,\phi_n(t)\,dt = \sum_{n=-\infty}^{\infty} m(nT_s)\cdot\int_{-\infty}^{\infty}\phi_n(t)\,\phi_n(t)\,dt = m(nT_s)\cdot T_s$$

Using relation $\int_{-\infty}^{\infty}\phi_n(t)\,\phi_k(t)\,dt = T_s\cdot\delta_{nk}$ where $\delta_{nk} = \begin{cases}1, & n=k\\ 0, & n\ne k\end{cases}$

Problem 5.11: A signal

$$m(t) = \cos 200\,\pi t + 2\cos 320\,\pi t$$

is ideally sampled at $f_s = 300$ Hz. If the sampled signal is passed through an ideal low-pass filter with a cutoff frequency of 250 Hz, what frequency components will appear in the output?

Solution: The spectrum of $m(t)$ can be expressed as,

$$M(f) = \frac{1}{2}[\delta(f - 100) + \delta(f + 100)] + [\delta(f - 160) + \delta(f + 160)]$$ as

depicted in Fig. 5.11 P. (a)

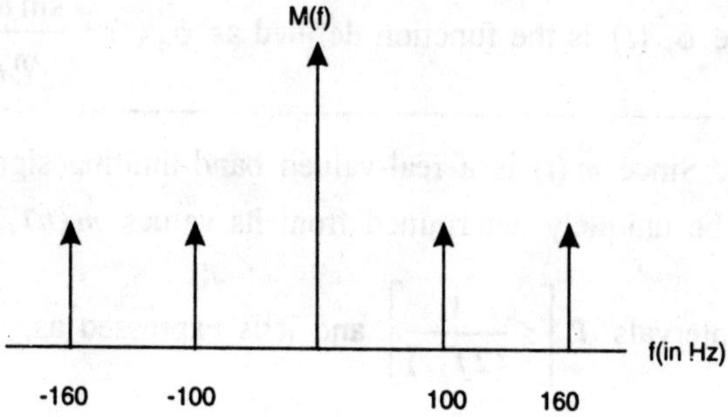

Fig. P. 5.11 (a)

Figure 5.11 (b) illustrated next shows spectrum $M_s(\omega)$ of the ideal sampled signal having sample frequency $f_s = 300$ Hz

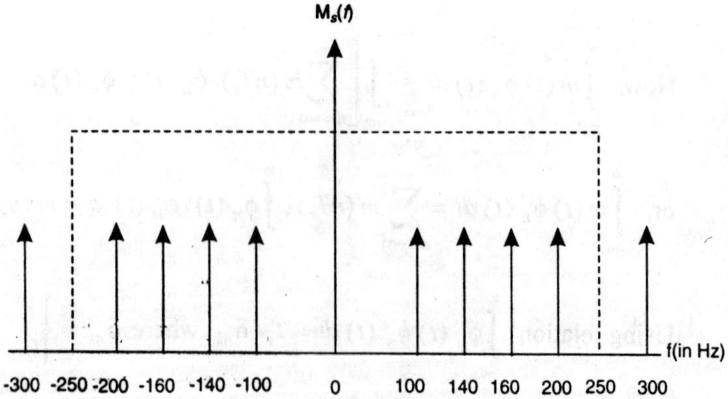

Fig. P. 5.11 (b)

Now, it can be inferred that, if sampled signal is passed through an ideal low-pass filter having cut-off frequency of 250 HZ as indicated by a dashed lined in the Fig. 5.11 P. (b), then frequency components having frequencies 100 Hz, 140 Hz, 160 Hz, and 200 Hz will be appear at the output.

Problem 5.12: American Standard Code for Information Interchange (ASCII) has 128 characters which are binary-coded. If a computer generates 100000 characters per second, determine.

(*i*) The number of bits required per character

(*ii*) The data rate (or bite rate) R_b required to transmit the computer output.

Solution: (*i*) If n be the number of bits required/character, then, we have

$$n = \log_2 (128) = 7 \ b/\text{character}$$

(*ii*) Duration of each bit is given by, $T_b = \frac{1}{7 \times 10^5} \text{ sec} = \frac{1}{.7} \ \mu \text{ sec.}$

Hence,data rate, $R_b = \frac{1}{T_b} = 0.7$ Mb/s.

Problem 5.13: A PCM system uses a uniform quantizer followed by a 7-b binary encoder. The bite rate of the system is 50 Mb/s. What is the maximum message bandwidth for which system operation is satisfactory?

Solution: As we know

$$nf_s \leq R_b$$

or, $f_s \leq \frac{R_b}{n} \leq \frac{50}{7} = 7.14$ [As given, $R_b = 50$ Mb/s, $n = 7$

Also, $2f_M \leq f_s$

or, $f_m \leq \frac{f_s}{2}$

Hence, maximum message bandwidth, $f_{\max} = \frac{f_s}{2} = 3.57$ MHz

Problem 5.14: Consider binary PCM transmission of a video signal with f_s = 10 MHz. Calculate the signaling rate needed to achieve $(\text{SNR})_0 \geq 45\,dB$.

Solution: For binary PCM, signal to noise ratio in dB,

$$\left(\frac{S}{N_q}\right)_{dB} = 1.76 + 6.02$$

Now given, that $[\text{SNR}]_0 \geq 45$ dB

then, $1.76 + 6.02\,n \geq 45$

or, $n \geq 7.18$

and number of binary digit, $n = 8$

Hence, signalling rate, $R_b = nf_s$

$R_b = 8 \times 10 = 80$ MHz

Problem 5.15: Show that in a PCM system, the output signal-to-quantizing-noise ratio can be expressed as

$$\left(\frac{S}{N_q}\right)_0 = \frac{3}{2}\left(4^{\frac{f_B}{f_m}}\right)$$

where f_B is the channel bandwidth and f_m is the message bandwidth.

Solution: In a binary PCM, the quantization levels are expressed by,

$$L = 2^n, \qquad \text{...(1)}$$

where, n = number of bits

and, the minimum required bandwidth for PCM is given by,

$$f_{\text{PCM}} = \frac{n}{2} f_s \geq f_m \text{ Hz.} \qquad \text{...(2)}$$

where f_s and f_m are sampling rate and message bandwidth respectively.

Now, signal-to-quantization ratio,

$$\left(\frac{S}{N_q}\right) = \frac{3}{2}L^2 \text{ or, } \left(\frac{S}{N_q}\right) = \frac{3}{2}2^{2n} \quad \text{Using equation (1)}$$

or, $$\left(\frac{S}{N_q}\right)_0 = \frac{3}{2}2^{\left(\frac{2f_B}{f_m}\right)} = \frac{3}{2}\left(4^{\frac{f_B}{f_m}}\right) \qquad \text{Here } f_{\text{PCM}} = f_B$$

Problem 5.16: The bandwidth of a TV radio plus audio signal is 4.5 MHz. If this signal is converted to PCM with 1024 quantizing levels, determine the bit rate of the resulting PCM signal. Assume that the signal is sampled at a rate 20 percent above the Nyquist rate.

Solution: Given, $L = 1024$

then, we have $n = \log_2 (1024) = 10$

and, Nyquist rate $= 2f_m = 2 \times 4.5$ MHz $= 9$ MHz

Hence, sampling rate $f_s = 9 \times 1.2$ MHz $= 10.8$ MHz

and, bit rate, $R_b = nf_s = 10 \times 10.8$ MHz $= 108$ Mb/s

Problem 5.17: Given the binary sequence 1101110, draw the transmitted pulse waveform for

(*i*) AMI RZ signalizing format and

(*ii*) split-phase (Manchester) signaling format.

Solution:

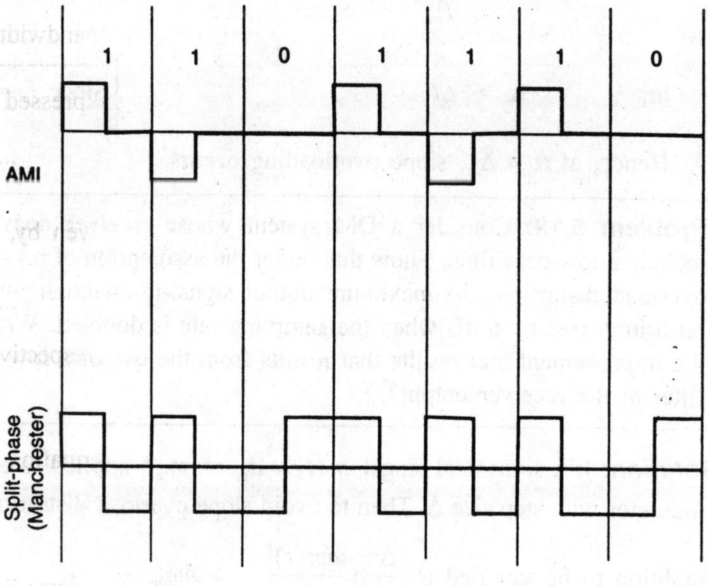

Fig. P. 5.17 (a)

(*i*) In AMI RZ signalling format, positive and negative pulses (of equal magnitude) are used alternatively for symbol 1, and no pulse is used for symbol 0. In either case pulse returns to zero before the end of bit interval as illustrated in Fig. P. 5.17 (a)

(*ii*) In split-phase signalling format, symbol 1 is represented by a positive pulse followed by a negative pulse, with both pulses being of equal amplitude and half-bit duration and for symbol 0, the polarities of these pulses are reversed as depicted in Fig.

Problem 5.18: A given DM system operates with a sampling ratio, f_s and a fixed size Δ. If the input to the system is

$$m(t) = \alpha t \text{ for } t > 0$$

Determine the value of α for which slope overload occurs.

Solution: For slope overloading to occur, the condition is,

$$\left|\frac{dm(t)}{dt}\right|_{\max} > \frac{\Delta}{T_s}$$

then, $$\alpha > \frac{\Delta}{T_s}$$

or, $$\alpha > \Delta f_s \qquad \left[\text{Since } f_s = \frac{1}{T_s}\right]$$

Hence, at $\alpha = \Delta f_s$, slope overloading occurs.

Problem 5.19: Consider a DM system whose receiver does not include a low-pass filter. Show that under the assumption of no slope overload distortion, the maximum output signal-to-quantizing-noise ratio increases by 6 dB when the sampling rate is doubled. What is the improvement that results that results from the use of a low-pass filter at the receiver output?

Solution: If a sinusoidal singal $m(t) = A_m \cos \omega_m t$ applied to a delta modulator with step size Δ. Then to avoid slope overload distortion, the condition to be satisfied is $\frac{\Delta}{T_s} \geq \left|\frac{dm(t)}{dt}\right|_{\max} = A\omega_m$

or $$A \leq \frac{\Delta}{\omega_m T_s} \leq \frac{\Delta}{\omega_m} \cdot f_s$$

Maximum permissible value of the output signal power is expressed by,

$$P_{max} = \frac{A^2}{2} = \frac{\Delta^2 f_s^2}{8\pi^2 f_m^2}$$

Mean-square quantizing error $< q_e^2 >= \frac{\Delta^2}{3}$.

Then signal-to-quantizing-noise ratio can be given as,

$$[\text{SNR}]_0 = \left(\frac{S}{N_q}\right)_0 = \frac{P_{max}}{\frac{\Delta^2}{3}} = \frac{3f_s^2}{8\pi^2 f_m^2} = Cf_s^2$$

whre $C = \frac{3}{8\pi^2 f_m^2}$

In dB, signal-to-noise ratio can be expressed as,

$$(\text{SNR})_{0\text{dB}} = \left(\frac{S}{N_q}\right)_{0dB} = 10 \log C + 20 \log (f_s)$$

Then, change in signal-to-quantizing-noise ratio after sampling rate is doubled is, given by,

$$\Delta[(\text{SNR})_{0d\text{B}}] = 20 \log 2f_s - 20 \log f_s$$

or, $$\Delta[(\text{SNR})_{0d\text{B}}] = 20 \log \left(\frac{2f_s}{f_s}\right) = 6 \text{ dB}$$

Let the bandwidth of a postreconstruction low-pass filter at the output, end of the receiver be $f_M \geq f_m$ and $f_M << f_s$. Then, assuming that the quantizing noise power N_q is distributed over the frequency band upto f_s, the output quantizing noise power within the bandwidth f_M is,

$$N_q = \left(\frac{\Delta^2}{3}\right)\frac{f_M}{f_s} \text{ then, } \left(\frac{S}{N_q}\right)_0 = \frac{P_{max}}{N_q} = \frac{3f_s^3}{8\pi^2 f_m^2 f_M} = c' f_s^3$$

where $C' = \frac{3}{8\pi^2 f_m^2 f_M}$

Expressing in decibels, we have $\left(\frac{S}{N_q}\right)_{0dB} = 10 \log C + 30 \log f_s$

Hence, change in signal to quantizing-noise ratio

$$= \Delta\,[(\text{SNR})_{0dB}] = 30 \log (2f_s) - 30 \log f_s = 9 \text{ dB}$$

Problem 5.20: Determine Nyquist interval.

(a) $g(t) = \sin c\,(200\,t) = \dfrac{\sin 200\,\pi t}{200\,\pi t} = \dfrac{1}{200} \cdot \left[\dfrac{\sin 200\,\pi t}{\pi t}\right]$

(b) $g(t) = \sin c^2\,(200\,t)$

(c) $g(t) = \sin c\,(200\,t) + \sin c^2\,(200\,t)$

Solution: The, Fourier transform of $g(t)$ is expressed by,

$$F\,[g(t)] = \frac{1}{200} \cdot P_a(\omega)$$

$$\text{where } P_a(\omega) = \begin{cases} 1, & |\omega| < 200\,\pi \\ 0, & |\omega| < 200\,\pi \end{cases}$$

Figure 5.20 (a) and Figure P. 5.20 (b) illustrates $g(t)$ and its spectrum.

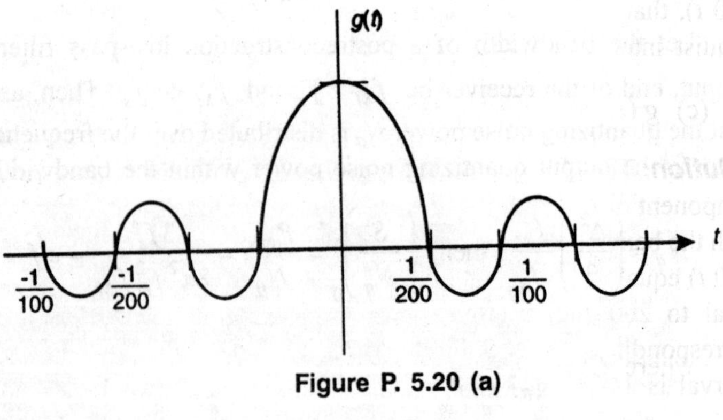

Figure P. 5.20 (a)

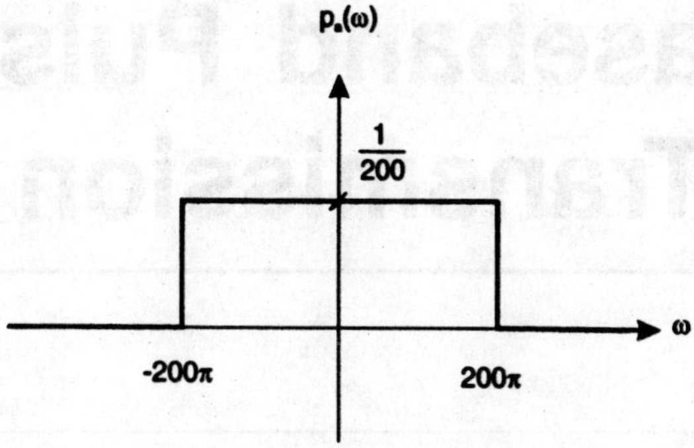

Fig. P. 5.20 (b)

Now, from the figure it can be inferred that, sampling rate = 200 Hz (Nyquist rate)

$$\text{Nyquist interval} = \frac{1}{200} \text{ sec.}$$

(b) $g(t) = \sin c^2 (200t)$

Solution: This signal can be expressed as the product of the sin *c* pulse and sin *c* (200 *t*) with itslef. Since multiplication in the time domain corresponds to convolution in the frequency domain, we find that the signal *g* (*t*) has a bandwidth equal to twice that of the sin *c* pulse sin (200 *t*), that is 200 Hz. Hence, Nyquist rate of *g* (*t*) is 400 Hz, and the Nyquist interval is 1/400 seconds.

(c) $g(t) = \sin c\,(200t) + \sin c^2 (200t)$

Solution: The bandwidth of *g* (*t*) is determined by the highest frequency component of sin *c* (200 *t*) or sin c^2 (200 *t*), whichever one is the largest. With the bandwidth (i.e., highest frequency component of) the sin *c* pulse (200 *t*) equal to 100 Hz and that of the squared sin *c* pulse sin c^2 (200 *t*), equal to 200 Hz, it follows that the bandwidth of *g* (*t*) is 200 Hz. Correspondingly, the Nyquist rate of *g* (*t*) is 400 Hz, and its Nyquist interval is 1/400 seconds.

Chapter 6

Baseband Pulse Transmission

Problem 6.1: Consider a rectangular pulse defined by

$$g(t) = \begin{cases} A, & 0 \le t \le T \\ 0, & \text{otherwise} \end{cases}$$

It is proposed to approximate the matched filter for $g(t)$ by an ideal low-pass filter of bandwidth B; maximization of the peak pulse signal-to-noise ratio is the primary objective.

(*a*) Determine the optimum value of B for which the ideal low-pass filter provides the best approximation to the matched filter.

(*b*) By how many decibels is the ideal low-pass filter worse off that the matched filter?

Solution: Ideal low-pass filter with variable bandwidth. The transfer function of the matched filter for a rectangular pulse of duration τ and amplitude A is expressed by,

$$H_{\text{opt}}(f) = \operatorname{sinc}(fT)\exp(-j\pi fT) \quad \text{...(1)}$$

The amplitude response $|H_{\text{opt}}(f)|$ of the matched filter is plotted in Fig. 6.1 (a). Response approximating filter with an ideal low-pass filter of bandwidth B is shown in Fig. 6.1 (b). The requirement is to determine the particular value of bandwidth B that can provide the best approximate to the matched filter.

The maximum value of the output signal, produced by an ideal low-pass filter in response to the rectangular pulse occurs at $t = \frac{T}{2}$ for

$BT \leq 1$. This maximum value, expressed in terms of the sine integral, is equal to $\left(\frac{2A}{\pi}\right) Si(\pi BT)$. The average noise power at the output of the ideal low–pass filter is equal to BN_0. The maximum output signal-to-noise ratio of the ideal low-pass filter, is then,

$$(\text{SNR})'_0 = \frac{\left(\frac{2A}{\pi}\right)^2 Si^2(\pi BT)}{BN_0} \qquad \ldots(2)$$

Using eqn (1) and eqn (2) and putting $AT = 1$, we have

$$\frac{(SNR)'_0}{(SNR)_0} = \frac{2}{\pi^2 BT} Si^2\,(\pi BT)$$

This ratio is plotted in Fig. 6.1 (c) as a function of the time-bandwidth product BT. The peak value on this curve occurs for $BT = 0.685$, for which we find that the maximum signal-to-noise ratio of the ideal low-pass filter is 0.84 dB below that of the true matched filter. Therefore, the "best" value for the bandwidth of the ideal low-pass filter characteristic of Fig. 6.1 (b) is $B = 0.685/T$.

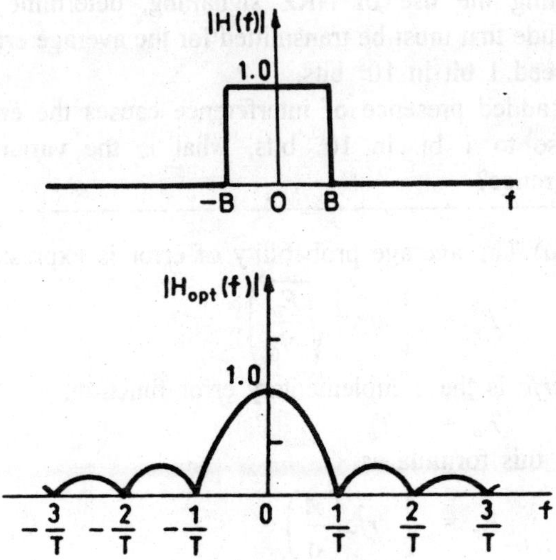

Fig. P. 6.1 (a) and (b)

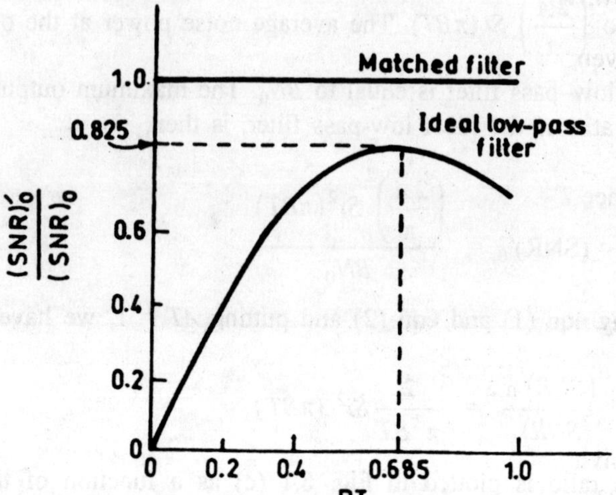

Fig. P. 6.1 (c)

Problem 6.2: A continuous-time signal is sampled and then transmitted as a PCM signal. The random variable at the input of the decision device in the receiver has a variance of 0.01 volts^2.

(*a*) Assuming the use of NRZ signalling, determine the pulse amplitude that must be transmitted for the average error rate not to exceed 1 bit in 10^8 bits.

(*b*) If the added presence of interference causes the error rate to increase to 1 bit in 10^6 bits, what is the variance of the interference?

Solution: (*a*) The average probability of error is expressed by,

$$P_e = \frac{1}{2}\, erfc\left(\sqrt{\frac{E_b}{N_0}}\right),$$

where *erfc* is the complementary error function.

where $E_b = A^2 T_b$

Rewrite this formula as,

$$P_e = \frac{1}{2}\, erfc\left(\frac{A}{\sigma}\right) \qquad ...(1)$$

where A is the pulse amplitude at $\sigma = \sqrt{N_0 T_b}$.

Now, let, $u = \sqrt{\frac{E_b}{N_0}} = \frac{A}{\sigma}$

Given,

$$\sigma^2 = 10^{-2} \text{ volts}^2,$$
$$\sigma = 0.1 \text{ volt}$$
$$P_e = 10^{-8}$$

Since P_e is quite small, then it can be approximated as follows,

$$erfc\,(u) = \frac{\exp(-u^2)}{\sqrt{\pi u}}$$

Rewriting eqn (1) with $P_e = 10^{-8}$, we get

$$\frac{\exp(-u^2)}{2}\sqrt{\pi u} = 10^{-8}$$

Solving this equation for u, obtain, $u = 3.97$

Than the corresponding value of the pulse amplitude is given by,

$$A = \sigma u = 0.1 \times 3.97 = 0.397 \text{ volts}$$

(*b*) Let σ_i^2 denote the combined variance due to noise and interference; that is

$$\sigma_T^2 = \sigma^2 + \sigma_i^2$$

where σ^2 is due to noise and σ_i^2 is due to the interference. The new value of the average probability of error is 10^{-6}. Hence

$$10^{-6} = \frac{1}{2}\, erfc\left(\frac{A}{\sigma_T}\right) = \frac{1}{2}\, erfc\,(u_T) \qquad \ldots(2)$$

where $u_T = \frac{A}{\sigma_T}$

Equation (2) may be approximated as (with $P_e = 10^{-6}$)

$$\frac{\exp\left(-u_T^2\right)}{2\sqrt{\pi}\, u_T} = 10^{-6}$$

Solving for u_T, we obtain, $u_T = 3.37$

The corresponding value of σ_T^2 is given by,

$$\sigma_T^2 = \left(\frac{A}{u_T}\right)^2 = \left(\frac{0.397}{3.37}\right)^2 = 0.0138 \text{ volts}^2$$

The variance of the interference is therefore

$$\sigma_i^2 = \sigma_T^2 - \sigma^2 = 0.0138 - 0.01 = 0.0038 \text{ volts}^2$$

Problem 6.3: In a binary PCM system, symbols 0 and 1 have *a priori probabilities* p_0 and p_1, respectively. The conditional probability density function of the random variable Y (with sample value y) obtained by sampling the matched filter output in the receiver of Fig. 6.3 at the end of a signaling interval, given that symbol 0 was transmitted, is denoted by $f_Y\left(\frac{y}{0}\right)$. Similarly, $f_Y\left(\frac{y}{1}\right)$ denotes the conditional probability density function of Y, given that symbol 1 was transmitted. Let λ denote the threshold used in the receiver, so that if the sample value y exceeds λ, the receiver decides in favour of symbol 1; otherwise, it decides in favour of symbol 0. Show that the optimum threshold λ_{opt}, for which the average probability of error is a minimum, is given by the solution of

$$\frac{f_Y(\lambda_{opt}|1)}{f_Y(\lambda_{opt}|0)} = \frac{p_0}{p_1}$$

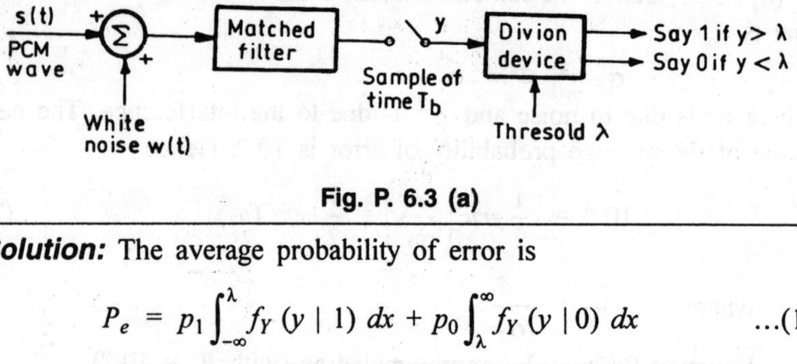

Fig. P. 6.3 (a)

Solution: The average probability of error is

$$P_e = p_1 \int_{-\infty}^{\lambda} f_Y(y \mid 1)\, dx + p_0 \int_{\lambda}^{\infty} f_Y(y \mid 0)\, dx \qquad \ldots(1)$$

An optimum choice of λ corresponds to minimum P_e. Differentiating Eq. (1) with respect to λ, we get:

$$\frac{\partial P_e}{\partial \lambda} = p_1 f_Y(\lambda \mid 1) - p_0 f_Y(\lambda \mid 0)$$

Setting $\frac{\partial P_e}{\partial \lambda} = 0$, we get the following condition for the optimum value of λ:

$$\frac{f_Y(\lambda_{opt} \mid 1)}{f_Y(\lambda_{opt} \mid 0)} = \frac{p_0}{p_1}$$ which is the desired result.

Problem 6.4: The overall pulse shape $p(t)$ of a baseband binary PAM system is defined by

$$p(t) = \text{sin}\,c\left(\frac{t}{T_b}\right)$$

where T_b is the bit duration of the input binary data. Ther amplitude levels at the pulse modulator output are + 1 or – 1, depending on whether the binary symbol at the input is 1 or 0, respectively. Sketch the waveform at the output of the receive filter in response to the input data 001101001.

Solution: The shape for symbol 1 is:

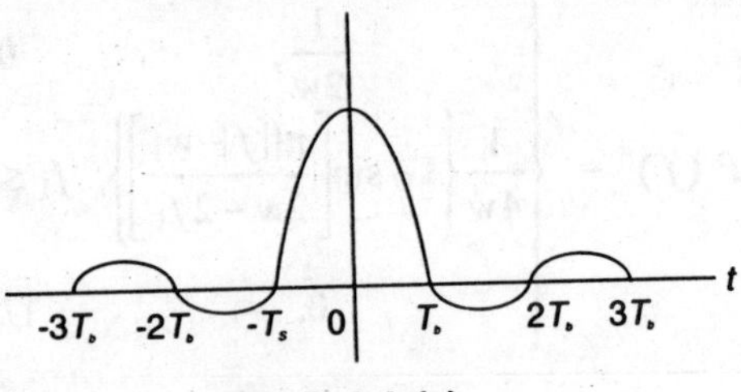

Fig. P. 6.4 (a)

The input data superimposed are depicted next,

Fig. P. 6.4 (b)

The resultant waveform is shown below,

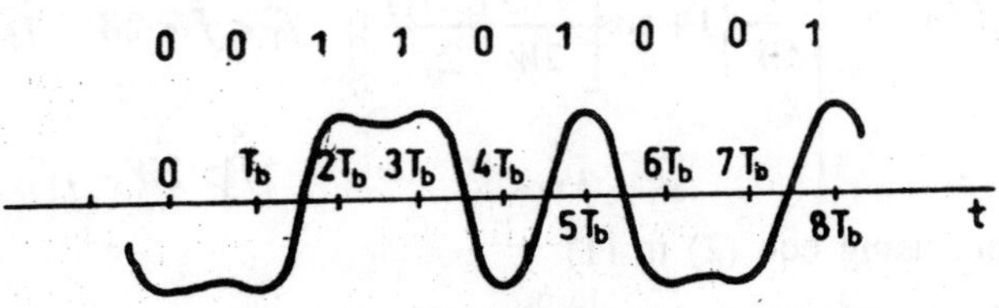

Fig. P. 6.4 (c)

(*a*) 2 amplitude levels are equivalent to $\log_2 2 = 1$ bit per pulse.

Therefore, 6 pulses are required per sample. $B_T = \dfrac{6}{2T_s} = 24$ kHz, ($\dfrac{1}{T_s}$ is the sampling rate).

(*b*) 4 amplitude levels are equivalent to 2 bits per pulse. $B_T = \frac{3}{2T_s}$ = 12 kHz.

(*c*) 8 amplitude levels are equivalent to 3 bits per pulse. $B_T = \frac{2}{2T_S}$ = 8 kHz.

Problem 6.5: Determine the inverse Fourier transform of the frequency function $P(f)$ defined in as

$$P(f) = \begin{cases} \frac{1}{2w}, & 0 \le |f| < f_1 \\ \frac{1}{4w}\left\{1 - \sin\left[\frac{\pi(|f| - w)}{2w - 2f_1}\right]\right\}, & f_1 \le |f| < 2w - f_1 \\ 0, & |f| \ge 2w - f_1 \end{cases}$$

Solution: Since $P(f)$ is an even real function, its inverse Fourier transform equals to,

$$p(t) = 2\int_0^\infty P(f)\cos(2\pi f t)\,df \qquad \text{...(1)}$$

The $P(f)$ defined is reproduced here in the form,

$$P(f) = \begin{cases} \frac{1}{2W}, & 0 < |f| < f_1 \\ \frac{1}{4W}\left\{1 + \cos\left[\frac{\pi(|f| - f_1)}{2W - 2f_1}\right]\right\}, & f_1 < f < 2W - f_1 \\ 0, & |f| > 2W - f_1 \end{cases} \qquad \text{...(2)}$$

Then, using eqn (2) in (1):

$$p(t) = \frac{1}{W}\int_0^{f_1} \cos(2\pi f t)\,df +$$

$$\frac{1}{2B}\int_{f_1}^{2W - f_1}\left[1 + \cos\left(\frac{\pi(f - f_1)}{2W\alpha}\right)\right]\cos(2\pi f t)\,df$$

$$= \left[\frac{\sin(2\pi ft)}{2\pi Wt}\right] + \left[\frac{\sin(2\pi ft)}{4\pi Wt}\right]_{f_1}^{2W-f_1} + \frac{1}{4}W\left[\frac{\sin\left(2\pi ft + \dfrac{\pi(f-f_1)}{2W\alpha}\right)}{2\pi t + \dfrac{\pi}{2}W\alpha}\right]_{f_1}^{2W-f_1}$$

$$+ \frac{1}{4W}\left[\frac{\sin\left(2\pi ft - \dfrac{\pi(f-f_1)}{2W\alpha}\right)}{2\pi t - \dfrac{\pi}{2}W\alpha}\right]_{f_1}^{2W-f_1}$$

$$= \frac{\sin(2\pi f_1 t)}{4\pi Wt} + \frac{\sin[2\pi t(2W-f_1)]}{4\pi Wt} - \frac{1}{4W}$$

$$\frac{\sin(2\pi f_1 t) + \sin[2\pi t(2W-f_1)]}{2\pi t - \dfrac{\pi}{2}W\alpha} + \frac{\sin(2\pi f_1 t) + \sin[2\pi t(2W - f_1 t)]}{2\pi t - \dfrac{\pi}{2}W\alpha}$$

$$= \frac{1}{W}[\sin(2\pi f_1 t) + \sin[2\pi t(2W-f_1)]]\left[\frac{1}{4\pi t} - \frac{\pi t}{(2\pi t)^2 - \left(\dfrac{\pi}{2}W\alpha\right)^2}\right]$$

$$= \frac{1}{W}[\sin(2\pi Wt)\cos(2\pi\alpha W]\left[\frac{-\left(\dfrac{\pi}{2}W\alpha\right)^2}{4\pi t\left[(2\pi t)^2 - \left(\dfrac{\pi}{2}W\alpha\right)^2\right]}\right]$$

$$= \sin c(2Wt)\cos(2\pi\alpha Wt)\left[\frac{1}{1-16\alpha^2W^2t^2}\right]$$

Problem 6.6: A computer puts out binary data at the rate of 56 kb/s. The computer output is transmitted using a baseband binary PAM system that is designed to have a raised-cosine spectrum. Determine the transmission bandwidth required for each of the following rolloff factors: $\alpha = 0.25, 0.5, 0.75, 1.0$.

Solution: The Bandwidth B of a raised cosine pulse spectrum is $2W - f_1$, where $W = \frac{1}{2T_b}$ and $f_1 = W(1 - \alpha)$. Thus $B = W(1 + \alpha)$. For a data rate of 56 kilobites per second, $W = 28$ kHz.

(*a*) For $\alpha = 0.25$

$B = 28 \text{ kHz} \times 1.25 = 35 \text{ kHz}$

(*b*) $B = 28 \text{ kHz} \times 1.5 = 42 \text{ kHz}$

(*c*) $B = 49 \text{ kHz}$

(*d*) $B = 56 \text{ kHz}$

> **Problem 6.7:** Repeat previous problem, given that each set of three successive binary digits in the computer output are coded into one of eight possible amplitude levels, and the resulting signal is transmitted using an eight-level PAM system designed to have a raised-cosine spectrum.

Solution: The use of eight amplitude levels ensures that 3 bits can be transmitted per pulse. The symbol period can be increased by a factor of 3. All four bandwidths in previous will be reduced to $\frac{1}{3}$ of their binary PAM values.

> **Problem 6.8:** An analog signal is sampled, quantized and encoded into a binary PCM wave. The number of representation levels used is 128. A synchronizing pulse is added at the end of each code word representing a sample of the analog signal. The resulting PCM wave is transmitted over a channel of band-width 12 kHz using a quaternary PAM system with raised-cosine spectrum. The rolloff factor is unity.
>
> (*a*) Find the rate $\left(\frac{b}{s}\right)$ at which information is transmitted through the channel.
>
> (*b*) Find the rate at which the analog signal is sampled. What is the maximum possible value for the highest frequency component of the analog signal?

Solution: (*a*) For a unity rolloff, raised cosine pulse spectrum, the bandwidth B equals $\frac{1}{T}$, where T is the pulse length. Therefore T in this case is $\frac{1}{12}$ kHz. Quartenary PAM ensures 2 bits per pulse, so the rate of information is

$$\frac{2 \text{ bits}}{T} = 24 \text{ kilobits per second}$$

(*b*) For 128 quantizing levels, 7 bits are required to transmit an amplitude. The additional bit for synchronization makes each code word 8 bits. The signal is transmitted at 24 kilobits/s, so it must be sampled at

$$\frac{24 \text{ kbits / s}}{8 \text{ bits / sample}} = 3 \text{ kHz.}$$

The maximum possible value for the signal's highest frequency component is 1.5 kHz, in order to avoid aliasing.

Problem 6.9: A binary PAM wave is to be transmitted over a baseband channel with an absolute maximum bandwidth of 75 kHz. The bit duration is 10 μs. Find a raised-cosine spectrum that satisfies these requirements.

Solution: The raised cosine pulse bandwidth $B = 2W - f_1$, where $W = \frac{1}{2T_b}$. For this channel, $B = 75$ kHz. For the given bit duration, $W = 50$ khz. Then,

$$f_1 = 2W - B = 25 \text{ kHz}$$

$$\alpha = 1 - \frac{f_1}{B_T} = 0.5$$

Problem 6.10: The binary data stream 001101001 is applied to the input of a duobinary system.

(*a*) Construct the duobinary coder output and corresponding receiver output, without a precoder.

(*b*) Suppose that owing to error during transmission, the level at the receiver input produced by the second digit is reduced to zero. Construct the new receiver output.

Solution:

(*a*) Binary sequence b_k	0	0	1	1	0	1	0	0	1
Polar representation	–1	–1	1	1	–1	1	–1	–1	1
Duobinary coder output c_k		–2	0	2	0	0	0	–2	0
Receiver output $\hat{b}_k$	–1	–1	1	1	–1	1	–1	–1	1
Output binary sequence	0	0	1	1	0	1	0	0	1
(*b*) Receiver intput	0	0	2	0	0	0	–0	2	
Receiver output $\hat{b}_k$	–1	1	–1	1	–1	1	–1	–1	1
Output binary sequence	0	1	0	1	0	1	0	0	1

We see that not only is the second digit in error, but also the error propagates.

Problem 6.11: Repeat the previous problem assuming the use of a precoder in the transmitter.

Solution:

(*a*) Binary sequence b_k		0	0	1	1	0	1	0	0	1
Coded sequence d_k	1	1	1	0	1	1	0	0	0	1
Polar representation	1	1	1	–1	1	1	–1	–1	–1	1
Duobinary coder output c_k		2	2	0	0	2	0	–2	–2	0
Receiver output		0	0	1	1	0	1	0	0	1
(*b*) Receiver intput		2	0	0	0	2	0	–2	–2	0
Receiver output		0	1	1	1	0	1	0	0	1

In this case we see that only the second digit is in error, and there is no error propagation.

Problem 6.12: The scheme shown in Fig. P. 6.12 may be viewed as a differential encoder (consisting of the modulo-2 adder and the 1-unit delay element) connected in cascade with a special form of correlative coder (consisting of the 1-unit delay element and summer). A single delay element is shown in Fig. P. 6.12 since it is common to both the differential encoder and the correlative coder. In this differential encoder, a transition is represented by symbol 0 and no transition by symbol 1.

(*a*) Find the frequency response and impulse response of the correlative coder part of the scheme shown in Fig. P. 6.12.

(*b*) Show that this scheme may be used to convert the on-off representation of a binary sequence (applied to the input) into the bipolar representation of the sequence at the output. You may illustrate this conversion by considering the sequence 010001101.

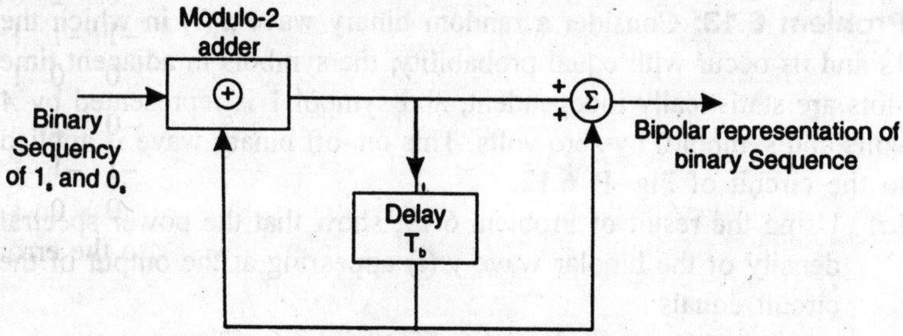

Fig. P. 6.12

Solution: (*a*) The correlative coder has output

$$z_n = y_n - y_{n-1}$$

Its impulse response is

$$h_k = \begin{cases} 1 & k = 0 \\ -1 & k = 1 \\ 0 & \text{otherwise} \end{cases}$$

The frequency response is

$$H(f) = \sum_{k=-\infty}^{\infty} h_k \exp(-j2\pi f k T_b) = 1 - \exp(-j2\pi f T_b)$$

(*b*) Let the input to the differential encoder be x_n, the input to the correlative coder by y_n, and the output of the correlative coder be z_n. Then, for the sequence 010001101 in its on-off form, we get,

x_n		0	1	0	0	0	1	1	0	1
y_n	1	1	0	0	0	0	1	0	0	1
z_n		0	–1	0	0	0	1	–1	0	1

Then z_n has the waveform as depicted below,

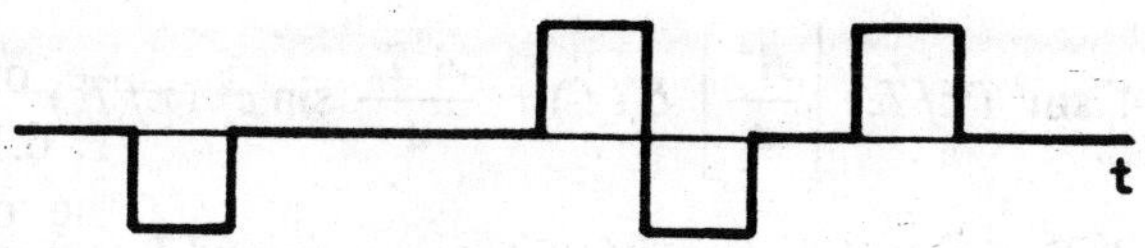

Fig. P. 6.12 (a)

The sequence z_n is a bipolar representation of the input sequence x_n.

Problem 6.13: Consider a random binary wave $x(t)$ in which the 1s and 0s occur with equal probability, the symbols in adjacent time slots are statistically independent, and symbol 1 is represented by A volts and symbol 0 by zero volts. This on–off binary wave is applied to the circuit of Fig. P. 6.12.

(*a*) Using the result of Problem 6.19, show that the power spectral density of the bipolar wave $y(t)$ appearing at the output of the circuit equals

$$S_Y(f) = T_b A^2 \sin^2(\pi f T_b) \sin c^2(\pi f T_b)$$

(*b*) Plot the power spectral densities of the on-off and bipolar binary waves, and compare them.

Solution: (*a*) The output symbols of the modulo-2 adder are independent because:

1. The input sequence to the adder has independent symbols, and therefore

2. knowing the previous value of the adder does not improve prediction of the

$$f(y_n \mid y_{n-1}) = f(y_n)$$

where y_n is the value of the adder output at time nT_b. The adder output sequence is another on-off binary wave with independent symbols. Such a wave has the power spectral density

$$S_Y(f) = \frac{A^2}{4}\delta(f) + \frac{A^2 T_b}{4} \sin c^2(f T_b)$$

The correlative coder has the transfer function

$$H(f) = 1 - \exp(-j2\pi f T_b),$$

Therefore, the output wave has the power spectral density

$$\begin{aligned} S_Z(f) &= |H(f)|^2 S_Y(f) \\ &= [1 - \exp(-j2\pi f T_b)]\,[1 - \exp(j2\pi f T_b)]\, S_Y(f) \\ &= [2 - 2\cos(2\pi f T_b)]\, S_Y(f) = 4\sin^2(\pi f T_b)\, S_Y(f) \\ &= 4\sin^2(\pi f T_b)\left[\frac{A^2}{4}\right]\delta(f) + \frac{A^2 T_b}{4} \sin c^2(\pi f T_b) \\ &= A^2 T_b \sin^2(\pi f T_b) \sin c^2(f T_b) \text{ [using } \sin(\pi f T_b = 0 \text{ at } f = 0)] \end{aligned}$$

(*b*)

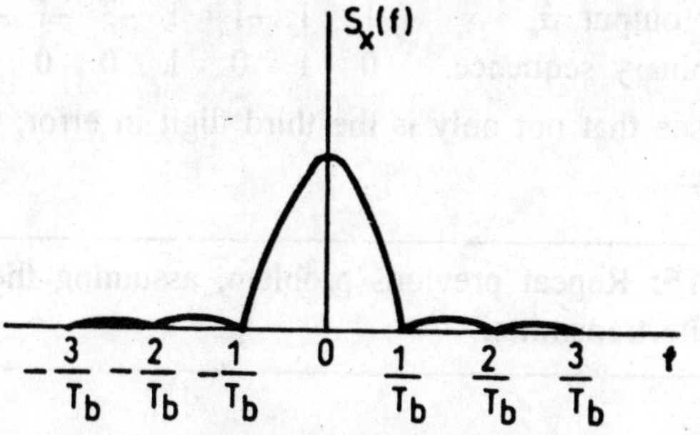

Fig. P. 6.13 (a)

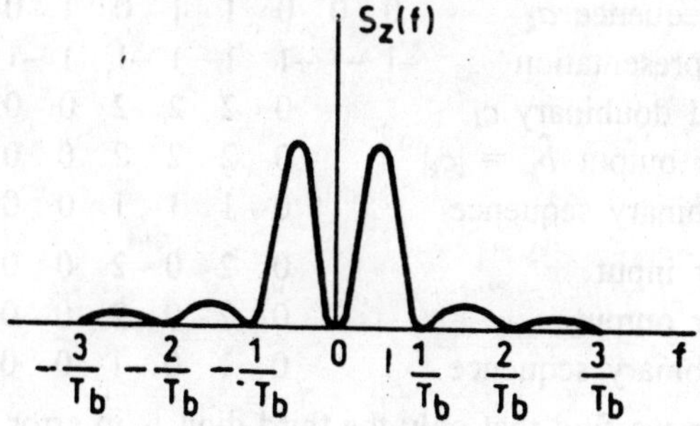

Fig. P. 6.13 (b)

Note that the bipolar wave has no dc component.

Problem 6.14: The binary data stream 011100101 is applied to the input of a modified duobinary system.
(*a*) Construct the modified duobinary coder output and corresponding receiver output, without a precoder.
(*b*) Suppose that due to error during transmission, the level produced by the third digit is reduced to zero. Construct the new receiver output.

Solution: The modified duobinary receiver estimate is

$$\hat{a}_k = c_k + \hat{a}_{k-2}$$

(*a*)

Binary sequence a_k	0	1	1	1	0	0	1	0	1
Bipolar representation	−1	1	1	1	−1	−1	1	−1	1
Modified duobinary c_k			2	0	−2	−2	2	0	0
Receiver output $\hat{a}_k$	−1	1	1	1	−1	−1	1	−1	1
Output binary sequence	0	1	1	1	0	0	1	0	1

(*b*)

Receiver input			0	0	−2	−2	2	0	0
Receiver output $\hat{a}_k$	(−1	1	−1	1	−3	−1	−1	−1	−1
Output binary sequence	0	1	0	1	0	0	0	0	0

Here we see that not only is the third digit in error, but also the error propagates.

> **Problem 6.15:** Repeat previous problem, assuming the use of a precoder in the transmitter.

Solution:

(*a*)

Binary sequence b_k			0	1	1	1	0	0	1	0	1
Coded sequence a_k	0	0	0	1	1	0	1	0	0	0	1
Polar representation	−1	−1	−1	1	1	−1	1	−1	−1	−1	1
Modified doubinary c_k			0	2	2	−2	0	0	−2	0	2
Receiver output $\hat{b}_k = \lvert c_k \rvert$			0	2	2	2	0	0	2	0	2
Output binary sequence			0	1	1	1	0	0	1	0	1

(*b*)

Receiver input	0	2	0	−2	0	0	−2	0	2
Receiver output	0	2	0	2	0	0	2	0	2
Output binary sequence	0	1	0	1	0	0	1	0	1

This time we find that only the third digit is in error, and there is no error propagation.

> **Problem 6.16:** Suppose that in a baseband *M*-ary PAM system with *M* equally likely amplitude levels, the average probability of symbol error P_e is less than 10^{-6} so as to make the occurrence of decoding errors negligible. Show that the minimum value of received singal-to-noise ratio in such a system is approximately given by
>
> $$(\text{SNR})_{R,\min} \cong 7.8\,(M^2 - 1)$$

Solution: The probability of error is (from the solution to problem 6.16)

$$P_e = \left(1 - \frac{1}{M}\right) erfc\left(\frac{A}{2\sqrt{2}\sigma}\right)$$

The received signal-to-noise ratio is

$$(\text{SNR})_R = \frac{A^2\left(M^2 - 1\right)}{12\,\sigma^2}$$

Now, using eqn (2) in eqn (1), we have

$$P_e = \left(1-\frac{1}{M}\right) erfc\left(\sqrt{\frac{3(SNR)_R}{2(M^2-1)}}\right)$$

With $P_e = 10^{-6}$, it can be written

$$10^{-6} = \left(1-\frac{1}{M}\right) erfc\,(u)$$

where

$$u^2 = \frac{3\,(SNR)_R}{2\,(M^2-1)}$$

For a specified value of m, Eq. (3) can be solved for the corresponding value of u and the following table can be constructed as,

M	u
2	3.37
4	3.42
8	3.45
16	3.46

Thus to a first degree of approximation, the minimum value of received signal-to-noise ratio required for $P_e < 10^{-6}$ is given by,

$$\frac{3\,(SNR)_{R,\min}}{2\,(M^2-1)} \cong (3.42)^2$$

That is, $(SNR)_{R,\min} \cong 7.8\,(M^2-1)$

Problem 6.17: Some radio systems suffer from *multipath distortion*, which is caused by the existence of more than one propagation path between the transmitter and the receiver. Consider a channel the output of which, in response to a signal $s\,(t)$, is defined by (in the absence of noise)

$$x\,(t) = K_1 s\,(t - t_{01}) + K_2 s\,(t - t_{02})$$

where K_1 and K_2 are constants, and t_{01} and t_{02} represent transmission delays. It is proposed to use the three-tap delay-line-filter of Fig. P. 7.4 to equalize the multipath distortion produced by this channel.

(*a*) Evaluate the transfer function of the channel.

(*b*) Evaluate the parameters of the tapped-delay-line filter in terms of K_1, K_2, t_{01}, and t_{02}, assuming that $K_2 \ll K_1$ and $t_{02} > t_{01}$.

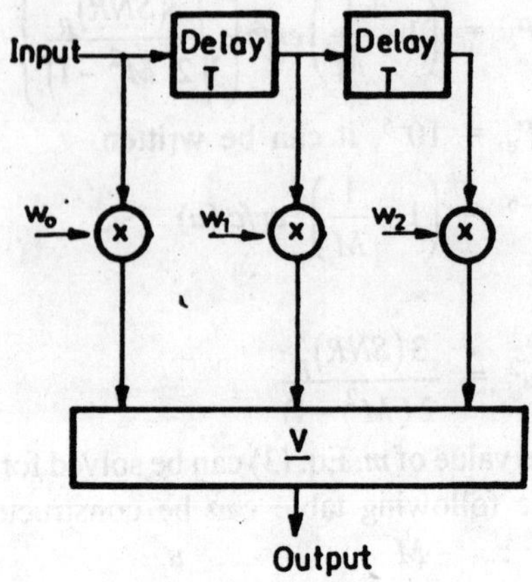

Fig. P. 6.17

Solution: (*a*) The channel output is

$$x(t) = K_1 s(t - t_{01}) + K_2 s(t - t_{02})$$

Taking the Fourier transform of both sides, we get

$$X(f) = K_1 \exp(-j2\pi f t_{01}) + K_2 \exp(-j2\pi f t_{02}) S(f)$$

The transfer function of the channel is therefore,

$$H_c(f) = \frac{X(f)}{S(f)} = K_1 \exp(-j2\pi f t_{01}) + K_2 \exp(-j2\pi f t_{02})$$

(*b*)

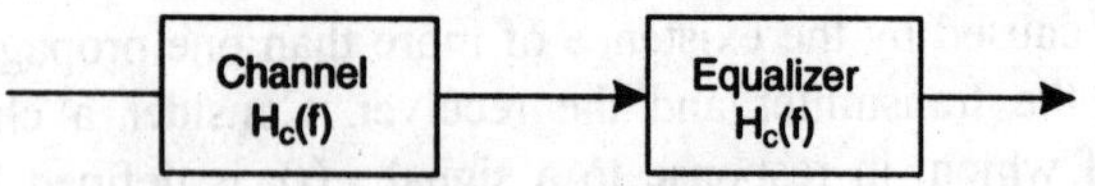

Fig. P. 6.17 (a)

Ideally, the equalizer should be designed so that

$$H_c(f)\ H_e(f) = K_0 \exp(-j2\pi f t_0)$$

Where K_0 is a constant gain and t_0 is the transmission delay. The transfer function of the equalizer is

$$H_e(f) = w_0 + w_1 \exp(-j2\pi fT) + w_2 \exp(-j4\pi fT)$$

$$= w_0 \left[1 + \frac{w_1}{w_0} \exp(-j2\pi fT) + \frac{w_2}{w_0} \exp(-j4\pi fT)\right] \quad \ldots(1)$$

Hence,

$$H_e(f) = \frac{k_0 \exp(-j2\pi f t_0)}{H_c(f)} = \frac{K_0 \exp(-j2\pi f t_0)}{K_1 \exp(-j2\pi f t_{01}) + K_2 \exp(-j2\pi f t_{02})}$$

$$= \frac{\left(\frac{K_0}{K_1}\right) \exp\left[-j2\pi f (t_0 - t_{01})\right]}{1 + \frac{K_2}{K_1} \exp\left[-j2\pi f (t_{02} - t_{01})\right]}$$

Since $K_2 \ll K_1$,
we may approximate $H_e(f)$ as follows

$$H_e(f) = \frac{K_0}{K_1} \exp[-j2\pi f (t_0 - t_{01})] \left\{1 - \frac{K_2}{K_1} \exp[-j2\pi f (t_{02} - t_{01})]\right.$$

$$\left. + \left(\frac{K_2}{K_1}\right)^2 \exp[-j4\pi f (t_{02} - t_{01})]\right\}$$

Comparing Eqs (1) and (2), it can be deduced that

$$\frac{K_0}{K_1} \cong w_0$$

$$t_0 - t_{01} \cong 0$$

$$-\frac{K_2}{K_1} \cong \frac{w_1}{w_0}$$

$$\left(\frac{K_2}{K_1}\right)^2 \cong \frac{w_2}{w_0}$$

$$T \cong t_{02} - t_{01}$$

Choosing $K_0 = K_1$, the tap weights of the equalizer are as follows,

$$w_0 = 1 \qquad w_1 = -\frac{K_2}{K_1} \qquad w_2 = \left(\frac{K_2}{K_1}\right)^2$$

Problem 6.18: Let the sequence $[x(nT)]$ denote the input applied to a tapped-delay-line equalizer. Show that intersymbol interference is eliminated completely by the equalizer provided that its transfer function satisfies the condition

$$H(f) = \frac{T}{\sum_k X\left(f - \frac{k}{T}\right)}$$

where T is the symbol duration.
As the number of taps in the equalizer approaches infinity, the transfer function of the equalizer becomes a Fourier series with real coefficients and can therefore approximate any function in the interval $\left(-\frac{1}{2}, \frac{1}{2T}\right)$.
Demonstrate this property of the equalizer.

Solution: Fourier transform of the tapped-dealy-line equalizer output is defined by

$$Y_{out}(f) = H(f)\, X_{in}(f) \quad \text{...(1)}$$

where $H(f)$ is the equalizer's transfer function and $X_{in}(f)$ is the Fourier transform of the input signal. The input signal consists of a uniform sequence of samples, denoted by $[x(nT)]$. We may therefore write:

$$X_{in}(f) = \frac{1}{T}\sum_k X\left(f - \frac{k}{T}\right) \quad \text{...(2)}$$

where T is the sampling period and $s(t)$ is the signal from which the sequence of samples is derived. For perfect equalization, we require that

$$Y_{out}(f) = 1 \text{ for all } f.$$

Using eqs. (1) and (2), we find that

$$H(f) = \frac{T}{\sum_k X\left(f - \frac{k}{T}\right)} \quad \text{...(3)}$$

Let the impulse response (sequence) of the equalizer be denoted by (w_n). Assuming an infinite number of taps, we have

$$H(f) = \sum_{n=-\infty}^{\infty} w_n \exp(j2\pi fT)$$

It can be seen here that $H(f)$ is in the form of a complex Fourier series with real coefficients defined by the tap weights of the equalizer. Then tap-weights are themselves defined as,

$$w_n = \frac{1}{T} \int_{-1/2T}^{1/2T} H(f) \exp(-j2\pi t/T), \ n = 0, +1, +2, \ldots$$

The transfer function $H(f)$ is itself defined in terms of the input signal by Eq. (3). Accordingly, tapped-delay-line equalizer of infinite length can approximate any function in the frequency interval $\left(-\frac{1}{2T}, \frac{1}{2T}\right)$.

Problem 6.19: White noise of two-sided spectral density 2×10^{-6} V^2/Hz is applied to a single R-C low pass filter whose 3dB cut off frequency is 4 kHz. Find the mean squared value of the noise output.

Solution: Frequency response H (ω) of an RC low-pass filter with 3-dB cut off frequency of 4 kHz is expressed by,

$$H(\omega) = \frac{1}{1 + j\omega/\omega_0}$$

Now, PSD at the output,

$$S_{yy}(\omega) = |H(\omega)|^2 \cdot S_{xx}(\omega)$$

or $$S_{yy}(\omega) = \frac{1}{1+(\omega/\omega_0)^2} \frac{\eta}{2}$$

Hence, the mean square value of the noise output is given by,

$$N_0 = E[n_0^2(t)]$$

or, $$N_0 = \frac{1}{2\pi} \cdot \int_{-\infty}^{\infty} S_{yy}(\omega) \cdot d\omega$$

or, $$N_0 = \frac{1}{2\pi} \cdot \int_{-\infty}^{\infty} \frac{\eta}{2} \cdot \frac{d\omega}{1+(\omega/\omega_0)^2}$$

or, $$N_0 = \frac{\omega_0^2 \eta}{4\pi} \int_{-\infty}^{\infty} \frac{d\omega}{\omega^2 + \omega_0^2}$$

$$\text{or,} \quad N_0 = \frac{\eta\omega_o^2}{4\pi}\frac{1}{\omega_0}\left[\tan^{-1}\frac{\omega}{\omega_o}\Big|_{-\infty}^{\infty}\right] = \frac{\eta\omega_o}{4\pi}\cdot\pi$$

Given $\eta = 2\times10^{-6}\ \text{V}^2/\text{Hz}$ and $\omega_0 = 2\pi\times4\times10^3$ Hz, we have

Hence, Noise Output $N_0 = \dfrac{2\times10^{-6}\times2\pi\times4\times10^3}{4} = 4\pi\times10^{-3}\ \text{V}^2$

Problem 6.20: A signal, $s(t) = e^{-at}u(t)$ where $u(t)$ is the unit step functio, is applied to the input of a low-pass filter having

$$|H(\omega)| = \frac{b}{\sqrt{\omega^2 + b^2}}$$

Calculate the value of the ratio $\dfrac{a}{b}$, for which 50% of the input signal energy is transferred to the output.

Solution: Given Input signal, $s(t) = e^{-at}\cdot u(t)$

and, its power spectral density, $S_{xx}(\omega) = \dfrac{1}{\jmath\omega + a}$.

At the filter output, power spectral density, is given by

$$S_{yy}(\omega) = S_{xx}(\omega)\cdot|H(\omega)|^2$$

$$S_{yy}(\omega) = \frac{b^2}{\omega^2 + b^2}\cdot\frac{1}{\jmath\omega + a}$$

Now, given,

$$\frac{1}{2}\left[\frac{1}{2\pi}\int_{-\infty}^{\infty}|S_{xx}(\omega)|^2\,d\omega\right] = \frac{1}{2\pi}\int_{-\infty}^{\infty}|S_{yy}(\omega)|^2\,d\omega$$

$$\text{then,} \quad \frac{1}{2}\cdot\int_{-\infty}^{\infty}\frac{1}{\omega^2 + a^2}\,d\omega = \frac{b^2}{\text{b}^2 - a^2}\int_{-\infty}^{\infty}\left[\frac{1}{\omega^2 + a^2} - \frac{1}{\omega^2 + b^2}\right]d\omega$$

$$\text{or,} \quad \frac{1}{2}\cdot\frac{1}{a}\left[\tan^{-1}\frac{\omega}{a}\int_{-\infty}^{\infty}\right] = \frac{b^2}{(b^2 - a^2)}\left[\frac{1}{a}\tan^{-1}\frac{\omega}{a}\Big|_{-\infty}^{\infty}\right] -$$

$$\frac{b^2}{(b^2-a^2)}\left[\frac{1}{b}\tan^{-1}\frac{\omega}{b}\int_{-\infty}^{\infty}\right]$$

or $$\frac{1}{2a}\cdot\pi = \frac{b^2}{b^2-a^2}\pi\left(\frac{1}{a}-\frac{1}{b}\right)$$

or, $$\frac{1}{2} = \frac{b}{a+b}$$

Hence, $$\frac{a}{b} = 1$$

Problem 6.21: The equivalent noise bandwidth of a system is defined as

$$B_{eq} = \frac{1}{2\pi}\frac{\int_0^{\infty}|H(\omega)|^2\,d\omega}{|H(\omega)|^2_{max}}\cdot\text{Hz}$$

where $|H(\omega)|^2_{max} = \max|H(\omega)|^2$

Determine the equivalent noise bandwidth of the ideal band-pass filter and that of a low pass RC filter.

Solution: Frequency response of an ideal band-pass filter is depicted below,

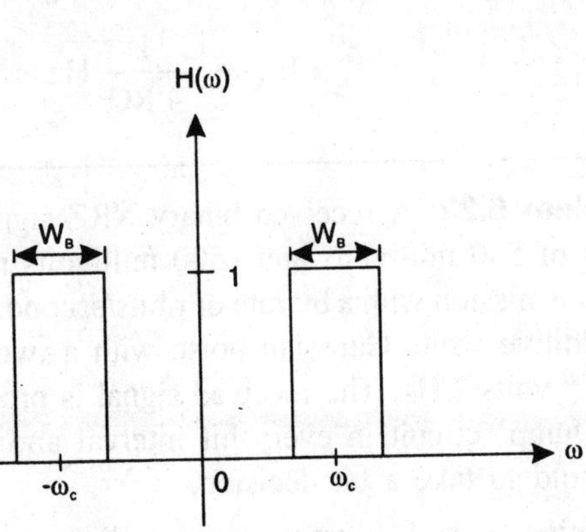

Fig. 6.21 (a)

From the figure, we have

$$\max|H(\omega)|^2 = 1$$

then $$B_{eq} = \frac{1}{2\pi}\cdot\frac{\int_0^\infty |H(\omega)|^2\, d\omega}{|H(\omega)|^2_{max}} = \frac{1}{2\pi}\cdot\frac{W_B}{1} = \frac{W_B}{2\pi}.$$

Since, integral is from 0 to ∞, then, $\int_0^\infty |H(\omega)|^2\, d\omega$ = area in only the quadrature.

For the low-pass RC filter, frequency response is expressed by,

$$H(\omega) = \frac{1}{1+j\omega RC}$$

then, $$\max|H(\omega)|^2 = |H(0)|^2 = 1$$

Hence, $$B_{eq} = \frac{1}{2\pi}\cdot\int_0^\infty |H(\omega)|^2\, d\omega$$

or, $$B_{eq} = \frac{1}{2\pi}\cdot\int_0^\infty \frac{1}{1+(\omega RC)^2}\, d\omega$$

or, $$B_{eq} = \frac{1}{2\pi}\cdot\frac{1}{RC}\left[\tan^{-1}\omega RC \Big|_0^\infty\right]$$

or, $$B_{eq} = \frac{1}{4\,RC}\ \text{Hz}$$

Problem 6.22: A received binary NRZ signal assumes the voltage levels of 500 millivolts and –500 millivolts respectively for '1' and '0' transmission with a bit rate or r bits/second. The signal is corrupted by additive white Gaussian noise with a two-sided spectral density of 10^{-6} volts 2/Hz. The received signal is processed by an 'Integrate and Dump' circuit in every bit interval and compared with a zero threshold to take a bit decision.

Assuming '1' and '0' transmission to be equally likely, determine the maximum value of r such that the bit error probability $\leq 10^{-5}$.

Given:

$$Q(x) = \frac{1}{\sqrt{2\pi}} \int_x^{\infty} e^{-Z^2/2} \cdot dz = 10^{-5} \text{ at } x = 4.27.$$

$$erfc(x) = \frac{2}{\sqrt{\pi}} \int_x^{\infty} e^{-Z^2/2} \cdot dz = 2 \times 10^{-5} \text{ at } x = 3.02$$

Solution:

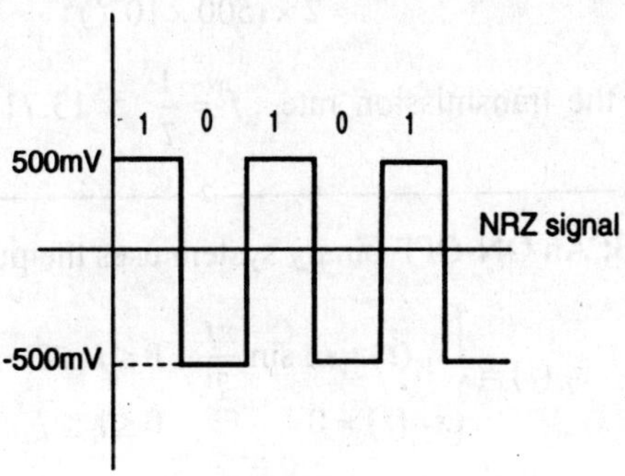

Fig. 6.22 (a)

From the figure drawn here, we can express the transmitted signal as,

$$S_i(t) = \begin{cases} s_1(t) = +A = +500 \text{ mV}, & 0 \le t \le T \\ s_2(t) = -A = -500 \text{ mV}, & 0 \le t \le T \end{cases}$$

$$S_i(t) = \int_0^T [s_1(t) - s_2(t)]^2 \, dt$$

$$E_d = \int_0^T (2A)^2 \, dt = 4A^2 T$$

Bit error probability, $P_e = Q\left(\sqrt{\frac{E_d}{2N_0}}\right)$

$$P_e = Q\left(\sqrt{\frac{2A^2T}{N_0}}\right)$$

Given, $P_e \leq 10^{-5}$

then, $$Q\left(\sqrt{\frac{2A^2T}{N_0}}\right) \leq 10^{-5}$$

or, $$\frac{2A^2T}{N_0} = 4.27$$

Now as, $\frac{N_o}{2} = 10^{-6}$ volts/Hz

or, $$T = \frac{2 \times 10^{-6} \times (4.27)^2}{2 \times (500 \times 10^{-3})^2} = 7.29 \times 10^{-5}$$

Therefore, the transmission rate, $f = \frac{1}{T} = 13.71$ kb/sec.

Problem 6.23: An ON-OFF binary system uses the pulse waveforms

$$s_i(t) = \begin{cases} s_1(t) = A \sin \dfrac{\pi t}{T} & 0 \leq t \leq T \\ s_2(t) = 0 & 0 \leq t \leq T \end{cases}$$

Let A = 0.2 μs and T = 2 μs. Additive white noise with a power spectral density $\frac{N_0}{2} = 10^{-15}$ W/Hz is added to the signal. Determine the probability of error when $P(s_1) = P(s_2) = \frac{1}{2}$.

Given, $Q(\sqrt{10}) = 7.83 \times 10^{-4}$.

Solution: Probability of error, $P_e = Q\left(\sqrt{\frac{E_d}{2N_0}}\right)$ (1)

where $Q()$ is complementary error function defined as,

$$Q(z) = \frac{1}{2\pi}\int_z^{\infty} e^{-\lambda^2/2} \cdot d\lambda$$

Energy of the difference signal at the filter input, is given by,

$$E_d = \int_0^T [(s_1(t) - s_2(t)]^2 dt$$

or, $$E_d = \int_0^T A^2 \sin^2 \frac{\pi t}{T} dt = \frac{A^2}{2}\int_0^T \left(1 - \cos\frac{2\pi t}{T}\right) dt$$

or, $$E_d = \frac{A^2}{2}\cdot\left[t - \frac{\sin 2\pi t/T}{2\pi/T}\Big|_0^T\right] = \frac{A^2 T}{2}$$

From equation (1), $P_e = Q\left(\sqrt{\frac{A^2T}{4N_0}}\right) = Q\left(\sqrt{\frac{(2\times10^{-4})^2\,(2\times10^{-6})}{4\,(2\times10^{-15})}}\right)$

or, $P_e = Q(\sqrt{10}) = 7.83\times10^{-4}$

Problem 6.24: The input $X(t)$ to an ideal bandpass filter having the frequency response as shown in the figure below is a white noise process. Determine the total noise power at the output of the filter.

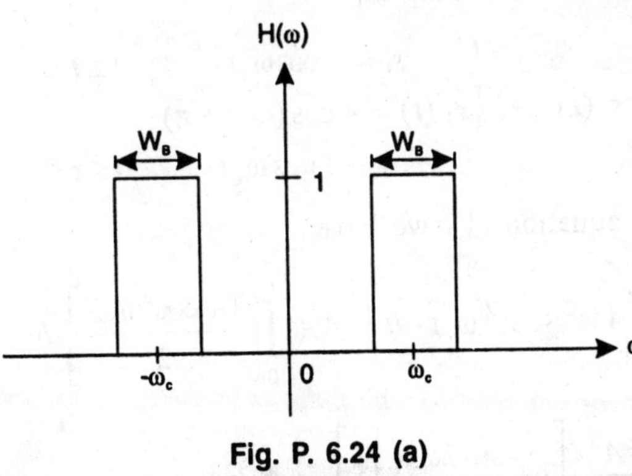

Fig. P. 6.24 (a)

Solution: Since $x(t)$ is white noise,

then, $S_{xx}(\omega) = \frac{N_0}{2}$

Then, PSD at output, $S_{yy}(\omega) = |H(\omega)|^2 S_{xx}(\omega) = \frac{N_0}{2} \cdot |H(\omega)|^2$

Hence, total noise power at the output of the filtern, is given by,

$$E[Y^2(t)] = \frac{1}{2\pi}\int_{-\infty}^{\infty} S_{yy}(\omega)\, d\omega = \frac{1}{2\pi}\frac{N_0}{2}\cdot\int_{-\infty}^{\infty}|H(\omega)|^2\, d\omega$$

$$= \frac{N_0}{2}\cdot\frac{1}{2\pi}(2W_B) = N_0 B \quad \text{where, } B = \frac{W_B}{2\pi}$$

Problem 6.25: In a PSK system, the received waveforms $s_1(t) = A\cos\omega_c t$ and $s_2(t) = -A\cos\omega_c t$ are coherently detected with a matched filter. The value of A is 20 mV, and the bit rate is 1 Mb/s. Assume that the noise power spectral density $\eta/2 = 10^{-11}$ W/Hz. Find the probability of error P_e.

Solution: Energy difference signal at the filter input is expressed as,

$$E_d = \int_0^T [s_1(t) - s_2(t)^2]\cdot dt \tag{1}$$

For PSK, transmitted signal,

$$s_i(t) = \begin{cases} s_1 = A\cos\omega_c t & 0 \le t \le T \\ s_2(t) = A\cos(\omega_c t + \pi) & \\ \quad = -A\cos\omega_c t & 0 \le t \le T \end{cases}$$

then, for equation (1), we have

$$E_d = \int_0^T 4A^2\cdot\cos^2\omega_c t\cdot dt = 4A^2\int_0^T\left[\frac{1+\cos^2\omega_c t}{2}\right]dt$$

$$= \frac{4A^2}{2}\cdot\left[t + \frac{\sin 2\omega_c t}{2\omega_c}\int_0^T\right] = 2A^2 T$$

Hence, probability of error,

$$P_e = Q\left(\sqrt{\frac{E_d}{2N_o}}\right) = Q\left(\sqrt{\frac{4^2 T}{N_o}}\right)$$

$$P_e = Q\left(\sqrt{\frac{(20\times 10^{-3})^2 \times 10^{-6}}{2\times 10^{-11}}}\right) = Q(\sqrt{20}) = 3.9\times 10^{-6}$$

Problem 6.26: Derive the expression for the probability of error of the bipolar baseband signal.

Solution: For bipolar baseband signalling, the input signal is expressed as,

$$s_i(t)\begin{cases} s_1(t) = +A, & 0\le t\le T \\ s_2(t) = -A, & 0\le t\le T \end{cases}$$

Then, at the filter input, energy of the difference signal is given by,

$$E_d = \int_0^T [s_1(t) - s_2(t)^2]\, dt$$

or $$E_d = \int_0^T (2A)^2\, dt = 4A^2T \qquad (1)$$

Since probability of error, $P_e = Q\left(\sqrt{\frac{E_d}{2\eta}}\right)$.

where $\eta/2$ is the PSD of noise at the filter input then from equation (1), we get

$$P_e = Q\left(\sqrt{\frac{4A^2T}{2\eta}}\right) = Q\left(\sqrt{\frac{2A^2T}{\eta}}\right)$$

Where $Q(.)$ is complementary error function.

Problem 6.27: It is desired to generate a random signal $x(t)$, with autocorrelation function $R_{xx}(T) = 5\eta e^{-5|\tau|}$, by passing a white noise $\eta(t)$, with power spectral density $S_{xx}(f) = \eta/2$ watts/Hz, through a LTI system. Obtain an expression for the transfer function $H(f)$ of the LTI system.

Solution: Power spectral density of signal $x(t)$ is given by,

$$S_{xx}(\omega) = \int_{-\infty}^{\infty} R_{xx}(\tau)\cdot e^{-j\omega\pi}\,d\tau = 5\eta\int_{-\infty}^{\infty} e^{-5|\tau|}\cdot e^{-j\omega\pi}\,d\tau$$

$$= 5\eta\int_{-\infty}^{0} e^{5\tau - j\omega\tau}d\tau + 5\eta\int_{0}^{\infty} e^{-5\tau - j\omega\tau}d\tau$$

$$= 5\eta\left[\left(\frac{e^{(5-j\omega)\tau}}{5-j\omega}\Big|_{-\infty}^{0}\right) + \left(\frac{e^{-(5+j\omega)\tau}}{5+j\omega}\Big|_{0}^{\infty}\right)\right]$$

$$= 5\eta\cdot\frac{1}{5-j\omega} + \frac{1}{5+j\omega}$$

$$S_{xx}(\omega) = \frac{50\,\eta}{25+\omega^2}$$

and output power spectral density is expressed by

$$S_{yy}(\omega) = |H(\omega)|^2\cdot S_{xx}(\omega)$$

$$\text{or,}\quad |H(\omega)|^2 = \frac{S_{yy}(\omega)}{S_{xx}(\omega)} = \frac{50\,\eta}{25+\omega^2}\cdot\frac{1}{\eta/2}$$

$$|H(\omega)|^2 = \frac{100}{25+\omega^2} \qquad \text{from eqn (1)}$$

$$\text{then,}\ |H(f)|^2 = \frac{100}{25+(2\pi f)^2}$$

$$\text{or,}\quad H(f) = \frac{10}{5+j2\pi f}$$

Problem 6.28: Prove that signal to noise ratio, $\left(\frac{S}{N}\right)_0 \leq \frac{2E}{\eta}$ where E is the energy of the input signal $s(t)$ and $\eta/2$ is the power spectral density of the input noise $\eta(t)$.

Solution: Let the frequency response of the linear filter is $H(\omega)$.

Then the matched filter output is given as

$$g_o(T) = k \int_{-\infty}^{\infty} H(\omega) \cdot s(\omega)\, e^{jwT}\, d\omega$$

where $s(\omega) = f\,[s(t)]$

Now, output noise power, $N_o = E[\eta_o^2(t)] = \frac{\eta}{2} \cdot \frac{1}{2\pi} \int_{-\infty}^{\infty} |H(\omega)^2 d\omega$

Hence, signal-to-noise ratio is given by

$$\left(\frac{S}{N}\right)_0 = \frac{\left[\frac{1}{(2\pi)}\right]^2 \left| \int_{-\infty}^{\infty} H(\omega)\, s(\omega)\, e^{j\omega T}\, d\omega \right|^2}{\left(\frac{\eta}{2}\right)\left[\frac{1}{2\pi}\right] \int_{-\infty}^{\infty} |H(\omega)|^2\, d\omega} \tag{1}$$

Now, using Schwarz inequality, we have

$$\left| \int_{-\infty}^{\infty} [H(\omega)\, s(\omega)\, e^{j\omega T}\, d\omega] \right|^2 \leq \int_{-\infty}^{\infty} |H(\omega)^2|\, d\omega \int_{-\infty}^{\infty} s(\omega)^2\, d\omega \tag{2}$$

Combination of eqn. (1) and eqn (2) gives,

$$\left(\frac{S}{N}\right)_0 \leq \frac{2}{\eta} \cdot \frac{1}{2\pi} \int_{-\infty}^{\infty} |s(\omega)^2 d\omega = \frac{2E}{\eta}$$

where $E = \frac{1}{2\pi} \int_{-\infty}^{\infty} |s(\omega)|^2\, d\omega$, energy of input signal.

Problem 6.29: Compute the matched filter output over (0, *T*) to the pulse waveform

$$s(t)\begin{cases} e^{-t} & 0 \le t \le T \\ 0 & \text{otherwise} \end{cases}$$

Solution: For the given *s* (*t*), the inpulse response of the matched filter is,

$$h(t) = s(T-t) = e^{-(T-t)}$$

Now, output

$$z(t) = s(t) * h(t) = \int_{-\infty}^{\infty} e^{-\tau} \cdot e^{-(T-t+\tau)} d\tau = e^{-T} \int_{0}^{t} e^{t-2\tau} \cdot d\tau$$

$$= -\frac{e^{-T}}{2} \cdot [e^{t-2\tau}]_0^t = e^{-T} \cdot \frac{e^{t} - e^{-t}}{2} = e^{-T} \sin ht$$

Problem 6.30: The output of a filter is given by

$$Y(t) = X(t+T) - X(t-T)$$

where $X(t)$ is a WSS process with power spectrum $S_{xx}(\omega)$ and *T* is constant. Find the power spectrum of $Y(t)$.

Solution: The output of the filter is

$$Y(t) = X(t+T) - X(t-T), \quad (1)$$

then inpulse response of the filter is given by,

$$h(t) = \delta(t) - \delta(t-T) \quad (2)$$

Taking Fourier transform on both sides of equation (2) we have

$$H(\omega) = 1 - e^{-j\omega T} \qquad [\text{As } \delta(t) \leftrightarrow 1 \text{ and } \delta(t-t_0) \leftrightarrow e^{-j\omega} t_0].$$

Hence, the power spectrum of $Y(t)$ is,

$$S_{yy}(\omega) = |H(\omega)|^2 S_{xx}(\omega) = |1 - e^{-j\omega T}|^2 \cdot S_{xx}(\omega)$$

$$= 2(1 - \cos \omega T) \cdot S_{xx}(\omega) = 4 \sin^2 \frac{\omega T}{2} \cdot S_{xx}(\omega)$$

Chapter 7

Digital Passband Transmission

Problem 7.1:

(*a*) Using the Gram-Schmidt orthogonalization procedure, find a set of orthonormal basis functions to represent the three signals $s_1(t)$, $s_2(t)$, and $s_3(t)$ shown in Fig. P. 7.1.

(*b*) Express each of these signals in terms of the set of basis functions found in part (*a*).

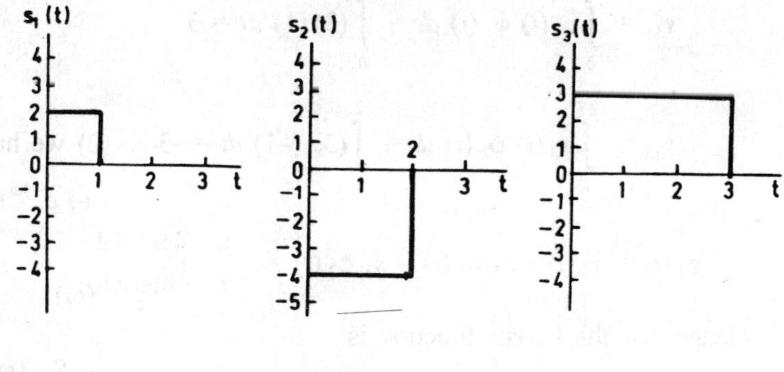

Fig. P. 7.1

Solution:

(*a*) We first observe that $s_1(t)$, $s_2(t)$ and $s_3(t)$ are linearly independent.

The energy of $s_1(t)$ is

$$E_1 = \int_0^1 (2)^2 \, dt = 4$$

The first basis function is therefore

$$\phi_1 = \frac{s_1(t)}{\sqrt{E_1}} = \begin{cases} 1, & 0 \le t \le 1 \\ 0, & \text{otherwise} \end{cases}$$

Define

$$s_{21} = \int_0^T s_2(t)\, \phi_1(t)\, dt = \int_0^1 (-4)\,(1)\, dt = -4$$

$$g_2(t) = s_2(t) - s_{21}\phi_1(t) = \begin{cases} -4, & 1 \le t \le 2 \\ 0, & \text{otherwise} \end{cases}$$

hence, the second basis function is

$$\phi_2(t) = \frac{g_2(t)}{\sqrt{\int_0^T g_2^2(t)dt}} = \begin{cases} -1, & 1 \le t \le 2 \\ 0, & \text{otherwise} \end{cases}$$

Define

$$s_{31} = \int_0^T s_3(t)\, \phi_1(t)\, dt = \int_0^1 (3)\,(1)\, dt = 3$$

$$s_{32} = \int_T^{2T} s_3(t)\, \phi_2(t)\, dt = \int_1^2 (3)\,(-1)\, dt = -3$$

$$g_3(t) = s_3(t) - s_{31}\phi_1(t) - s_{32}\phi_2(t) = \begin{cases} 3, & 2 \le t \le 3 \\ 0. & \text{otherwise} \end{cases}$$

Hence, the third basis function is

$$\phi_3(t) = \frac{g_3(t)}{\sqrt{\int_0^T g_3^2(t)\, dt}} = \begin{cases} 1, & 2 \le t \le 3 \\ 0, & \text{otherwise} \end{cases}$$

The three basis functions are as follows (graphically)

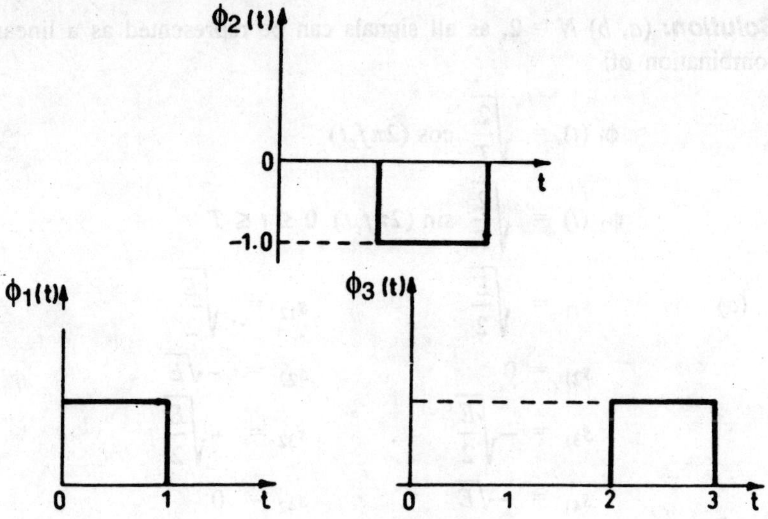

Fig. P. 7.1 (a)

(*b*)
$$s_1(t) = 2\phi_1(t)$$
$$s_2(t) = -4\phi(t) + 4\phi_2(t)$$
$$s_3(t) = 3\phi_1(t) - 3\phi_2(t) + 3\phi_3(t)$$

Problem 7.2: Consider the set of signals

$$s_1(t) = \begin{cases} \dfrac{2E}{T}\cos\left(2\pi f_c t + i\dfrac{\pi}{4}\right), & 0 \le t \le T \\ 0, & \text{elsewhere} \end{cases}$$

where $i = 1, 2, 3, 4$, and $f_c = \dfrac{n_c}{T}$ for some fixed integer n_c.

(*a*) What is the dimensionality, N, of the space spanned by this set of signals?

(*b*) Find a set of orthonormal basis functions to represent this set of signals.

(*c*) using the expansion, $s_1(t) = \sum_{j=1}^{N} s_{ij}\phi_j(t), \quad i = 1, 2, 3, 4$

find the coefficients s_{ij}

(*d*) Plot the locations of $s_i(t)$, $i = 1, 2, 3, 4$, in the signals space, using the results of parts (*b*) (*c*).

Solution: (*a*, *b*) $N = 2$, as all signals can be represented as a linear combination of:

$$\phi_1(t) = \sqrt{\frac{2}{T}} \cos(2\pi f_c t)$$

$$\phi_2(t) = \sqrt{\frac{2}{T}} \sin(2\pi f_c t) \quad 0 \le t \le T$$

(*c*)

$$s_{11} = \sqrt{\frac{E}{2}} \qquad s_{12} = \sqrt{\frac{E}{2}}$$

$$s_{21} = 0 \qquad s_{22} = -\sqrt{E}$$

$$s_{31} = -\sqrt{\frac{E}{2}} \qquad s_{32} = -\sqrt{\frac{E}{2}}$$

$$s_{41} = -\sqrt{E} \qquad s_{42} = 0$$

(*d*)

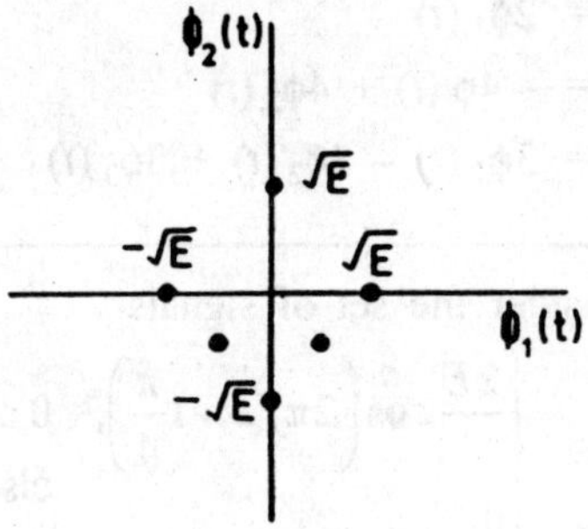

Fig. P. 7.2 (a)

Problem 7.3: Given two real-valued vectors x and y, prove Schwarz's inequality,

$$|x^T y| \le \|x\| \, \|y\|$$

where $|(x^T y)|$ is the absolute value of the inner product of x and y, respectively and $\|x\|$ and $\|y\|$ are its lengths of x and y respectively.

Solution:

$$\|(x + ay)\|^2 = \|x\|^2 + a^2 \|y\|^2 + 2a \, |(x, y)|$$

$$= c + A s^2 + 2Ba$$

where $\quad c = \| x \|^2, \quad A = \| y \|^2$, and $B = | (x, y) |$

This is a quadratic function in a since $\| (x + ay) \|^2 \geq 0$, the quadratic must have no real roots, except possibly a double root. This is equivalent to stating that the discriminant $AB^2 - 4Ac$ must be less than or equal to 0.

Therefore, $4B^2 \leq 4Ac$

or $\quad 4 \, | (x, y) |^2 \leq 4 \, \| x \|^2 \, \| y \|^2 \quad$ or $\quad | x, y | \leq \| x \| \, \| y \|$

Problem 7.4: Consider a random process $X(t)$ expanded in the form

$$X(t) = \sum_{j=1}^{N} X_j \phi_j(t) + W'(t), \; 0 \leq t \leq T$$

where $W'(t)$ is a remainder noise term. The $\{\phi_j(t) | \, j = 1, 2, \ldots, N\}$ form an orthonormal set, and the X_J are defined by

$$X_j = \int_0^T X(t) \, \phi_j(t) \, dt$$

Let $W'(t_k)$ denote a random variable obtained by observing $W'(t)$ at time $t = t_k$. Show that

$$E[X_j W'(t_k)] = 0, \; \begin{cases} j = 1,2,\ldots,N \\ 0 \leq t_k \leq T \end{cases}$$

Solution:

$$E[x_j W'(t_k)] - E[(S_{ij} \mid W_j) \, W'(t_k)]$$

$$E[S_{ij} W'(t_k)] = S_{ij} E[W'(t_k)] = 0$$

We also note that

$$W'(t_k) = W(t_k) - \sum_{j=1}^{N} W_i \phi_i(t_k)$$

we therefore have

$$E[X_j W'(t_k)] = E[W_j W'(t_k)] = E[W_j W(t_k) - \sum_{j=1}^{N} \phi_i(t_k) \, E[W_j W_i]]$$

But $\quad \mathrm{E}[W_j W(t_k)] = E[W(t_k) \int_0^T W(t) \, \phi_j(t) \, dt]$

$$= \int_0^T \phi_j(t)\, E[W(t_k)\, W(t)]\, dt$$

$$= \int_0^T \phi_j(t) \cdot \frac{N_0}{2}\, \delta(t - t_k)\, dt = \frac{N_0}{2} \phi_j(t_k)$$

$$E[W_j W_i] = \begin{cases} \dfrac{N_0}{2}, & i = j \\ 0, & i \neq j \end{cases}$$

Hence, we get the final result

$$E[X_j W'(t_k)] = \frac{N_0}{2} \phi_j(t_k) - \frac{N_0}{2} \phi_j(t_k) = 0$$

Problem 7.5: A PSK signal is applied to a correlator supplied with a phase reference that lies within ϕ radians of the exact carrier phase. Determine the effect of the phase error ϕ on the average probability of error of the system.

Solution:

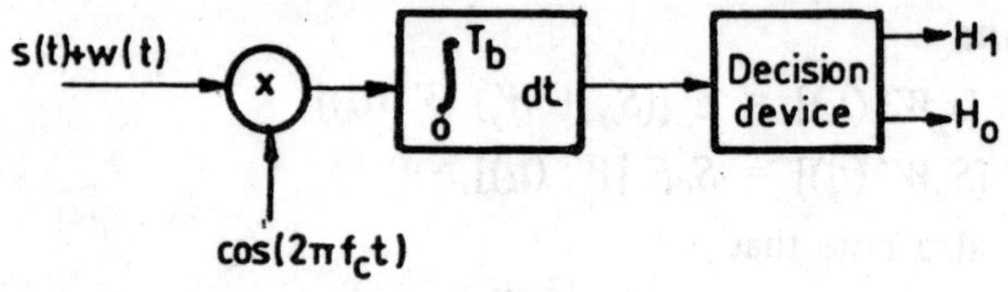

Fig. P. 7.5

With $S(t) = \pm A_c \cos(2\pi f_c t)$,

we find that the receiver output is

$$l = \pm \frac{A_c T_b}{2} \cos\phi + \int_0^{T_b} w(t) \cos(2\pi f_c t + \phi)\, dt$$

$$= \pm \frac{A_C' T_b}{2} + \int_0^{T_b} w(t) \cos(2\pi f_c t + \phi)\, dt$$

where $A_c' = A_c \cos\phi$.

The average probability of error of the system is therefore

$$P_e = \frac{1}{2} erfc\left(\sqrt{\frac{E_b'}{N_0}}\right)$$

Where $E_b' = \frac{T_b}{2}(A_c')^2 = \frac{A_c^2 T_b}{2} \cos\phi$, and $\frac{1}{2} N_0$ is the power spectral density of $w(t)$.

Therefore,

$$P_e = \frac{1}{2} erfc\left(\sqrt{\frac{E_b}{N_0}} \cos\phi\right)$$

where $E_b = \frac{1}{2} A_c^2 T_b$ is the transmitted signal energy.

Problem 7.6: The signal vectors s_1 and s_2 are used to represent binary symbols 1 and 0, respectively, in a coherent binary FSK system. The receiver decides in favor of symbol 1 when

$$x^T s_1 < x^T s_2$$

where $x^T s_i$ is the inner product of the observation vector x and the signal vector s_i, where $i = 1, 2$. Show that this decision rule is equivalent to the condition $x_1 > x_2$, where x_1 and x_2 are the elements of the observation vector x. Assume that the signal vectors s_1 and s_2 have equal energy.

Solution: For binary FSK, the two signal vectors are,

$$\underline{s}_1 = \begin{bmatrix} \sqrt{E_b} \\ 0 \end{bmatrix} \qquad \underline{s}_2 = \begin{bmatrix} 0 \\ \sqrt{E_b} \end{bmatrix}$$

Where E_b is the signal energy per bit. The inner product of these two signal vectors with the observation vector.

$$\underline{x} = \begin{bmatrix} x_1 \\ x_2 \end{bmatrix}$$

are as follows respectively,

$$(\underline{x}\ \underline{s}_1) = \sqrt{E_b}\, x_1$$

$$(\underline{x}, \underline{s}_2) = \sqrt{E_b}\, x_2$$

where $(x, s_i) = x^T s_i$ for $i = 1, 2$. The condition

$$x^T s_1 > x^T s_2$$

is therefore equivalent to

$$\sqrt{E_b}\, x_1 > \sqrt{E_b}\, x_2$$

Cancelling the common factor ..., we get

$$x_1 > x_2$$

which is the desired condition for making a decision in favor of symbol 1.

Problem 7.7: Consider a phase-locked loop consisting of a multiplier, loop filter, and voltage-controlled oscillator (VCO). Let the signal applied to the multiplier input be a PSK signal defined by

$$s(t) = A_c \cos [2\pi f_c t + k_p m(t)]$$

where k_p is the phase sensitivity, and the data signal $m(t)$ takes on the value +1 for binary symbol 1 and –1 for binary symbol 0. The VCO output is

$$r(t) = A_c \sin [2\pi f_c t + \theta(t)]$$

(*a*) Evaluate the loop filter output, assuming that this filter removes only modulated components with carrier frequency $2f_c$.

(*b*) Show that this output is proportional to the data signal $m(t)$ when the loop is phase locked, that is, $\theta(t) = 0$.

Solution: (a) The noiseless PSK signal is given by

$$S(t) = A_c \cos [2\pi f_c t + k_p m(t)]$$

$$= A_c \cos (2\pi f_c t) \cos [k_p m(t)] - A_c \sin (2\pi f_c t) \sin [k_p m(t)]$$

Since $m(t) = \pm 1$, it is follows that

$$\cos [k_p m(t)] = \cos (\pm k_p) = \cos (k_p)$$

$$\sin [k_p m(t)] = \sin (\pm k_p) = \pm \sin (k_p) = m(t) \sin (k_p)$$

Therefore,

$$S(t) = A_c \cos (k_p) \cos (2\pi f_c t) - A_c m(t) \sin (k_p) \sin (2\pi f_c t) \quad ...(1)$$

The VCO output is

$$r(t) = A_v \sin [2\pi f_c t + \theta(t)]$$

The multiplier output is therefore

$$r(t)\,S(0) = \frac{1}{2} A_c\, A_v \cos(k_p)\,\{\sin[\theta(t)] + \sin[4\pi f_c t + \theta(t)]\} -$$

$$\frac{1}{2} A_c A_v m(t) \sin(k_p)\,\{\cos[\theta(t)] + \cos[4\pi f_c t + \theta(t)]\}$$

The loop filter removes the double-frequency components, producing the output

$$e(t) = \frac{1}{2} A_c A_v \cos(k_p) \sin[\theta(t)] - \frac{1}{2} A_c A_v m(t) \sin(k_p) \cos[\theta(t)]$$

Note that if $k_p = \frac{\pi}{2}$ (i.e., the carrier is fully deviated), there would be no carrier component for the PLL to track.

(*b*) Since the error signal tends to drive the loop lock (i.e., $\theta(t)$ approaches zero), the loop filter output reduces to

$$e(t) = -\frac{1}{2} A_c A_v \sin(k_p)\, m(t)$$

which is proportional to the desired data signal $m(t)$. Hence, the phase-looked loop may be used to recover $m(t)$.

Problem 7.8: The signal component of a coherent PSK system is defined by

$$s(t) = A_c k \sin(2\pi f_c t) \pm A_c \sqrt{1-k^2} \cos(2\pi f_c t)$$

where $0 \le t \le T_b$, and the plus sign corresponds to symbol 1 and the minus sign corresponds to symbol 0. The first term represents a carrier component included for the purpose of synchronizing the receiver to the transmitter.

(*a*) Draw a signal-space diagram for the scheme described here; what observations can you make about this diagram?

(*b*) Show that, in the presence of additive white Gaussian noise of zero mean and power spectral density $\frac{N_0}{2}$, the average probability of error is

$$P_e = \frac{1}{2}\, erfc\left(\sqrt{\frac{E_b}{N_0}\left(1-k^2\right)}\right)$$

where

$$E_b = \frac{1}{2}A_c^2T_b$$

(*c*) Suppose that 10 percent of the transmitted signal power is allocated to the carrier component. Determine the $\frac{E_b}{N_0}$ required to realize a probability of error equal to 10^{-4}.

(*d*) Compare this value of $\frac{E_b}{N_0}$ with that required for a conventional PSK system with the same probability of error.

Solution: (*a*) The signal-space diagram of the scheme described in this problem is two-dimensional, as shown by

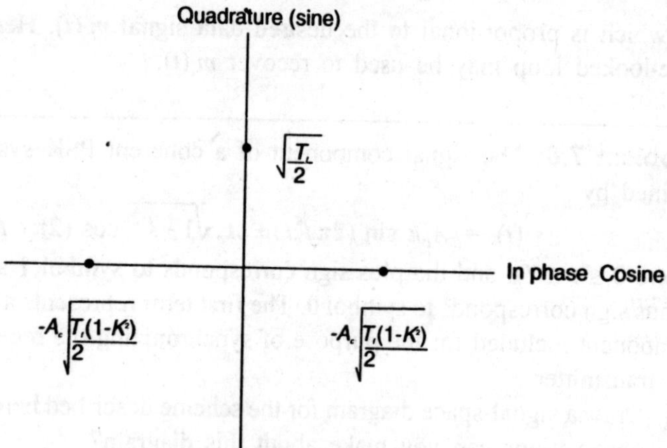

Fig. P. 7.8 (a)

This signal-space diagram differes from that of the conventional PSK signaling scheme in that it is two-dimensional, with a new signal point on the quadrature axis at $A_ck\sqrt{\frac{T_b}{2}}$. If k is reduced to zero, the above diagram reduces to the same form as that shown in Fig. P. 7.8 (a).

(*b*)

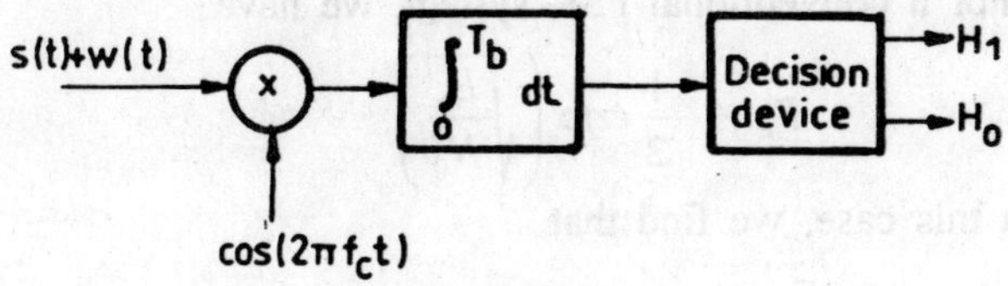

Fig. P. 7.8 (b)

The signal at the decision device input is

$$l = \pm\frac{A_c}{2}\sqrt{1-k^2}\ \ T_b + \int_0^{T_b} w\,(t)\,\cos\,(2\pi f_c t)\,dt$$

Therefore, following a proc=dure similar to that used for evaluating the probability of error for a conventional PSK system, we find that for the system defin eq. (1) that average probability of error is

$$P_e = \frac{1}{2}\,erfc\left(\sqrt{\frac{E_b\left(1-k^2\right)}{N_0}}\right)$$

where $E_b = \frac{1}{2}A_c^2 T_b$.

(*c*) For the case when $P_e = 10^{-4}$

and $k^2 = 0.1$, we get $10^{-4} = \frac{1}{2}\,erfc\,(u)$

where $u^2 = \frac{0.9\,E_b}{N_0}$

Using the approximation

$$erfc\,(u) \cong \frac{\exp\,(-u^2)}{\sqrt{\pi}\,u}$$

We obtain

$$\exp\,(-u)^2 - 2\sqrt{\pi} \times 10^{-4}\,u = 0$$

The solution to this equation is $u = 2.64$. The corresponding value of $\frac{E_b}{N_0}$ is

$$\frac{E_b}{N_0} = \frac{(2.64)^2}{0.9} = 7.74$$

Expressed in decibels, this value corresponds to 8.9 dB.

(*d*) For a conventional PSK system, we have

$$P_e = \frac{1}{2} erfc\left(\sqrt{\frac{E_b}{N_0}}\right)$$

In this case, we find that

$$\frac{E_b}{N_0} = (2.64)^2 = 6.92$$

Expressed in decibels, this value corresponds to 8.4 dB. Thus, the conventional PSk system requires 0.5 dB less in $\frac{E_b}{N_0}$ then the modified scheme described herein.

Problem 7.9: An FSK system transmits binary data at the rate of 2.5×10^6 bits per second. During the course of transmission, white Gaussian noise of zero mean and power spectral density 10^{-20} watts per hertz is added to the signal. In the absence of noise, the amplitude of the received sinusoidal wave for digit 1 or 0 is 1 microvolt. Determine the average probability of symbol error for the following system configurations:

(*a*) Coherent binary FSK.

(*b*) Coherent MSK.

(*c*) Noncoherent binary FSK.

Solution: bit duration is

$$T_b = \frac{1}{2.5 \times 10^6 \text{Hz}} = 0.4\ \mu s$$

The signal energy per bit is

$$E_b = \frac{1}{2} A_c^2 T_b = \frac{1}{2} (10^{-6})^2 \times 0.4 \times 10^{-6} = 2 \times 10^{-19} \text{ joules}$$

(*a*) Coherent Binary FSK

The average probability of error is

$$P_c = \frac{1}{2} erfc\left(\sqrt{\frac{E_b}{2N_0}}\right) = \frac{1}{2} erfc\left(\sqrt{\frac{2 \times 10^{-19}}{4 \times 10^{-20}}}\right) = \frac{1}{2} erfc\ (\sqrt{5})$$

using the approximation

$$erfc\ (u) \cong \frac{\exp(-u)^2}{\sqrt{\pi}\ u}$$

We obtain the result

$$P_e = \frac{1}{2}\ \frac{\exp(-5)}{\sqrt{5\pi}} = 0.85 \times 10^{-3}$$

(*b*) MSK

$$P_e = erfc\left(\sqrt{\frac{E_b}{N_0}}\right) = erfc\left(\sqrt{10}\right) \cong \frac{\exp(-10)}{\sqrt{10\pi}} = 0.81 \times 10^{-5}$$

(*c*) Noncoherent binary FSK

$$P_e = \frac{1}{2}\exp\left(-\frac{E_b}{N_0}\right) = \frac{1}{2}\ \exp(-5) = 3.37 \times 10^{-3}$$

Problem 7.10: (*a*) In a coherent FSK system, the signals $s_1(t)$ and $s_2(t)$ representing symbols 1 and 0, respectively, are defined by

$$s_1(t),\ s_2(t) = A_c \cos\left[2\pi\left(f_c \pm \frac{\Delta f}{2}\right)t\right],\ 0 \le t \le T_b$$

Assumming that $f_c > \Delta f$, show that the correlation coefficient of the signals $s_1(t)$ and $s_2(t)$ is approximately given by

$$\rho = \frac{\int_0^{T_b} s_1(t)\, s_2(t)\, dt}{\int_0^{T_b} s_1^2(t)\, dt} \cong \text{sinc}\,(2\Delta f T_b)$$

(*b*) What is the minimum value of frequency shift Δf for which the signals $s_1(t)$ and $s_2(t)$ are orthogonal?

(*c*) What is the value of Δf that minimizes the average probability of symbol error?

(*d*) For the value of Δf obtained in part (*c*), determine the increase in $\frac{E_b}{N_0}$ required so that this cohereint FSK system has the same noise performance as a coherent binary PSK system.

Solution:

(*a*) The correlation coefficient of the signals s_0 (*t*) and s_1 (*t*) is

$$= \frac{\int_0^{T_b} s_0(t)\, s_1(t)\, dt}{\left[\int_0^{T_b} s_0^2(t)\, dt\right]^{\frac{1}{2}} \left[\int_0^{T_b} s_1^2(t)\, dt\right]^{\frac{1}{2}}}$$

$$= \frac{A_c^2 \int_0^{T_b} \cos\left[2\pi\left(f_c + \frac{1}{2}\Delta f\right)t\right] \cos\left[2\pi\left(f_c - \frac{1}{2}\Delta f\right)t\right] dt}{\left[\frac{1}{2} A_c^2 T_b\right]^{\frac{1}{2}} \left[\frac{1}{2} A_c^2 T_b\right]^{\frac{1}{2}}}$$

$$= \frac{1}{T_b} \int_0^{T_b} \cos(2\pi \Delta f t) + \cos(4\pi f_c t)\, dt$$

$$= \frac{1}{2\pi T_b}\left[\frac{\sin(2\pi \Delta f T_b)}{\Delta f} + \frac{\sin(4\pi f_c T_b)}{2 f_c}\right]$$

since $f_c \gg \Delta f$, then we may ignore the second term in eq. (1), obtaining

$$\rho \cong \frac{\sin(2\pi \Delta f T_b)}{2\pi T_b \Delta f} = \text{sinc}\,(2\pi f T_b)$$

(*b*) The dependence of ρ on Δf is as shown below

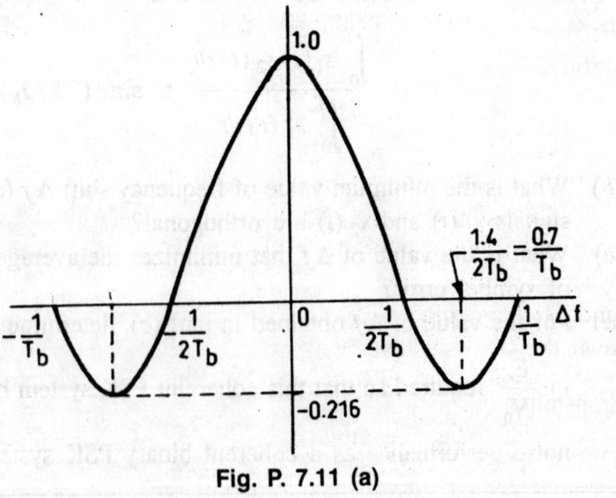

Fig. P. 7.11 (a)

$s_0(t)$ and $s_1(t)$ are othogonal when $\rho = 0$. therefore, the minimum value of Δf for which they are orthogonal, is $\frac{1}{2T_b}$

(*c*) The average probability of error is given by

$$E_b = \frac{1}{2}\, erfc\left(\sqrt{\frac{E_b(1-p)}{2N_0}}\right)$$

The most negative value of ρ is – 0.216, occurring at

$$\Delta f = \frac{0.7}{T_b}$$

The minimum value of p_e is therefore

$$p_{e,\,\min} = \frac{1}{2}\, erfc\left(\sqrt{0.608\frac{E_b}{N_0}}\right)$$

(*d*) For a coherent binary PSK system, the average probability of error is

$$P_e = \frac{1}{2}\, erfc\left(\sqrt{\frac{E_b}{N_0}}\right)$$

Therefore, the $\frac{E_b}{N_0}$ of this coherent binary FSK system must be increased by the factor 1/0.608 = 1.645 (or 2.16 dB) so as to realize the same average probability of error as a coherent binary PSK system.

Problem 7.12: A binary FSK singal with *discontinuous phase* is defined by

$$s(t) = \begin{cases} \sqrt{\frac{2E_b}{T_b}}\cos\left[2\pi\left(f_c + \frac{\Delta f}{2}\right)t + \theta_1\right] & \text{for symbol 1} \\ \sqrt{\frac{2E_b}{T_b}}\cos\left[2\pi\left(f_c - \frac{\Delta f}{2}\right)t + \theta_2\right] & \text{for symbol 0} \end{cases}$$

where E_b is the signal energy per bit, T_b is the bit duration, and θ_1 and θ_2 are sample values of uniformly distributed random variables over the interval 0 to 2π. In effect, the two oscillators supplying the transmitted frequencies $f_c \pm \Delta\frac{f}{2}$ operate independently of each other. Assume that $f_c \gg \Delta f$.

(*a*) Evaluate the power spectral density of the FSK singal.
(*b*) Show that for frequencies far removed from the carrier frequency f_c, the power spectral density falls off as the inverse square of frequency.

Solution: (*a*)

Since the two oscillators used to represent symbols 1 and 0 are independent, we may view that resulting binary FSK wave as the sum of two on-off keying (00k) signals one 00*k* signal operates with the oscilaltor of frequency f_1. The second 00*k* signal operates with the oscillator of frequency f_2.

The power spectral density of a random binary wave $x_1(t)$, in which symbol 1 is represented by *A* volts and symbol 0 by zero volts, is given by

$$S_{x_1}(f) = \frac{A^2}{4}\delta(f) + \frac{A^2 T_b}{4}\operatorname{sinc}^2(fT_b)$$

Where T_b is the bit duration, when this binary wave is multiplied by a sinusoidal wave of unit amplitude and frequency $f_c + \Delta\frac{f}{2}$, we get the first 00*k* signal with

$$A = \sqrt{2\frac{E_b}{T_b}}$$

The power spectral density of this 00*k* signal equals

$$S_1(f) = \frac{1}{4}\left[S_{x_1}\left(f - f_c - \frac{\Delta f}{2}\right) + S_{x_1}\left(f + f_c + \frac{\Delta f}{2}\right)\right]$$

The power spectral density of the random binary wave $x_2(t) = x_1(t)$, in which symbol 1 is represented by zero volts and symbol 0 by *A* volts, is given by

$$S_{x_2}(f) = S_{x_1}(f)$$

When $X_2(t)$ is multiplied by the second sinusoidal wave of unit amplitude and frequency $f_c - \Delta\frac{f}{2}$, we get the second 00*k* signal whose power spectral density equal

$$S_2(f) = \frac{1}{4}\left[S_{x_2}\left(f - f_c + \frac{\Delta f}{2}\right) + S_{x_2}\left(f + f_c - \frac{\Delta f}{2}\right)\right]$$

The power spectral density of the FSK signal equals:

$$S_{FKS}(f) = S_1(f) + S_2(f)$$

$$= \frac{E_b}{8T_b}\left[\delta\left(f - f_c - \frac{\Delta f}{2}\right) + \delta\left(f + f_c + \frac{\Delta f}{2}\right) + \delta\left(f - f_c + \frac{\Delta f}{2}\right) + \delta\left(f + f_c - \frac{\Delta f}{2}\right)\right]$$

$$+ \frac{E_b}{8}\left\{\sin c^2\left[T_b\left(f - f_c - \frac{\Delta f}{2}\right)\right] + \sin c^2\left[T_b\left(f + f_c + \frac{\Delta f}{2}\right)\right] + \sin c^2\left[T_b\left(f - f_c + \frac{\Delta f}{2}\right)\right] + \sin c^2\left[T_b\left(f + f_c - \frac{\Delta f}{2}\right)\right]\right\}$$

This result shows that the power spectrum of this binary FKS wave contains delta function at

$$f = f_c \pm \Delta\frac{f}{2}$$

(*b*) At high values of *x*, the function sin *c* (*x*) falls off as $\frac{1}{x}$. Hence, at high frequencies, S_{FKS} falls off as $\frac{1}{f^2}$

Problem 7.12: Set up a block diagram for the generation of Sunde's FSK signal *s* (*t*) with continuous phase by using the representation given in by

$$s(t) = \sqrt{\frac{2E_b}{T_b}}\cos\left(\frac{\pi t}{T_b}\right)\cos(2\pi f_c t) \mp \sqrt{\frac{2E_b}{T_b}}\sin\left(\frac{\pi t}{T_b}\right)\sin(2\pi f_c t)$$

Solution:

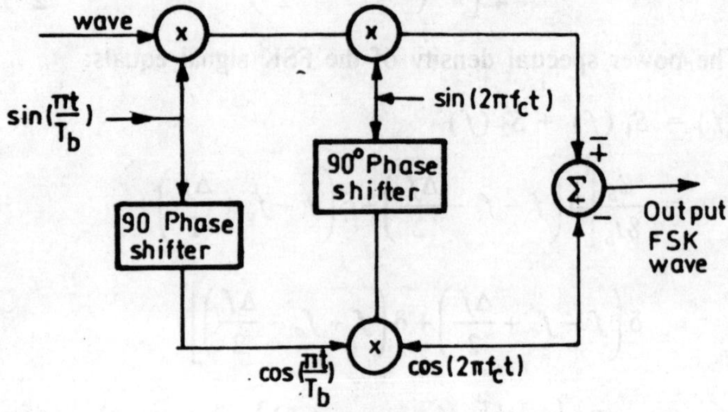

Fig. P. 7.12 (a)

Problem 7.13: In the on-off keying version of an ASK system, symbol 1 is represented by transmitting a sinusoidal carrier of amplitude $\sqrt{2\frac{E_b}{T_b}}$, where E_b is the signal energy per bit and T_b is the bit duration. Symbol 0 is represented by switching off the carrier. Assume that symbols 1 and 0 occur with equal probability.
For and AWGN channel, determine the average probability of error for this ASK system, assuming:
(*a*) Cohereint reception.
(*b*) Noncoherent reception, operating with a large value of bit energy-to-noise density ratio $\frac{E_b}{E_0}$.

Note: When *x* is large, the modified Bessel function of the first kind of zero order may be approximated as follows

$$I_0(x) \cong \frac{\exp(x)}{\sqrt{2\pi x}}$$

Solution: (*a*) ASK with coherent reception

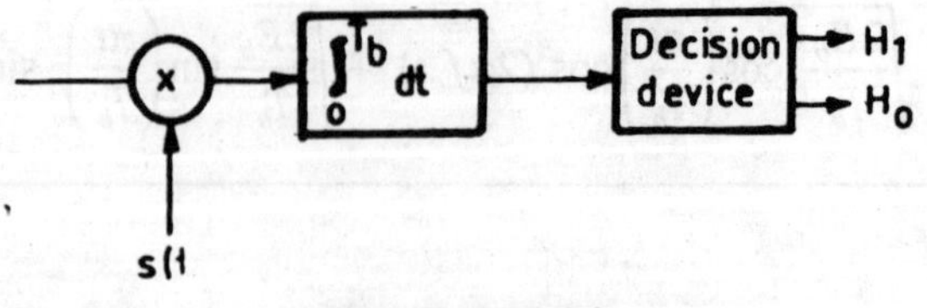

Fig. P. 7.13 (a)

Denoting the presence of symbol 1 or symbol 0 by hypothesis H_1 or H_0, respectively, we may write

$$H_1 : x(t) = s(t) + w(t)$$
$$H_0 : x(t) = w(t)$$

where $s(t) = A_c \cos(2\pi f_c t)$, with $A_c = \sqrt{2\frac{E_b}{T_b}}$.

therefore

$$l = \int_0^{T_b} x(t)\, s(t)\, dt$$

If $l > \frac{E_b}{2}$, the receiver decides in favour of symbol 1.

If $l < \frac{E_b}{2}$, it decides in favour of symbol 0.

The conditional probability density function of the random variable L, whose value is denoted by l, are defined by

$$f_{L|0}(l|0) = \frac{1}{\sqrt{\pi N_0 E_b}} \exp\left(-\frac{l^2}{N_0 E_b}\right)$$

$$f_{L|1}(l|1) = \frac{1}{\sqrt{\pi N_0 E_b}} \exp\left[-\frac{(l-E_b)^2}{N_0 E_b}\right]$$

The average probability of error is therefore,

$$P_e = p_0 \int_{E_{b/2}}^{\infty} f_{L|0}(l|0)\, dl + p_0 \int_{-\infty}^{E_{b/2}} f_{L|0}(l|1)\, dl$$

$$= \frac{1}{2} \int_{E_b/2}^{\infty} \frac{1}{\sqrt{\pi N_0 E_b}} \exp\left(-\frac{l^2}{N_0 E_b}\right) dl$$

$$\frac{1}{2} \int_{-\infty}^{E_b/2} \frac{1}{\sqrt{\pi N_0 E_b}} \exp\left(-\frac{(l-E_b)^2}{N_0 E_b}\right) dl$$

$$= \frac{1}{\sqrt{\pi N_0 E_b}} \int_{\frac{E_b}{2}}^{\infty} \exp\left(-\frac{l^2}{N_0 E_b}\right) dl = \frac{1}{2}\, erfc\left(\frac{1}{2}\sqrt{\frac{E_b}{N_0}}\right)$$

(*b*) ASK with noncoherent reception

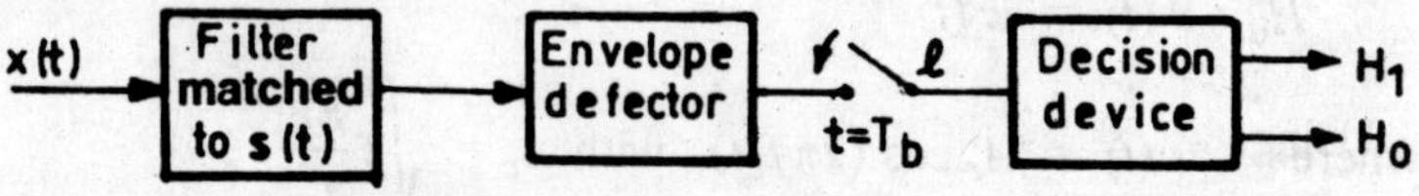

Fig. P. 7.13 (b)

In this case, the signal $s(t)$ is defined by

$$s(t) = A_c \cos(2\pi f_c t + \theta)$$

Where $$A_c = \sqrt{2\frac{E_b}{T_b}}, \text{ and } f_\theta(\theta) = \begin{cases} \frac{1}{2\pi}, & 0 \le \theta \le 2\pi \\ 0, & \text{otherwise} \end{cases}$$

For the case when symbol 0 is transmitted that is, under hypothesis H_0, we find that the random variable L, at the input of the decision device, is Rayleigh-distributed:

$$f_{L|0}(l \mid 0) = \frac{4l}{N_0 T_b} \exp\left(-\frac{2l^2}{N_0 T_b}\right)$$

For the case when symbol 1 is transmitted, that is under hypothesis H_1. We find that the random variable L is Rician-distributed

$$f_{L|1}(l|r) = \frac{4l}{N_0 T_b} \exp\left(-\frac{l^2 + A_c^2 \frac{T_b^2}{4}}{N_0 \frac{T_b}{2}}\right) I_0\left(\frac{2lA_c}{N_0}\right)$$

where $I_0\left(2l\frac{A_c}{N_0}\right)$ is the modified Bessel function of the first kind of zero order.

Before we can obtain a solution for the error performance of the receiver, we have to determine a value for the threshold. Since symbols 1 and 0 occur with equal probability, the minimum probability of error criterion yields:

$$\exp\left(-\frac{A_c^2 T_b}{2N_0}\right) I_0\left(\frac{2lA_c}{N_0}\right) \underset{H_0}{\overset{H_1}{\gtrless}} 1 \qquad \ldots(1)$$

For large values of $\frac{E_b}{N_0}$, we may approximate $I_0\left(\frac{2lA_c}{N_0}\right)$ as follows:

$$I_0\left(\frac{2lA_c}{N_0}\right) \equiv \frac{\exp\left(\frac{2lA_c}{N_0}\right)}{\sqrt{\frac{4\pi lA_c}{N_0}}}$$

Using this approximation, we may write eq. (1) as follows:

$$\exp\left[\frac{A_c(4 - A_cT_b)}{2N_0}\right] \underset{H_0}{\overset{H_1}{\gtrless}} \sqrt{\frac{4\pi lA_c}{N_0}}$$

Taking the logarighm of both sides of this relation, we get

$$l \underset{H_0}{\overset{H_1}{\gtrless}} \frac{A_cT_b}{4} + \frac{1}{2}\sqrt{\frac{\pi lN_0}{A_c}}$$

neglecting the second term on the right hand side of this relation, and using hte fact that

$$E_b = \frac{A_c^2T_b}{2}$$

We may write

$$l \underset{H_0}{\overset{H_1}{\gtrless}} \frac{1}{2}\sqrt{\frac{E_bT_b}{2}}$$

The threshold $\frac{1}{2}\sqrt{\frac{E_bT_b}{2}}$ is at the point corresponding to the crossover between the two probability density function, as illustrated below.

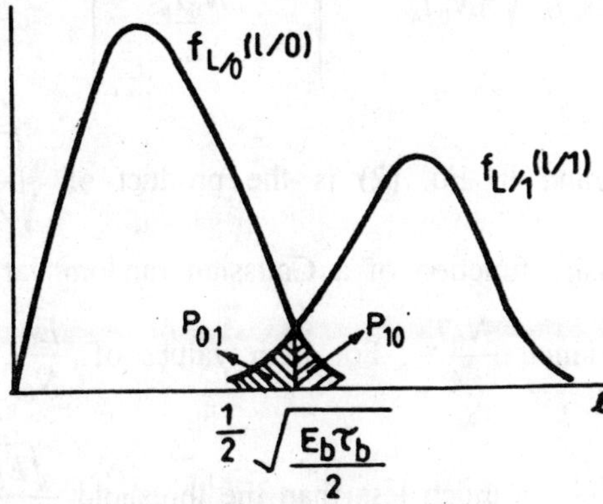

Fig. P. 7.13 (c)

The average probability of error is therefore

$$P_e = P_0 P_{10} + P_1 P_{01}$$

Where

$$P_{10} = \int_{\frac{\sqrt{E_b T_b}}{2\sqrt{2}}}^{\infty} f_{L|0}(l|0)\, dl = \int_{\frac{\sqrt{E_b T_b}}{2\sqrt{2}}}^{\infty} \frac{4l}{N_0 T_b} \exp\left(-\frac{2l^2}{n_0 T_b}\right) dl$$

$$= \left[-\exp\left(-\frac{2l^2}{N_0 T_b}\right)\right]_{\frac{\sqrt{E_b T_b}}{2\sqrt{2}}}^{\infty} = \exp\left(-\frac{E_b}{4N_0}\right)$$

$$P_{01} = \int_0^{\frac{\sqrt{E_b T_b}}{2\sqrt{2}}} f_{L|1}(l|1)\, dl = \int_0^{\frac{\sqrt{E_b T_b}}{2\sqrt{2}}} \frac{4l}{N_0 T_b} \exp\left(-\frac{l^2 + \frac{A_c^2 T_b^2}{4}}{\frac{N_0 T_b}{4}}\right) I_0\left(\frac{2lA}{N_0}\right) dl$$

$$= \int_0^{\frac{\sqrt{E_b T_b}}{2\sqrt{2}}} \frac{4l}{N_0 T_b} \exp\left(-\frac{l^2 + \frac{A_c^2 T_b^2}{4}}{\frac{N_0 T_b}{2}}\right) \cdot \frac{\exp\left(\frac{2lA_c}{N_0}\right)}{\sqrt{\frac{4\pi l A_c}{N_0}}}\, dl$$

$$= \int_0^{\frac{\sqrt{E_b T_b}}{2\sqrt{2}}} \sqrt{\frac{2l}{A_c T_b}} \sqrt{\frac{2}{\pi N_0 T_b}} \exp\left[-\frac{\left(l - \frac{A_c T_b}{2}\right)^2}{\frac{N_0 T_b}{2}}\right] dl \qquad \ldots(2)$$

The integrand in Eq. (2) is the product of $\sqrt{\frac{2l}{A_c T_b}}$ and the probability density function of a Gaussian random variable of mean $\frac{A_c T_b}{2}$ and variance $\frac{N_0 T_b}{4}$. For high values of $\frac{E_0}{N_0}$, the standard deviation $\sqrt{\frac{N_0 T_b}{4}}$ is much less than the threshold $\frac{\sqrt{E_b T_b}}{2\sqrt{2}}$

Consequently, the area under the portion of the curve from 0 to $\frac{\sqrt{E_b T_b}}{2\sqrt{2}}$ is quite small, that is, $P_{01} \cong 0$. Then, we may approximate the average probability of error as

$$P_e \cong P_0 P_{10} = \frac{1}{2}\exp\left(-\frac{E_b}{4N_0}\right)$$

Where it is assumed that symbols 0 and 1 occur with equal probability.

Problem 7.14: The purpose of a *radar system* is basically to detect the presence of a target and to extract useful information about the target. Supoose that in such a system, hypothesis H_0 is that there is no target present, so that the received signal $x(t) = w(t)$, wehre $w(t)$ is white Gaussian noise of zero mean and power spectral density $\frac{N_0}{2}$. For hypothesis H_1, a target is present, and $x(t) = w(t) + s(t)$, where $s(t)$ is an echo produced by the target. Assume that $s(t)$ is completely known. Evaluate:

(*a*) The *probability of false alarm* defined as the probability that the receiver decides that a target is present when it is not.

(*b*) The *probabilityo f detection* defined as the probability that the receiver decides that a target is present when it is.

Solution: Define the test statistic (receover output) as

$$L = \int_0^T s(t)\, x(t)\, dt$$

where T is the duration of the echo signal $s(t)$. With either $x(t) = w(t)$ or $x(t) = s(t) + w(t)$, and with $w(t)$ representing a Gaussian noise process, we find that $x(t)$ is also a Gaussian process. Since L is a linear function of $x(t)$, it follows that L is a Gaussian random variable.

The mean value of L is hypothesis-dependent. When no target is present, i.e., under hypothesis H_0, $x(t) = w(t)$, and since $w(t)$ has zero mean, we obtain

$$E\left[L|H_0\right] = E\left[\int_0^T s(t)\,w(t)\,dt\right] = 0$$

When a target is present, i.e., under hypothesis H_1,
We have $x(t) = s(t) + w(t)$, and so

$$E\left[L|H_1\right] = E\left[\int_0^T s(t)\,[s(t) + w(t)]\,dt\right] = \int_0^T s^2(t)\,dt = E$$

Where E is the energy of the target echo $s(t)$. However, the variance of L is the same under both hypothesis. Specifically, if H_0 is true, we have

$$\text{Var}\left[L|H_0\right] = E\left[\int_0^T\int_0^T s(t)\,s(\tau)\,w(t)\,w(\tau)\,dt\,d\tau\right]$$

$$= \int_0^T\int_0^T s(t)\,s(\tau)\,E\left[w(t)\,w(\tau)\right]dt\,d\tau$$

$$= \int_0^T\int_0^T s(t)\,s(\tau)\,R_w(t-\tau)\,dt\,d\tau$$

Where $R_w(\tau)$ is the autocorrelation function of $w(t)$. Since $w(t)$ is a with noise process of power spectral density $\frac{N_0}{2}$, we have

$$R_w(\tau) = \frac{N_0}{2}\,\delta(\tau)$$

Therefore,

$$\text{Var}\left[L|H_0\right] = \frac{N_0}{2}\int_0^T\int_0^T s(t)\,s(\tau)\,\delta(t-\tau)\,dt\,d\tau = \frac{N_0}{2}\int_0^T s^2(t)\,dt = \frac{N_0E}{2}$$

Similarly, we may show that

$$\text{Var}\left[L|H_1\right] = \frac{N_0E}{2}$$

We may thus express the probability density function of L, depending on whether H_0 or H_1 is true, as follows:

$$f_{L|H_0}(l|H_0) = \frac{1}{\sqrt{\pi N_0 E}} \exp\left(-\frac{l^2}{N_0 E}\right)$$

$$f_{L|H_1}(l|H_1) = \frac{1}{\sqrt{\pi N_0 E}} \exp\left(-\frac{(l-E)^2}{N_0 E}\right)$$

(*a*) The probability of false alarm P_F is defined by the sheded area shown below:

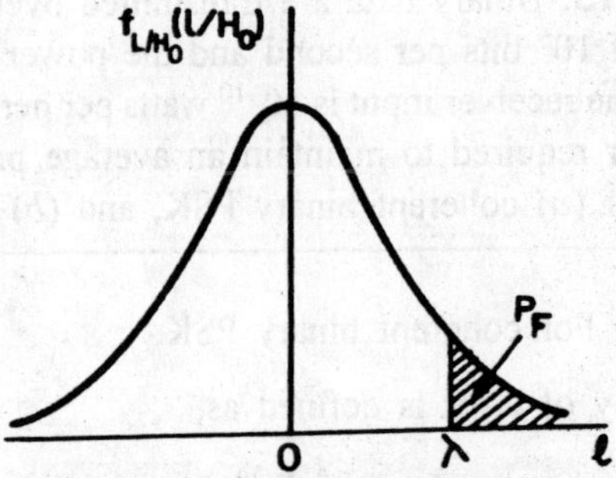

Fig. P. 7.14 (a)

Hence, denoting the threshold by *x*, we may write

$$P_F = P(L > \lambda \mid H_0) = \int_{\lambda}^{\infty} f_{L|H_0}(l|H_0)dl$$

$$= \frac{1}{\sqrt{\pi N_0 E}} \int_{\lambda}^{\infty} \exp\left(-\frac{l^2}{N_0 E}\right) dl = \frac{1}{2}\, erfc \left(\frac{\lambda}{\sqrt{N_0 E}}\right)$$

(*b*) The probability of detection P_D is denoted by the shaded area shown below:

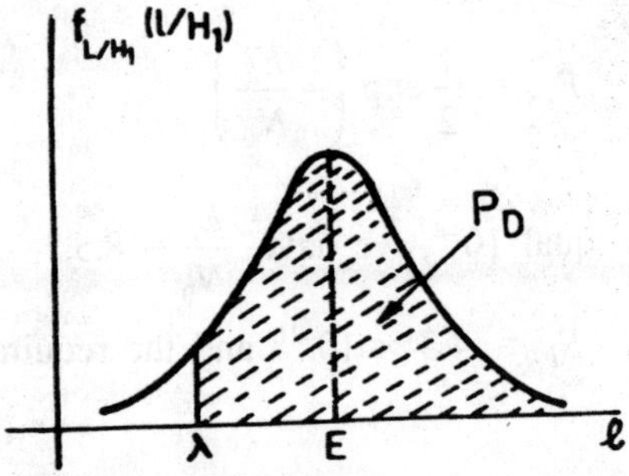

Fig. P. 7.14 (b)

Hence we may write

$$P_D = P(L > \lambda \mid H_1) = \int_{\lambda}^{\infty} f_{L|H_1}(l \mid H_1)\, dl$$

$$= \frac{1}{\sqrt{\pi N_0 E}} \int_{\lambda}^{\infty} \exp\left[-\frac{(l-E)^2}{N_0 E}\right] dl = \frac{1}{2}\, erfc\left(\frac{\lambda}{\sqrt{N_0 E}} - \sqrt{\frac{E}{N_0}}\right)$$

> **Problem 7.15:** Binary data are transmitted over a microwave link at the rate of 10^6 bits per second and the power spectral density of the noise at the receiver input is 10^{-10} watts per hertz. Find the average carrier power required to maintain an average probabilityo of error $P_e \le 10^{-4}$ for (*a*) coherent binary PSK, and (*b*) DPSK.

Solution: (*a*) For coherent binary PSK,

Probability of error is defined as,

$$P_e = \frac{1}{2}\, erfc\left(\frac{E_b}{N_0}\right).$$

Where E_b is the signal energy/bit.

For P_e to equal 10^{-4}, $\sqrt{\frac{E_b}{N_0}} = 2.64$, which gives

$\frac{E_b}{N_0} = 7.0$. Hence $E_b = 3.5 \times 10^{-10}$.

Hence the required average carrire power is 0.35 mW.

(*b*) For DPSK, the probability of error is defined as,

$$P_e = \frac{1}{2} \exp\left(-\frac{E_b}{N_0}\right)$$

For P_e to equal 10^{-4}, we have $\frac{E_b}{N_0} = 8.5$.

Therefore $E_b = 4.3 \times 10^{-10}$ and the required average power is 0.43 mW.

Problem 7.16: The binary sequence 1100100010 is applied to the DPSK transmitter of Fig. P. 7.16 (a).

(*a*) Sketch the resulting waveform at the transmitter output.

(*b*) Applying this waveform to the DPSK receiver of Fig. P. 7.16 (b), show that, in the absence of noise, the original binary sequence is reconstructed at the receiver output.

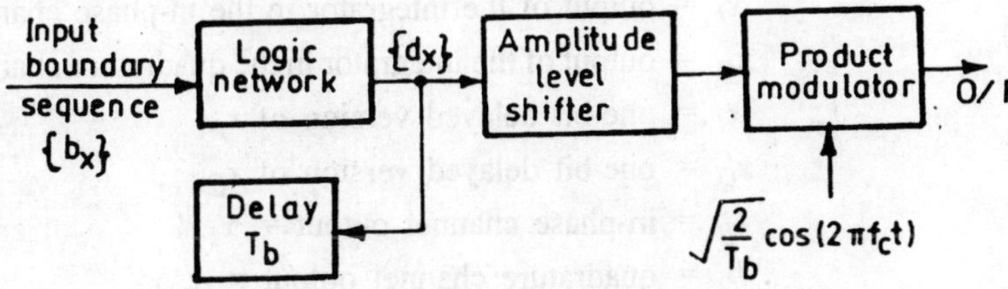

Fig. P. 7.16 (a)

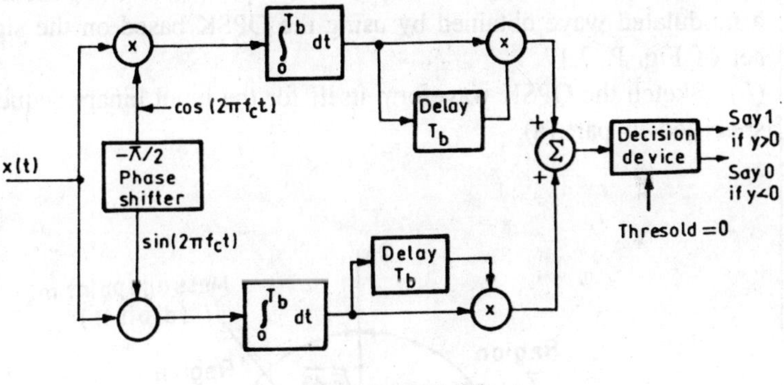

Fig. P. 7.16 (b)

Solution: (*a*) Table given below illustrates the generation of DPSK signal

b_k		1	1	0	0	1	0	0	0	1	0
d_{k-1}		1	1	1	0	1	1	0	1	0	0
d_k	1	1	1	0	1	1	0	1	0	0	1
Transmitted phase	0	0	0	π	0	0	π	0	π	π	0

The waveform of the DPSK signal is thus as follows:

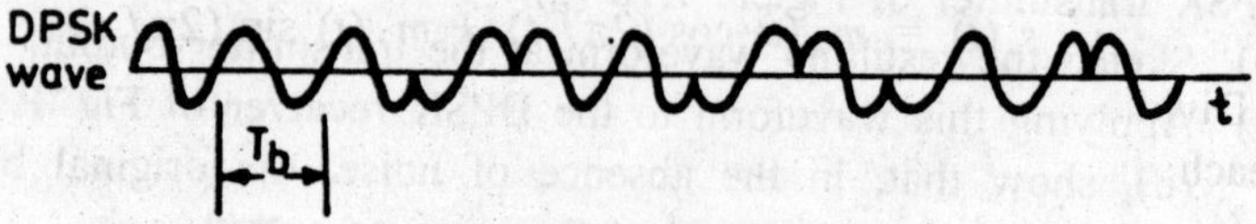

Fig. P. 7.16 (c)

(*b*) Let

$$x_I = \text{output of the integrator in the in-phase channel}$$
$$x_Q = \text{output of the integrator in the quadrature channel}$$
$$x_I = \text{one-bit delayed version of } x_I.$$
$$x'_Q = \text{one-bit delayed version of } x_Q.$$
$$I_Q = \text{in-phase channel output} = x_I x'_I$$
$$I_Q = \text{quadrature channel output} = x_Q x'_Q$$
$$y = I_I + I_Q$$

Problem 7.17: (*a*) Given the input binary sequence 1100100010, sketch the waveforms of the in-phase and quadrature components of a modulated wave obtained by using the QPSK based on the signal set of Fig. P. 7.17.

(*b*) Sketch the QPSK waveform itself for the input binary sequence specified in part (a).

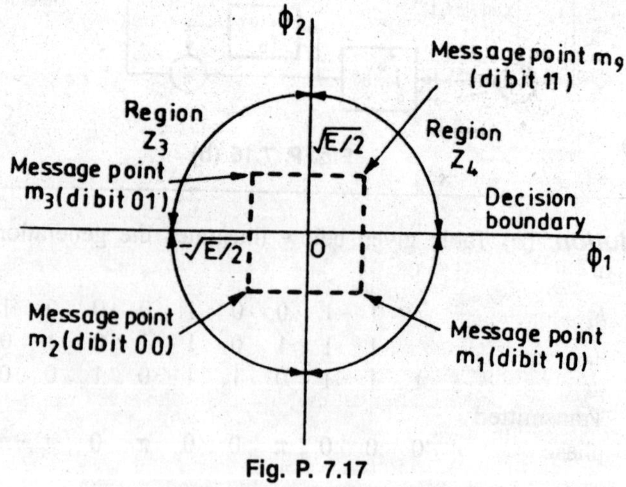

Fig. P. 7.17

Solution: (*a*) The quadrature phase shifting key (QPSK) is given by,

$$s(t) = m_1(t)\cos(2\pi f_c t) + m_2(t)\sin(2\pi f_c t)$$

Dividing the binary wave into dibits and finding $m_1(t)$ and $m_2(t)$ for each digit, we have,

digit	11	00	10	00	10
$m_1(t)$	$\sqrt{\frac{E}{T}}$	$-\sqrt{\frac{E}{T}}$	$\sqrt{\frac{E}{T}}$	$-\sqrt{\frac{E}{T}}$	$\sqrt{\frac{E}{T}}$
$m_2(t)$	$\sqrt{\frac{E}{T}}$	$-\sqrt{\frac{E}{T}}$	$-\sqrt{\frac{E}{T}}$	$-\sqrt{\frac{E}{T}}$	$-\sqrt{\frac{E}{T}}$

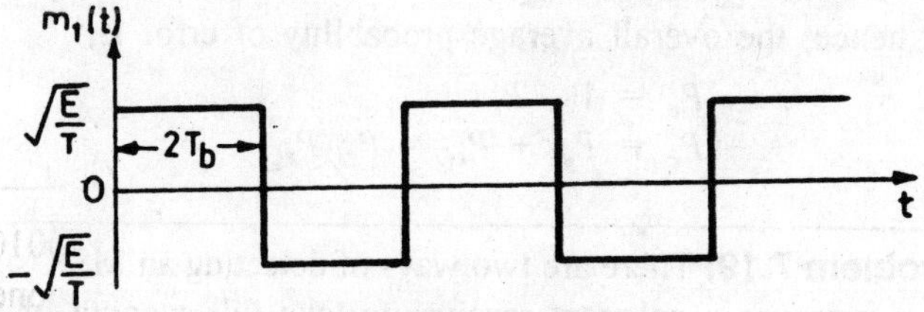

Fig. P. 7.17 (a)

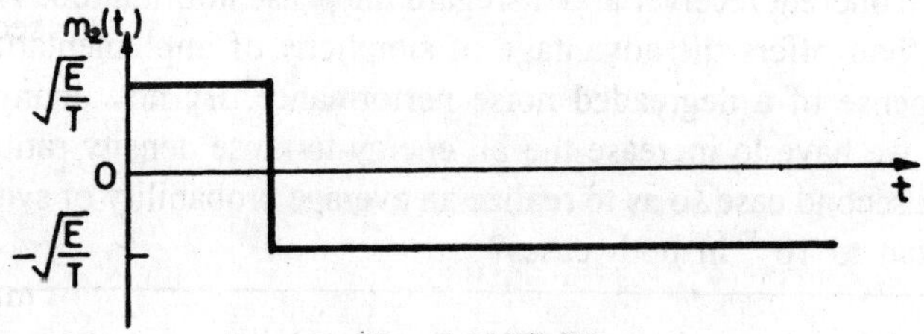

Fig. P. 7.17 (b)

(*b*)

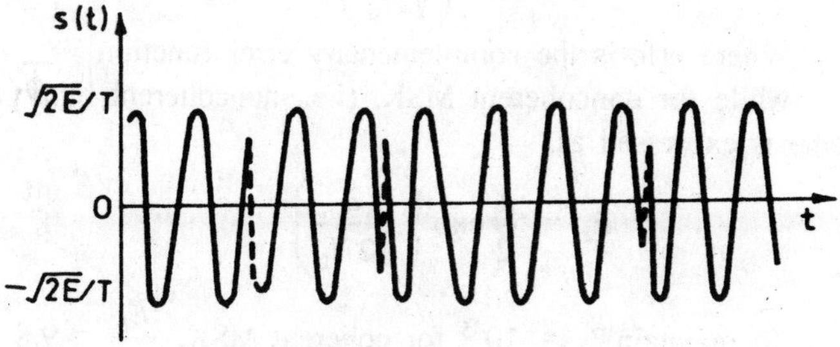

Fig. P. 7.17 (c)

Problem 7.18: Let P_{eI} and P_{eQ} denote the probabilities of symbol error for the in-phase and quadrature channels of a narrow-band system. Show that the average probability of symbol error for the overall system is given by

$$P_e = P_{eI} + P_{eQ} - P_{eI}P_{eQ}$$

Solution: Let P_{eI} and P_{eQ} are the average probability of symbol error in to the in-phase channel and in the quadrature channel respectively.

Since the individual outputs of the in-phase and quadrature channels are statisticallfy independent, the overall average probability of correct reception is

$$P_c = (1 - P_{eI})(1 - P_{eQ}) = 1 - P_{eI} - P_{eQ} - P_{eI} P_{eQ}$$

hence, the overall average probability of error is,

$$P_e = 1 - P_c$$

$$P_e = P_{eI} + P_{eQ} - P_{eI} P_{eQ}$$

Problem 7.19: There are two ways of detecting an MSK signal. One way is to use a coherent receiver to take full account of the phase information content of the MSK signal. Another way is to use a noncoherent receiver and disregard the phase information. The second method offers the advantage of simplicity of implementation, at the expense of a degreaded noise performance. By how many decibels do we have to increase the bit energy-to-noise density ratio E_b/N_0 in the second case so as to realize an average probability of symbol error equal to 10^{-5} in both cases?

Solution: For coherent MSK, the probability of error is given by

$$P_e = erfc\left(\sqrt{\frac{E_b}{N_0}}\right),$$

Where erfc is the complementary error function

while for noncoherent MSK, (i.e., noncoherent binary FSK), the same is expressed as,

$$P_e = \frac{1}{2}\exp\left(-\frac{E_b}{2N_0}\right)$$

To maintain $P_e = 10^{-5}$ for coherent MSK, $\frac{E_b}{N_0} = 9.8.$

Now to maintain the same probability of symbol error for noncoherent MSK, we have

$$\frac{E_b}{N_0} = 21.6, \text{ which is an increase of 3.4 dB.}$$

Problem 7.20: (*a*) Sketch the waveforms of the in-phase and quadrature components of the MSK signal in response to the input binary sequence 1100100010.

(*b*) Sketch the MSK waveform itself for the binary sequence specified in part (*a*).

Solution:

(*a*)

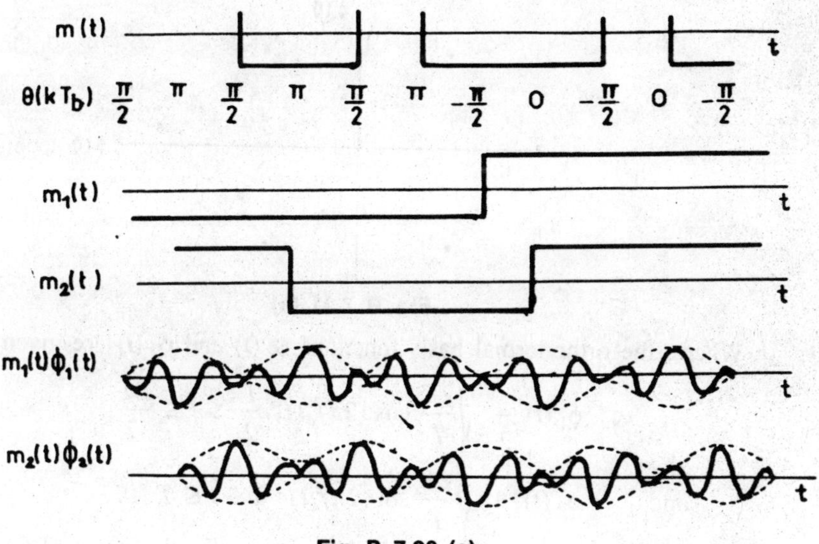

Fig. P. 7.20 (a)

(*b*)

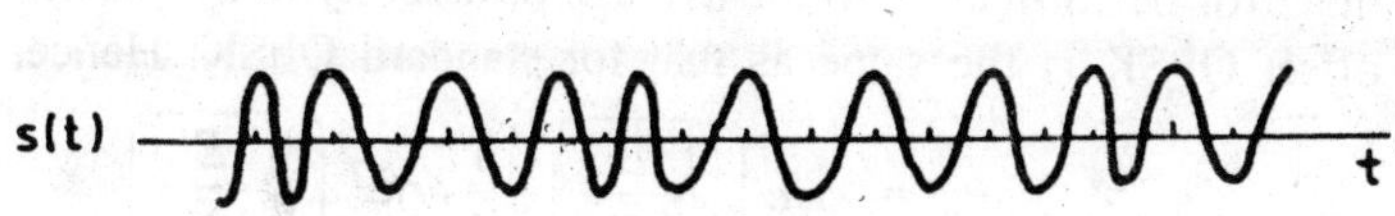

Fig. P. 7.20 (b)

Problem 7.21: In a special form of quadriphase-shift keying known as the offset PSK, the in-phase data stream is delayed relative to the quadrature data stream by half a symbol period $\frac{T}{2}$.

(*a*) What is the average probability oof symbol error for an offset QPSK system?

(*b*) What is the power spectral density of an offset QPSK signal produced by a random binary sequence in which symbols 1 and 0 (represented by ±1) are equally likely, and the symbols in different time slots are statistically independent and identically distributed?

(*c*) What are the similarities between the offset QPSK and MSK, and what features distinguish them?

Solution: (*a*)The signal space diagram for offset QPSK is depicted here,

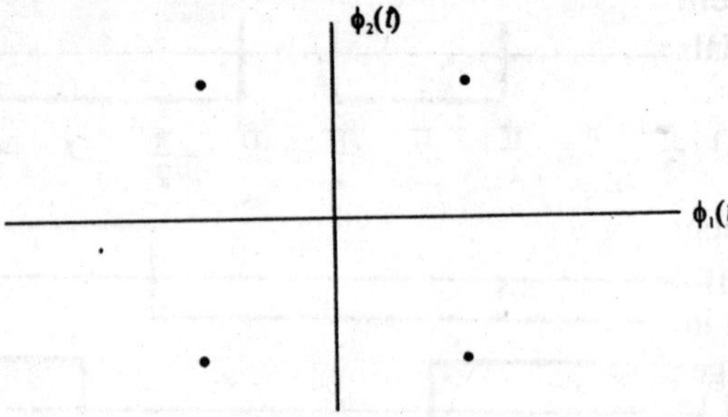

Fig. P. 7.21 (a)

Where, the orthonormal basis functions $\phi_1(t)$ and $\phi_2(t)$ are given by,

$$\phi_1(t) = \sqrt{\frac{2E}{T}} \cos(2\pi f_c t), \quad \frac{T}{2} \le t \le \frac{3T}{2}$$

and $$\phi_2(t) = \sqrt{\frac{2E}{T}} \sin(2\pi f_c t), \quad 0 \le t \le T$$

The singal space diagram is the same as for the standard QSPK, except $\phi_1(t)$ is defined over a different time interval. This will not affect the error performance, so the average probability of symbol error P_e for offset QPSK is the same as that for standard QPSK. Hence,

$$P_e = erfc\left(\sqrt{\frac{E}{2N_0}}\right) - \frac{1}{4}\, erfc^2\left(\sqrt{\frac{E}{2N_0}}\right)$$

(*b*) Because symbols in different time slots are independent, the in-phase and quadrature components are statistically independent. The baseband power spectral density is the sum of the power spectral densities of the in-phase and quadrature components.

Therefore, the base power spectral density can be expressed by,

$$S_B(f) = 2E\,\text{sinc}^2(fT).$$

hence, the power spectral density of the offset QPSK is

$$S(f) = \frac{E}{2}\{\text{sinc}^2[(f - f_c)T] + \text{sinc}^2[(f + f_c)T]\}$$

(*c*) The similarities between offset QPSK and MSK are that both have a half-symbol delay between the in-phase and quadrature components of each data symbol, and both have the same probability of error.

The differences between the two techniques are:

(1) The basis functions for offset QPSK are sinusoids multiplied by a rectangle function, while the basis functions for MSK are sinusoids multiplied by half a cosine pulse, and (2) offset QPSK is a form of phase modulation while MSK is a form of frequency modulation.

Problem 7.22: Equation for average probability of symbol error for coherent *M*-ary PSK,

$$P_e \cong erfc\left(\sqrt{\frac{E}{N_0}}\sin\left(\frac{\pi}{M}\right)\right)$$

is an approximate formula for the average probability of symbol error for coherent *M*-ary PSK. This formula was derived using the union bound in light of the signal-space diagram of Fig. P. 7.22. Given that message point m_1 was transmitted, show that the approximate formula of Eq. may be derived directly from Fig. P. 7.22.

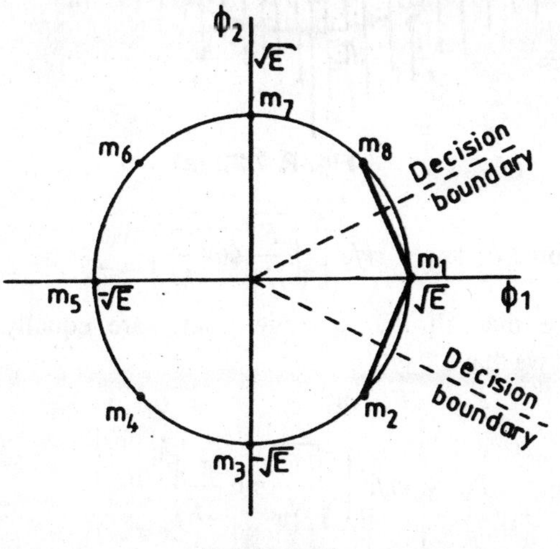

Fig. P. 7.22

Solution: Let r denote the received signal vector. Suppose that the signal correspond to message point m_1 is transmitted. Then, referring to the signal-space diagram of Fig. P. 7.22 (a), the functions probability of error is given

$$P_e|m_1 = P\ (r \text{ lies in shaded region})$$
$$= P\ (r \text{ lies in } \equiv) + P\ (R \text{ lies in } \|\ \|) - P\ (r \text{ lies in } \|\ \|)$$
$$= \frac{1}{2}\, erfc\left(\sqrt{\frac{E}{N_0}}\sin\frac{\pi}{M}\right) + \frac{1}{2}\, erfc\left(\sqrt{\frac{E}{N_0}}\sin\frac{\pi}{M}\right) - P\ (r \text{ lies in } \|\ \|)$$

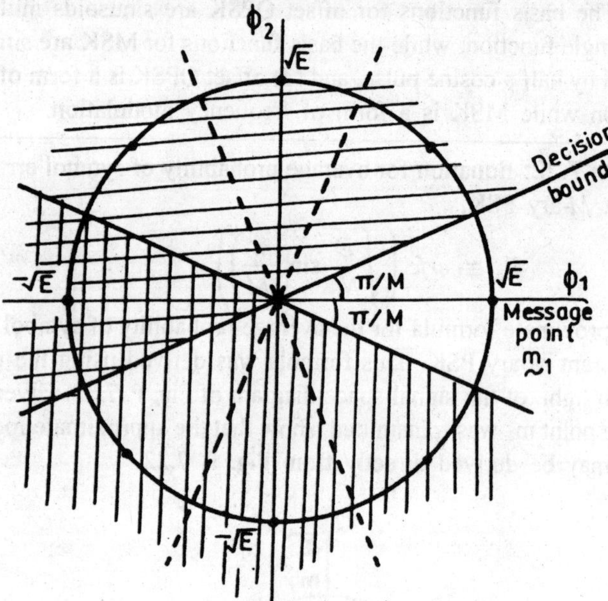

Fig. P. 7.22 (a)

Therefore, $P_e\ |m_1 < erfc\left(\sqrt{\frac{E}{N_0}}\sin\frac{\pi}{M}\right)$

Suppose that all the message points are equally likely to be transmitted, we have

$$P_e = P_e\ |\ m_1$$

and so $\quad P_e < erfc\left(\sqrt{\frac{E}{N_0}}\sin\frac{\pi}{M}\right)$

Problem 7.23: Consider an *M*-ary QAM with an in-phase and a quadrature component. The signal constellation of each of these two components has a geometry similar to that of *M*-ary PAM with a corresponding number of amplitude levels. Using this relationship, derive the formula for P'_e which is expressed as

$$P'_e = \left(1-\frac{1}{L}\right) erfc\left(\sqrt{\frac{E}{N_0}}\right)$$

and that defines the average probability of symbol error for either compoment of *M*-ary QAM.

Solution: The signal constellation for the in-phase or quadrature component of *M*-ary QAM has a geometry similar to that of discrete pulse-amplitude modulation (PAM) with a corresponding number of amplitude levels, as illustrated in the following figure for the case of $L = 8$ levels:

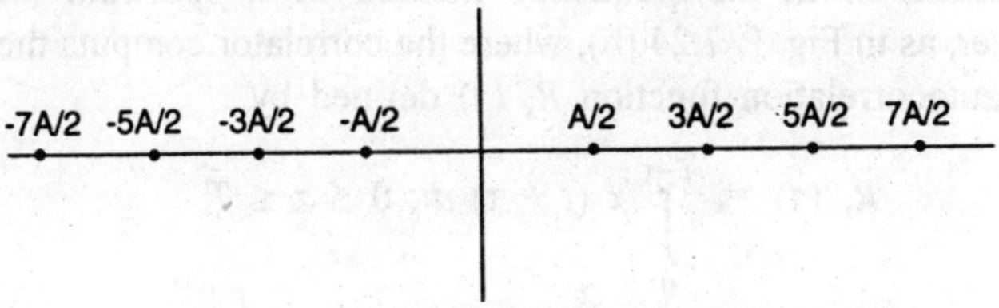

Fig. P. 7.23 (a)

In this example, the threshold levels used in the decision-making process are set at 0, $\pm A$, $\pm 2A$, $\pm 3A$.

Now, P'_e can be given by,

$$P'_e = \left(1-\frac{1}{L}\right) erfc\left(\frac{A}{2\sqrt{2}\sigma}\right) \qquad \ldots(1)$$

where the amplitude A is indicated in the above figure and the noise variance σ^2 is defined as,

$$\sigma^2 = \frac{N_0}{2T} \qquad \ldots(2)$$

where $\frac{N_0}{T}$ is the noise spectral density and T is the symbol duration. The energy of the lowest amplitude level is

$$E_0 = \left(\frac{A}{2}\right)^2 T \qquad \ldots(3)$$

From eqs. (2) and (3) the ratio $\frac{A}{2\sqrt{2}\sigma}$ can be expressed as,

$$\frac{A}{2\sqrt{2}\sigma} = \sqrt{\frac{E_0}{N_0}} \qquad \text{...(4)}$$

Finally, substituting Eq. (4) into (1), we obtain,

$$P_e' = \left(1 - \frac{1}{L}\right) erfc\left(\sqrt{\frac{E_0}{N_0}}\right)$$

which is desired result.

Problem 7.24: Figure P. 7.24 shows a noncoherent receiver using a matched filter for the detection of a sinusoidal signal of known frequency but random phase, in the presence of additive white Gaussian noise. An alternative implementation of this receiver is its mechanization in the frequency domain as a spectrum analyzer receiver, as in Fig. P. 7.24 (b), where the correlator computs the finite time autocorrelation function $R_x(\tau)$ defined by

$$R_x(\tau) = \int_0^{T-\tau} x(t+\tau)\, dt, \; 0 \le \tau \le T$$

Show that the square-law envelope detector output sampled at time $l = T$ in Fig. P. 7.24 (a) is twice the spectral output of the Fourier transformer sampled at frequency $f = f_c$ in Fig. P. 7.24 (b).

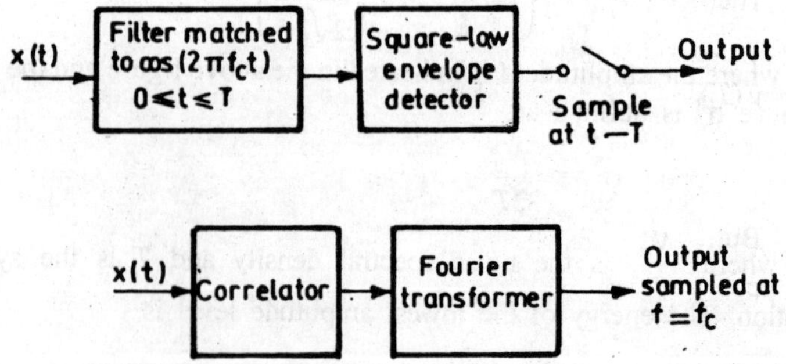

Fig. P. 7.24

Solution: Suppose that

$$x(t) = A_c \cos(2\pi f_c t + \theta)$$
$$= A_c \cos(2\pi f_c t)\cos\theta - A_c \sin(2\pi f_c t)\sin\theta$$

The output of the square-law envelope detector in Fig. P. 7.24, sampled at time $t = T$, is expressed as,

$$y(T) = [\int_0^T x(t)\cos(2\pi f_c t)]\,dt]^2 + [\int_0^T x(t)\sin(2\pi f_c t)\,dt]^2$$

which can also be expressed as,

$$y(T) = \int_0^T\int_0^T x(t_1)\,x(t_2)\,[\cos(2\pi f_c t_1)\cos(2\pi f_c t_2)$$
$$+ \sin(2\pi f_c t_1)\sin(2\pi f_c t_2)]\,dt_1\,dt_2 \qquad \ldots(1)$$

By substituting

$$t_1 = t, \text{ and } t_2 = t + \tau.$$

the resultant transformation is depicted below,

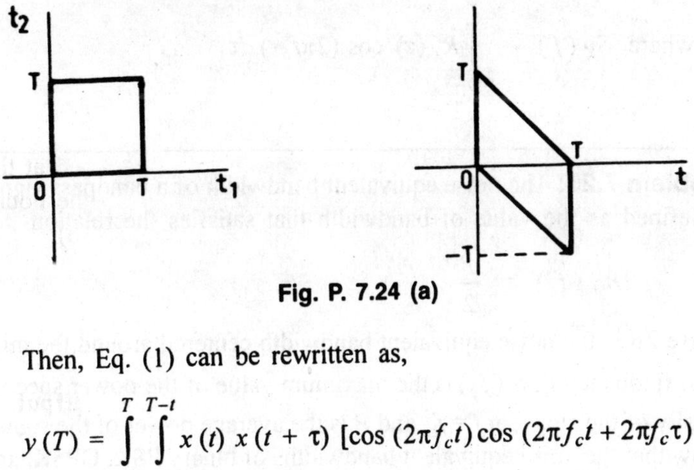

Fig. P. 7.24 (a)

Then, Eq. (1) can be rewritten as,

$$y(T) = \int_0^T\int_{-t}^{T-t} x(t)\,x(t+\tau)\,[\cos(2\pi f_c t)\cos(2\pi f_c t + 2\pi f_c \tau) +$$
$$\sin(2\pi f_c t + 2\pi f_c \tau)]\,dt\,d\tau \qquad \ldots(2)$$

But,

$$\cos(2\pi f_c t)\cos(2\pi f_c t + 2\pi f_c \tau) + \sin(2\pi f_c t)\sin(2\pi f_c t + 2\pi f_c \tau)$$
$$= \cos(2\pi f_c t)$$

Therefore, eqn (2) in simplified form can be written as,

$$y(T) = \int_0^T \int_{-t}^{T-t} x(t)\, x(t+\tau) \cos(2\pi f_c \tau)\, d\tau\, dt$$

$$= 2\int_0^T \int_{-t}^{T-t} x(t)\, x(t+\tau) \cos(2\pi f_c \tau)\, d\tau\, dt, \quad 0 \le \tau \le T \qquad \text{...(3)}$$

Defining the autocorrelation function as

$$R_X(\tau) = \int_{-t}^{T-t} x(t)\, x(t+\tau)\, dt \qquad 0 \le \tau \le T$$

Now, we may write eq. (3) in terms of $R_X(\tau)$ as,

$$y(T) = 2\int_0^T R_X(\tau) \cos(2\pi f_c t)\, d\tau = 2\, S_X(f_c)$$

$$\text{where } S_X(f) = \int_0^T R_X(\tau) \cos(2\pi f_c \tau)\, d\tau$$

Problem 7.25: The noise equivalent bandwidth of a bandpass signal is defined as the value of bandwidth that satisfies the relation

$$2BS(f_c) = \frac{P}{2}$$

where $2B$ is the noise equivalent bandwidth centered around the mid-band frequency f_c, $S(f_c)$ is the maximum value of the power spectral density of the singal at $f = f_c$, and P is the average power of the signal. Show that the noise equivalent bandwidths of binary PSK, QPSK, and MSK are as follows:

Type of Modulation	*Noise Bandwidth/Bit Rate*
Binary PSK	1.0
QPSK	0.5
MSK	0.62

Solution: The average power for any modulation scheme is given by,

$$P = \frac{E_b}{T_b}$$

which can be demonstrated for the three types given by integrating their power spectral densities from $-\infty$ to ∞,

$$P = \int_{-\infty}^{\infty} S(f)\,df = \frac{1}{4}\int_{-\infty}^{\infty} [S_B(f - f_c) + S_B(f + f_c)]\,df$$

$$= \frac{1}{2}\int_{-\infty}^{\infty} S_B(f)\,df.$$

The baseband power spectral densities for each of the modulation techniques are as follows,

	PSK	QPSK	MSK
$S_B(f)$	$2E_b \operatorname{sinc}^2(fT_b)$	$4E_b \operatorname{sinc}^2(2fT_b)$	$\frac{32E_b}{\pi^2}\frac{\cos(2\pi fT_b)^2}{16f^2T_b^2 - 1}$

Since $\int_{-\infty}^{\infty} a \sin c^2\,dx = 1$, $P = \frac{E_b}{T_b}$ is easily shown for PSK and QPSK. For MSK, we have

$$P = \frac{16E_b}{\pi^2}\int_{-\infty}^{\infty}\left[\frac{\cos(2\pi fT_b)}{16f^2T_b^2 - 1}\right]^2 df = \frac{16E_b}{\pi^2 T_b}\int_{-\infty}^{\infty}\frac{\cos^2(2\pi x)}{(16x^2 - 1)^2}\,dx$$

$$= \frac{8E_b}{\pi^2 T_b}\int_{-\infty}^{\infty}\frac{1 + \cos(4\pi x)}{16x^2\left(x^2 - \frac{1}{16}\right)}\,dx = \frac{E_b}{16\pi^2 T_b}\int_{-\infty}^{\infty}\frac{\cos 0 + \cos(4\pi x)}{\left(x^2 - \frac{1}{16}\right)^2}\,dx$$

From integral tables,

$$\int_0^x \frac{\cos(ax)\,dx}{(b^2 - x^2)^2} = \frac{\pi}{4b^3}[\sin(ab) - ab\cos(ab)]$$

For $a = 0$, the integral is 0.

For $a = 4\pi$,

$$b = \frac{1}{4}, \text{ we have}$$

$$P = \frac{E_b}{16\pi^2 T_b} \int_{-\infty}^{\infty} \frac{\cos(ax)}{(b^2 - x^2)^2} dx = \frac{E_b}{T_b}$$

Now, for the three schemes, the values of $S(f_c)$ are as follows:

	PSK	QPSK	MSK
$S(f_c)$	$\frac{E_b}{2}$	E_b	$\frac{8E_b}{\pi^2}$

Hence, the noise equivalent bandwidth for each technique is as follows:

	PSK	QPSK	MSK
Bandwidth	$\frac{1}{T_b}$	$\frac{1}{2T_b}$	$\frac{0.62}{T_b}$

Chapter 8

Spread-spectrum Modulation

Problem 8.1: A pseudo-noise (PN) sequenc eis generated using a feedback shift register of length $m = 4$. The chip rate is 10^7 chips per second. Find the following parameters:

(*a*) PN sequence length.

(*b*) Chip duration of the PN sequence.

(*c*) PN sequence period.

Solution: (*a*) The PN sequence length is

$$\begin{aligned} N &= 2^m - 1 \\ &= 2^4 - 1 \\ &= 15 \end{aligned}$$

(*b*) The chip duration is

$$\begin{aligned} T_c &= \frac{1}{10^7} \text{ s} \\ &= 0.1 \ \mu\text{s} \end{aligned}$$

(*c*) The period of the PN sequence is

$$\begin{aligned} T &= NTc \\ &= 15 \times 0.1 \\ &= 1.5 \ \mu\text{s} \end{aligned}$$

Problem 8.2: Fig. P. 8.2 shows a four-stage feedback shift register. The initial state of the register is 1000. Find the output sequence of the shift register.

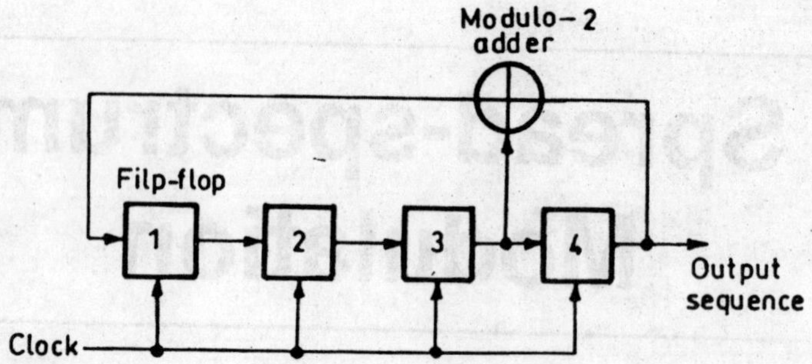

Fig. P. 8.2

Solution:

Shift Number	*Shift-register contents*	*modulo-2 adder output*	*shift-register output*
0	1000		
1	0100	0+0=0	0
2	0010	0+0=0	0
3	1001	1+0=1	0
4	1100	0+1=1	1
5	0110	0+0=1	1
6	1011	1+0=1	0
7	0101	1+1=0	1
8	1010	0+1=1	1
9	1101	1+0=1	1
10	1110	0+1=1	1
11	1111	1+0=1	0
12	0111	1+1=0	1
13	0011	1+1=0	1
14	0001	1+1=0	1
15	1000	0+1=1	1

The output sequence is therefore

$$11\underbrace{000100110101111}_{\text{one period}}0001$$

Problem 8.3: Show that the truth table given in Table 1 can be constructed by combining the following two steps:

(*a*) The message signal $b(t)$ and PN signal $c(t)$ are added modulo-2.

(*b*) Symbols 0 and 1 at the modulo-2 adder output are represented by phase shifts of 0 and 180 degrees, respectively.

Table 1: Polarity of Data sequence $b(t)$ at Time t

		+	−
Polarity of PN Sequence $c(t)$ at time t	+	0	π
	−	π	0

Solution: (*a*) The modulo–2 of $b(t)$ and $c(t)$, on a pulse-by-pulse basis is as follows:

		$b(t)$ 0	$b(t)$ 1
$c(t)$	0	0	1
	1	1	0

(*b*) If symbol 0 is represented by a sinusoid of zero phase shift, and symbol 1 is represented by a sinusoid of 180° phase shift, the output of the modulo–2 adder takes on the same form as that described in Table 1 of the text.

Problem 8.4: A single-tone jammer

$$j(t) = \sqrt{2j}\cos(2\pi f_c t + \theta)$$

is applied to a DS/BPSK system. The N-dimensional transmitted signal $x(t)$ is described by Eq. (1). Find the $2N$ coordinates of the jammer $j(t)$.

$$x(t) = c(t)\,s(t) \pm \sqrt{\frac{2E_b}{T_b}}\,c(t)\cos(2\pi f_c t)$$

$$= \pm\sqrt{\frac{E_b}{N}}\sum_{k=0}^{N-1} c_k \phi_k(t),\ 0 \le t \le T_b \qquad (1)$$

Solution: $j(t) = \sqrt{2j}\cos(2\pi f_c t + \theta)$

the basis functions are

$$\phi_k(t) = \begin{cases} \sqrt{\dfrac{2}{T_c}} \cos(2\pi f_c t), & kT_c \le t \le (k+1)\,T_c \\ 0, & \text{otherwise} \end{cases}$$

$$\tilde{\phi}_k(t) = \begin{cases} \sqrt{\dfrac{2}{T_c}} \sin(2\pi f_c t), & kT_c \le t \le (k+1)\,T_c \\ 0, & \text{otherwise} \end{cases}$$

Hence, we may express the jamming signal $j(t)$ as

$$j(t) = \sqrt{jT_c}\cos\theta \sum_{k=0}^{N-1} \phi_k(t) - \sqrt{jT_c}\sin \sum_{k=0}^{N-1} \tilde{\phi}_k(t)$$

Problem 8.5: The processing gain of a spread-spectrum system may be expressed as the ratio of the spread bandwidth of the transmitted signal to the despread bandwidth of the received signal. Justify this statement for the DS/BPSK system.

Solution:

Processing gain is $\dfrac{T_b}{T_c} = \dfrac{1/T_c}{1/T_b}$

The spread bandwidth of the transmitted signal is proportional to $\dfrac{1}{T_c}$. The despread bandwidth of the received signal is proportional to $\dfrac{1}{T_b}$. Hence,

$$\text{Processing gain} = \frac{\text{spread bandwidth of transmitted signal}}{\text{despread bandwidth of received signal}}$$

Problem 8.6: A direct-sequence spread binary phase-shift keying system uses a feedback shift register of length 19 for the generation of the PN sequence. Calculate the processing gain of the system.

Solution: $m = 19$

$$N = z^m - 1 = z^{19} - 1 \cong 2^{19}$$

The processing gain is

$$10\log_{10} N \cong 10\log_{10} 2^{19} = 190 \times 0.3 = 57 \text{ dB}$$

Problem 8.7: In a DS/BPSK system, the feedback shift register used to generate the PN sequence has length $m = 19$. The system is required to have an average probability of symbol error due to externally generated interfering signals that does not exceed 10^{-5}. Calculate the following system parameters in decibels:

(*a*) Processing gain. (*b*) Antijam margin.

Solution: (*a*) processing gain

$$= 10 \text{ lgo}_{10} (2^m - 1) = 10 \log_{10} (z^{19} - 1) = 57 \text{ dB}$$

(*b*) Antijam margin = (Processing gain) – $10 \log_{10} \left(\frac{E_b}{N_0}\right)$

The probability of error is

$$P_e = \left(\sqrt{\frac{E_b}{N_0}}\right)$$

with $P_e = 10^{-5}$, we have $\frac{E_b}{N_0} = 9.$

Hence,

Antijam margin = 57 – 10 $\log_{10}$ 9 = 57 – 9.5 = 47.5 dB **Ans.**

Problem 8.8: A fast FH/MFSK system has the following parameters:

Number of bits per MFSK symbol = 4

Number of hops per MFSK symbol = 4

Calculate the processing gain of the system.

Solution: The processing gain is $PG = 4 \times 4 = 16$

Hence, in decibels, $PG = 10 \log_{10} 16 = 12$ dB **Ans.**

Problem 8.9: A slow FH/MFSK system has the following parameters:

Number of bits per MFSK symbol = 4

Number of MFSK symbols per hop = 5

Calculate the processing gain of the system.

Solution: The processing gain (PG) is

$$\text{PG} = \frac{\text{FH bandwidth}}{\text{symbol rate}} = \frac{W_c}{R_s} = 5 \times 4 = 20$$

Hence in decibels PG = 10 $\log_{10}$ 20 = 25 dB **Ans.**

Chapter 9

Fundamental Limits in Information Theory

Problem 9.1: Consider the following binary sequence

111010011000101110100...

Use the Lempel-Ziv algorithm to encode this sequence. Assume that the binary symbols 0 and 1 are already in the codebook.

Solution: Using the Lampel–Ziv algorithm, the steps are given as below,

Initial step

Subsequences stored: 0

Data to be parsed: 1 1 1 0 1 0 0 1 1 0 0 0 1 0 1 1 0 1 0 0 ...

Step 1

Subsequences stored: 0, 1, 11

Date to be parsed: 1 0 1 0 0 1 1 0 0 0 1 0 1 1 0 1 0 0

Step 2

Subsequences stored: 0, 1, 11, 10

Date to be parsed: 1 0 0 1 1 0 0 0 1 0 1 1 0 1 0 0 ...

Step 3

Subsequences stored: 0, 1, 11, 10, 100

Data to be parsed: 1 1 0 0 0 1 0 1 1 0 1 0 0 ...

Step 4

Subsequences stored: 0, 1, 11, 10, 100, 110

Data to be parsed: 0 0 1 0 1 1 0 1 0 0 ...

Problem 9.2: Consider the transition probability diagram of a binary symmetric channel shown in Fig. 9.2. Find the probabilities of the binary symbols 0 and 1 appearing at the channel output.

When, given that, the input binary symbols 0 and 1 occur with probabilities 1/4 and 3/4, respectively.

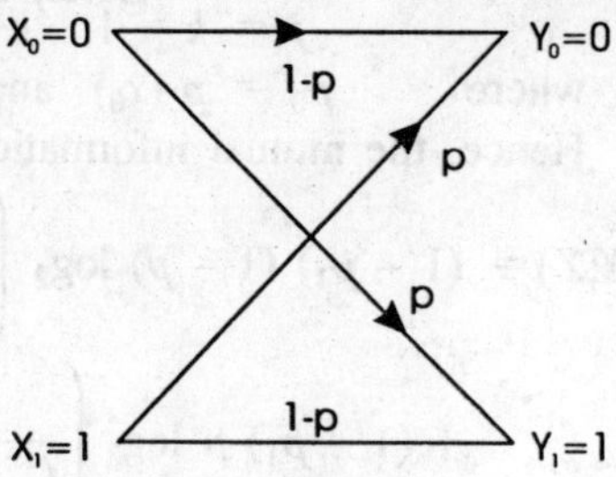

Fig. P. 9.2

Solution: The probability of the event x_0 occurs at channel input, and, that of the event x_1 occurs at channel intput.

$$p(x_0) = \frac{1}{4} \qquad p(x_1) = \frac{3}{4}$$

Then, probability of event $p(y_0) = (1-p)\left(\frac{1}{4}\right) + p\left(\frac{3}{4}\right)$

$$y_0 = \frac{1}{4} + \frac{p}{2}$$

and, probability of event y_1

$$p(y_i) = p\left(\frac{1}{4}\right) + (1-p)\left(\frac{3}{4}\right) = \frac{3}{4} - \frac{P}{2}$$

Problem 9.3: Consider a binary symmetric channel characterized by the transition probability p, plot the mutual information of the channel as a function of probability p_1.

Solution: By definition, the mutual information of th channel can be expressed as,

$$I(X, Y) = \sum_{j=0}^{1} \sum_{k=0}^{1} p(x_j, y_k) \log_2 \left(\frac{p(x_j, y_k)}{p(x_j)\, p(y_k)} \right)$$

The joint probability $p(x_j, y_k)$ has the following four possible values as next given,

$$j = k: \quad p(x_0, y_k) = p_0(1-p) = (1-p_1)(1-p)$$
$$j = 0, k = 1: \quad p(x_0, y_1) = p_0 p = (1-p)\, p$$
$$j = 1, k = 0: \quad p(x_1, y_0) = p_1 p$$

$$j = k = 1: \quad p(x_1, y_1) = p(1 - p_1)$$

where $\quad p_0 = p(x_0)$ and $p_1 = p(x_1)$

Hence, the mutual information is,

$$I(X;Y) = (1 - p_1)(1 - p)\log_2\left(\frac{(1-p_1)(1-p)}{(1-p_1)[(1-p_1)(1-p)+p_1p]}\right)$$

$$+ (1 - p_1)\,p\log_2\left(\frac{(1-p_1)\,p}{(1-p_1)[(1-p_1)\,p+p_1(1-p)]}\right)$$

$$+ p_1p\log_2\left(\frac{p_1p}{p_1[(1-p_1)(1-p)+p_1p]}\right)$$

$$+ p_1(1 - p)\log_2\left(\frac{p_1(1-p)}{p_1[(1-p_1)\,p+p_1(1-p)]}\right)$$

Now, by rearrangement of terms and then expanding algorithms this we get,

$$I(X;Y) = p\log_2 p + (1 - p)\log_2(1 - p) - [p_1(1 - p) + (1 - p_1)p] \times \log_2[p_1(1 - p) + (1 - p_1)p] - [p_1p + (1 - p_1)(1 - p)] \log_2[p_1p + (1 - p_1)(1 - p)]$$

Now, treating the transition probability p of the channel as a running parameter, the following numerical evaluations can be carried out as next given,

$$\boldsymbol{p = 0:}$$

$$I(X;Y) = -p_1\log_2 p_1 - (1 - p_1)\log_2(1 - p_1)$$

$$p_1 = 0.5,\ I(X;Y) = 1.0$$

$$\boldsymbol{p = 01:}$$

$$I(X;Y) = -0.469 - (0.1 + 0.8\,p_1)\log_2(0.1 + 0.8\,p_1) - (0.9 - 0.8\,p_1)\log_2(0.9 - 0.9\,p_1)$$

$$p_1 = 0.5,\ I(X;Y) = 0.531$$

$$\boldsymbol{p = 0.2:}$$

$$I(X;Y) = -0.7219 - (0.2 + 0.6\,p_1)\log_2(0.2 + 0.6\,p_1) - (0.8 - 0.6\,p_1)\log_2(0.8 - 0.6\,p_1)$$

$$p_1 = 0.5,\ I(X;Y) = 0.278$$

$$\boldsymbol{p = 0.3:}$$

$$I(X;Y) = -0.88129 - (0.3 + 0.4\,p_1)\log_2(0.3 + 0.4\,p_1) - (0.7 - 0.4\,p_1)\log_2(0.7 - 0.4\,p_1)$$

$$p_1 = 0.5,\ I(X;Y) = 0.1187$$
$$p = 0.5:\ I(X;Y) = 0$$

Hence, treating the a priori probability p_1 as a variable and the transition probability p as a running parameter, the following plots can be plotted.

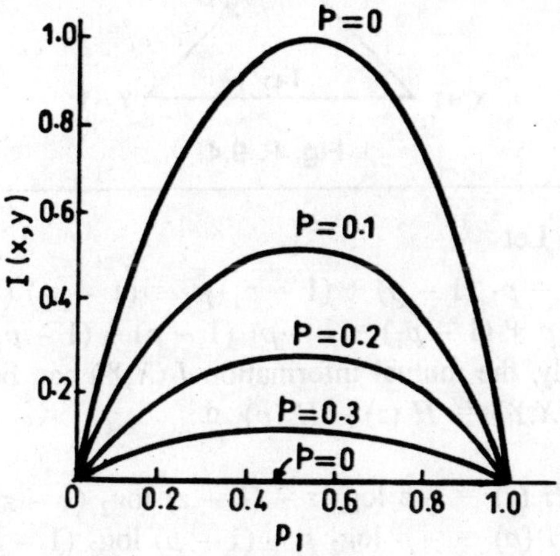

Fig. P. 9.3

Problem 9.4: Consider the binary symmetric channel described in Fig. 9.4. Let p_0 denote the probability of choosing binary symbol $x_0 = 0$, and let $p_1 = 1 - p_0$ denote the probability of choosing binary symbol $x_1 = 1$. Let p denote the transition probability of the channel.

(*a*) Show that the average mutual information between the channel input and channel output is given by

$$I(X;Y) = H(z) - H(p)$$

where $$H(z) = z \log_2\left(\frac{1}{z}\right) + (1 - z) \log_2\left(\frac{1}{1-z}\right)$$

$$z = p_0 p + (1 - p_0)(1 - p)$$

and $$H(p) = p \log_2\left(\frac{1}{p}\right) + (1 - p) \log_2\left(\frac{1}{1-p}\right)$$

(*b*) Show that the value of p_0 that maximizes $I(H;Y)$ is equal to $\frac{1}{2}$.

(*c*) Show that the channel capacity equals

$$C = 1 - H(p)$$

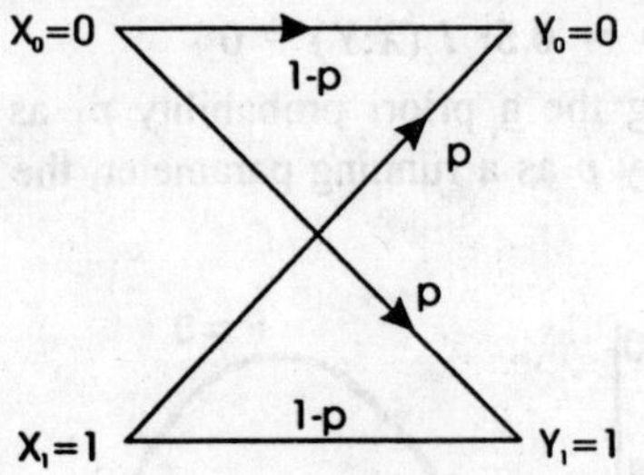

Fig. P. 9.4

Solution: (*a*) Let

$$z = p_1\,(1 - p) + (1 - p_1)\,p_1 = (1 - p_0)\,(1 - p) + p_0 p$$

then, $\quad p_1 p + (1 - p_1) = 1 - p_1\,(1 - p) - (1 - p_1)\,p = 1 - z$

Correspondingly, the mutual information $I\,(X;Y)$ can be expressed as,

$$I\,(X;Y) = H\,(z) - H\,(p)$$

where

$$H\,(z) = -z \log_2 z - (1 - z) \log_2 (1 - z)$$
$$H\,(p) = -p \log_2 p - (1 - p) \log_2 (1 - p)$$

(*b*) Differentiating $I\,(X;Y)$ with respect to p_0 (or p_1) and setting the result equal to zero, $I\,(X;Y)$ attains its maximum value at $p_0 = p_1 = \frac{1}{2}$.

(*c*) Setting $p_0 = p_1 - \frac{1}{2}$ in the expression for the variable z, we get:

$$z = 1 - z = \frac{1}{2}$$

and, correspondingly,

$$H\,(z) = 1$$

Hence, the following value for the channel capacity:

$$C = I(X;Y)\Big|_{p_0 = p_1 = 1/2} = 1 - H\,(p)$$

where $H\,(p)$ is the entropy function of the channel transition probability p.

Problem 9.5: Two binary symmetric channels are connected in cascade, as shown in Fig. P. 9.5. Find the overall channel capacity of the cascaded connection, assuming that both channels have the same transition probability diagram shown in Fig. 9.5 (a).

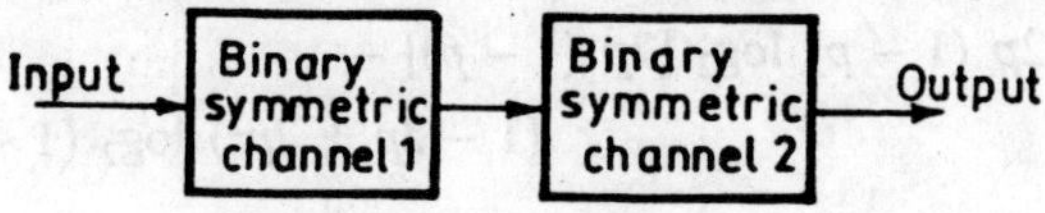

Fig. P. 9.5

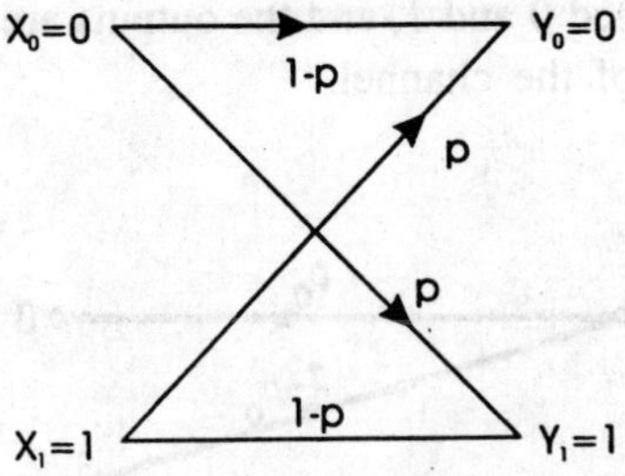

Fig. P. 9.5 (a)

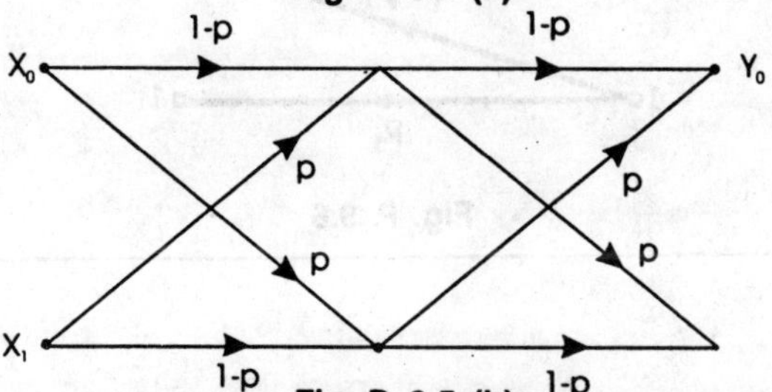

Fig. P. 9.5 (b)

Solution: From the diagram depicted above, we get (by inspection),

$$p\,(y_0 \mid x_0) \;=\; (1-p)^2 + p^2 = 1 - 2p\,(1-p)$$

$$p\,(y_0 \mid x_1) \;=\; (1-p) + (1-p)\,p = 2p\,(1-p)$$

Now, the cascade of two binary symmetric channels with a transition probability p is equivalent to a single binary symmetric channel with a transition probability equal to $2p\,(1-p)$, as shown below:

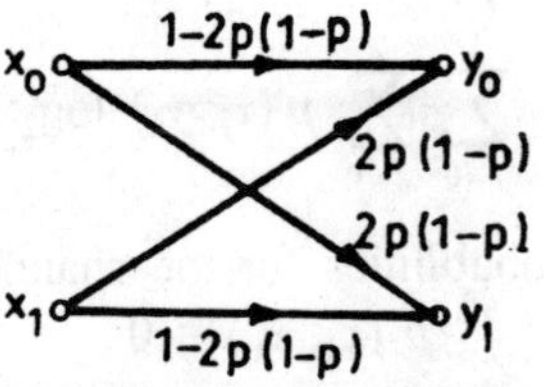

Fig. P. 9.5 (c)

Correspondingly, the channel capacity of the cascade is,

$$C = 1 - H[2p(1-p)]$$
$$= 1 - 2p(1-p)\log_2[2p(1-p)] - (1 - 2p + 2p^2)\log_2(1 - 2p + 2p^2)$$

Problem 9.6: The binary erasure channel is described in Fig. P. 9.6. The inputs are labeled 0 and 1, and the outputs are labeled 0, 1 and?. Find the capacity of the channel.

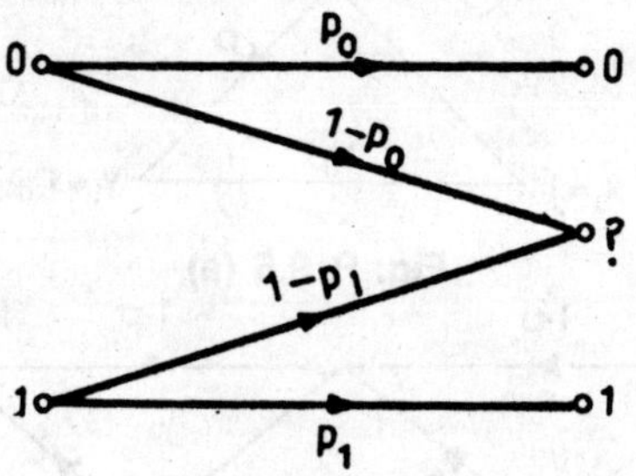

Fig. P. 9.6

Solution:

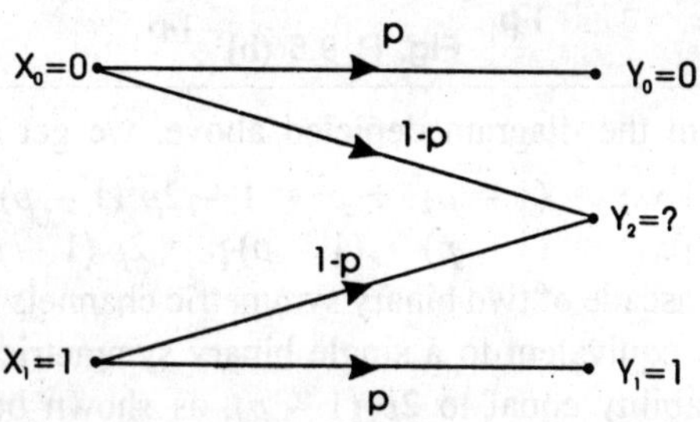

Fig. P. 9.6 (a)

The mutual information for the erasure channel is expressed as,

$$I(X;Y) = \sum_{j=0}^{1}\sum_{k=0}^{2} p(x_j, y_k)\log_2\left(\frac{p(x_j, y_k)}{p(x_j)\,p(y_k)}\right) \quad \ldots(1)$$

Then the joint probabilities for the channel can be given as,

$p(x_0, y_0) = p\,p_0 \qquad p(x_1, y_0) = 0 \qquad p(x_0, y_2) = p_0(1-p)$

$p(x_0, y_1) = 0 \qquad p(x_1, y_1) = p\,p_1 \qquad p(x_1, y_2) = p_1(1 - p)$

where $p_0 + p_1 = 1$.

Substituting these values in equation (1), we obtain,

$$I(X;Y) = p\left[p_0 \log_2\left(\frac{1}{p_0}\right) + (1 - p_0)\log_2\left(\frac{1}{1 - p_0}\right)\right] = pH(p_0)$$

Since the transition probability p is fixed, the mutual information $I(X;Y)$ can be maximized by choosing a priori probability p_0 to maximize $H(p_0)$ and this maximization occurs at $p_0 = \frac{1}{2}$, for which $H(p_0) = 1$. Therefore, the channel capacity C of the erasure channel is p.

Problem 9.7: Consider a digital communication system that uses a repetition code for the channel encoding/decoding. In particular, each transmission is repeated n times, where $n = 2m + 1$ is an odd integer. The decoder operates as follows. If in a block of n received bits, the number of 0s exceeds the number of 1s, the decoder decides in favor of a 0. Otherwise, it decides in favor of a 1. An error occurs when $m + 1$ or more transmissions out f $n = 2m + 1$ are incorrect. Assume a binary symmetric channel.

(*a*) For $n = 3$, show that the average probability of error is given by

$$P_e = 3p^2(1 - p) + p^3$$

where p is the transition probability of the channel.

(*b*) For $n = 5$, show that the average probability of error is given by

$$P_e = 10p^3(1 - p)^2 + 5p^4(1 - p) + p^5$$

(*c*) For the general case, show that the average probability of error is given by

$$p_e = \sum_{i=m+1}^{n} \binom{n}{i} p^i (1 - p)^{n-i}$$

Solution: (*a*) When each symbol is repeated three times, we have

Messages	*Unused signals*	*Channel outputs*
000	001	000
	010	001
	011	010
	100	100
	101	101
	110	110
111		111

We get

1. The probability that no errors occur in the transmission of three 0s or three 1s is $(1 - p)^3$.
2. The probability of just one error occuring is $3p\,(1 - p)^2$.
3. The probability of two errors occuring is $3p^2\,(1 - p)$.
4. The probability of receiving all three bits in error is p^3.

With the decision–making based on a majority vote it can be inferred that contributions 3 and 4 lead to the probability of error as,

$$p_3 = 3p^2\,(1 - p) + p^3$$

(*b*) Now, when each symbol is transmitted five times, then

Messages	*Unused signals*	*Channel outputs*
00000		00000
	00001	00001
	00010	00010
	00011	00011
	00011	00011
	00011	00011
	00011	00011
	11110	11110
11111		11111

The probability of zero, one, two, three, four, or five bit errors in transmission is as follows, respectively:

$$(1 - p^5$$
$$5p\,(1 - p))^4$$
$$10p^2\,(1 - p)^3$$
$$10p^3\,(1 - p)^2$$
$$5p^4\,(1 - p)$$
$$p^5$$

The last three contributions constitute the probability of error

$$p_e = p^5 + 5p^4 (1 - p) + 10p^3 (1 - p)^2$$

(*a*) For the general case of $n = 2m + 1$ it should be noted that the decision–making process (based on a majority vote) makes an error when $m + 1$ bits or more out of the n bits of a message are received in error. The probability of i message bits being received in error is

$$\binom{n}{l} \cdot p^i (1 - p)^{n-i}.$$

Therefore the probability of error is (in general)

$$p_e = \sum_{i=m+1}^{n} \binom{n}{i} p_i (1 - p)^{n-i}$$

Problem 9.8: Let $X_1, X_2, \ldots, X_n$ denote the elements of a Gaussian vector X. The X_i are independent with mean μ_i and variance σ_i^2, $i = 1, 2, \ldots, n$. Show that the differential entropy of the vector X equals

$$h(X) = \frac{n}{2} \log_2 [2\pi e (\sigma_1^2 \sigma_2^2 \ldots \sigma_n^2)^{1/n}]$$

What does $h(X)$ reduce to if the variances are equal?

Solution: We know that, the differential entropy of a random variable is independent of its mean. Now, to determine the differential entropy of a Gaussian vector X, consisting of the components $X_1, X_2, \ldots, X_n$, we set the mean of X equal to zero. Under this condition, the joint probability density function of the Gaussian vector X can be expressed as,

$$f_x(x) = \frac{1}{\left(\sqrt{2\pi}\right)^n \sigma_1 \sigma_2 \ldots \sigma_n} \exp\left(-\frac{x_1^2}{2\sigma_1^2} - \frac{x_2^2}{2\sigma_2^2} - \ldots - \frac{x_n^2}{2\sigma_n^2}\right) \quad \ldots(1)$$

Taking logrithm to both sides of eqn (1), we have,

$$\log_2 f_x(x) = -\log_2 [(2\pi)^{n/2} \sigma_1 \sigma_2 \ldots \sigma_n] - \left(-\frac{x_1^2}{2\sigma_1^2} - \frac{x_2^2}{2\sigma_2^2} - \ldots - \frac{x_n^2}{2\sigma_n^2}\right) \log_2 e$$

Therefore the differential entropy of X is

$$h(X) = -\int\int \ldots \int f_x(x) \log_2 (f_x(x))\, dx$$

$$= \log_2 [(2\pi)^{n/2} \sigma_1 \sigma_2 \ldots \sigma_n] \int\int \ldots \int f_x(x)\, dx$$

$$+ \log_2 e \int\int \ldots \int \left(\frac{x_1^2}{2\sigma_1^2} + \frac{x_2^2}{2\sigma_2^2} + \ldots + \frac{x_n^2}{2\sigma_n^2} \right) f_x(x)\, dx \quad \ldots(2)$$

Next, it can be noted that,

$$\int\int \ldots f_x(x)\, dx = 1$$

$$\int\int \ldots \int x_i^2 f_x(x)\, dx = \sigma_i^2$$

$$i = 1, 2, \ldots, n$$

Then eqn (2) in simplified form can be written as,

$$h(X) = \log_2 [(2\pi)^{n/2} \sigma_1 \sigma_2 \ldots \sigma_n] + \frac{n}{2} \log_2 e$$

$$= \log_2 [2\pi (\sigma_1^2 \sigma_2^2 \ldots \sigma_n^2)^{1/n}]^{n/2} + \frac{n}{2} \log_2 e$$

$$= \frac{n}{2} [2\pi (\sigma_1^2 \sigma_2^2 \ldots \sigma_n^2)^{1/n}] + \frac{n}{2} \log_2 e$$

$$= \frac{n}{2} \log_2 [2\pi e (\sigma_1^2 \sigma_1^2 \ldots \sigma_n^2)^{1/n}] \quad \ldots(3)$$

When the individual variances are equal, then

$$\sigma_1^2 = \sigma_2^2 = \ldots \sigma_n^2 = \sigma^2$$

$$(\sigma_1^2 \sigma_2^2 \ldots \sigma_n^2)^{1/n} = \sigma^2$$

Accordingly, the differential entropy of X is written as,

$$h(X) = \frac{n}{2} \log_2 (2\pi e \sigma^2)$$

Problem 9.9: A continuous random variable X is constrained to a peak magnitude M; that is, $-M < X < M$.

(*a*) Show that the differential entropy of X is maximum when it is uniformly distributed, as shown by

$$f_x(x) = \begin{cases} \frac{1}{2M}, & -M < x \leq M \\ 0, & \text{otherwise} \end{cases}$$

(*b*) Show that the maximum differential entropy of X is $\log_2 2M$.

Solution: (*a*) The differential entropy of a random variable X is expressed by,

$$h(X) = -\int_{-\infty}^{\infty} f_x(x) \log_2 f_x(x)\, dx$$

The constraint on the value x of the random variable X is

$$|x| \le M$$

Using the method of Lagrange multipliers, it can be inferred that under this constraint, $h(X)$ is maximized when

$$\int_{-M}^{M} [-f_x(x) \log_2 f_x(x) + \lambda f_X(x)]\, dx$$

is stationary. Differentiating $-f_X(x)\log_2 f_X(x) + \lambda f_X(x)$ with respect to $f_X(x)$, and then setting the result equal to zero, we obtain,

$$-\log_2 e + \lambda = \log_2 f_x(x)$$

It shows that $f_X(x)$ is independent of x. Therefore for the differential entropy $h(X)$ under the constraints $|x| \le M$ and $\int_{-\infty}^{\infty} f_X(x)\, dx = 1$ to be maximum, the random variable X must be uniformly distributed, i.e.,

$$f_X(x) = \begin{cases} \dfrac{1}{2M}, & -M < x \le M \\ 0, & \text{otherwise} \end{cases} \qquad \ldots(1)$$

(*b*) The maximum differential entropy of the uniformly distributed random variable X is expressed as

$$h(x) = \int_{-\infty}^{\infty} f_x(x) \log_2 \left[\frac{1}{f_x(x)}\right] dx \qquad \ldots(2)$$

using eqn (1) in eqn (2), we get,

$$h(x) = \int_{-M}^{M} \frac{1}{2M} \log_2 [2M]\, dx = \frac{1}{2M} \log_2 [2M] \int_{-M}^{M} dx = \log_2 [2M]$$

Problem 9.10: Prove the following property for the mutual information, $I(X; Y)$

(*a*) $I(X;Y) = I(Y; X)$ (b) $I(X;Y) \ge 0$

(*c*) $I(X;Y) = h(X) - h(Y|X) = h(Y) - h(Y|X)$

Solution: (*a*) The mutual information between the random variables X and Y can be expressed as,

$$I(X;Y) = \int_{-\infty}^{\infty}\int_{-\infty}^{\infty} f_{X,Y}(x,y) \log_2 \left[\frac{f_X(x|y)}{f_X(x)}\right] dx\, dy \qquad \ldots(1)$$

$$\text{and, } I(Y;X) = \int_{-\infty}^{\infty}\int_{-\infty}^{\infty} f_{X,Y}(x,y) \log_2 \left[\frac{f_Y(y|x)}{f_Y(y)}\right] dx\, dy \qquad \ldots(2)$$

Using Bayes' rule, we have

$$\frac{f_X(x|y)}{f_X(x)} = \frac{f_Y(y|x)}{f_Y(y)}$$

Then, from eqn (1) and eqn (2), we have,

$$I(X;Y) = I(Y;X)$$

(*b*) It is noted that,

$$f_{X,Y}(x,y) = f_X(x \mid y)\, f_Y(y)$$

Rewriting eqn (1) as,

$$I(X;Y) = \int_{-\infty}^{\infty}\int_{-\infty}^{\infty} f_{X,Y}(x,y) \log_2 \left[\frac{f_{X,Y}(x,y)}{f_X(x) f_y(y)}\right] dx\, dy \geq 0$$

By the continuous version of the fundamental inequality,

$$\int_{-\infty}^{\infty} f_{X,Y}(x,y) \log_2 \left[\frac{f_{X,Y}(x,y)}{f_x(x) f_y(y)}\right] dx\, dy \geq 0$$

which is satisfied with equality if and only if

$$f_{X,Y}(x,y) = f_X(x)\, f_Y(y)$$

therefore,

$$I(X;Y) \geq 0$$

(*c*) By definition, the conditional differential entropy of X is given by,

$$h(X \mid Y) = \int_{-\infty}^{\infty}\int_{-\infty}^{\infty} f_{X,Y}(x,y) \log_2 \left[\frac{1}{f_X(x|y)}\right] dx\, dy \qquad \ldots(3)$$

Also, by definition, the differential entropy of X is expressed by,

$$h(X) = \int_{-\infty}^{\infty} f_X(x) \log_2 \left[\frac{1}{f_X(x)}\right] dx$$

Since

$$\int_{-\infty}^{\infty} f_Y(y|x)\,dy = 1,$$

the expression for $h(X)$ can be rewritten as,

$$h(X) = \int_{-\infty}^{\infty} f_X \log_2\left[\frac{1}{f_X(x)}\right] dx \int_{-\infty}^{\infty} f_Y(y \mid x)\,dx$$

$$= \int_{-\infty}^{\infty}\int_{-\infty}^{\infty} f_Y(y \mid x)\, f_X(x) \log_2\left[\frac{1}{f_X(x)}\right] dx\,dy$$

But

$$f_Y(y \mid x)\, f_X(x) = f_{X,Y}(x, y)$$

Hence,

$$h(X) = \int_{-\infty}^{\infty}\int_{-\infty}^{\infty} f_{X,Y}(x, y) \log_2\left[\frac{1}{f_X(x)}\right] dx \quad \text{...(4)}$$

Now subtracting eqn (3) from eqn (4), we get,

$$h(X) - h(X|Y) = \int_{-\infty}^{\infty}\int_{-\infty}^{\infty} f_{X,Y}(x, y)\left[\log_2 \frac{1}{f_X(x)} - \log_2 \frac{1}{f_X(x|y)}\right] dx\,dy$$

$$= \int_{-\infty}^{\infty}\int_{-\infty}^{\infty} f_{X,Y}(x, y) \log_2\left[\frac{f_X(x|y)}{f_X(x)}\right] dx\,dy = I(X;Y)$$

(*d*) Using the symmetric property derived in part (*a*), we have

$$I(Y;X) = h(Y) - h(Y|X)$$

Problem 9.11: Consider the continuous random variable Y defined by

$$Y = X + N$$

where X and N are statistically independent. Show that the conditional differential entropy of Y, given X, equals

$$h(Y|X) = h(N)$$

where $h(N)$ is the differential entropy of N.

Solution: By definition conditional differential entropy of X is expressed as,

$$h(Y|X) = \int_{-\infty}^{\infty} f_{X,Y}(x, y) \log_2 \left[\frac{1}{f_Y(y|x)}\right] dx\, dy \quad ...(1)$$

Since

$$f_{X,Y}(x, y) = f_Y(y|x)\, f_X(x)$$

then eqn (1) can be written as,

$$h(Y|X) = \int_{-\infty}^{\infty} f_X(x)\, dx \int_{-\infty}^{\infty} f_Y(y_1, x) \log_2 \left[\frac{1}{f_Y(y|x)}\right] dy \quad ...(2)$$

The variable Y is related to X as

$$Y = X + N$$

Hence, the conditional probability density function $f_Y(y|x)$ is identical to that of N except for a translation of x, the given value of X. If $f_N(n)$ denote the probability density function of N. Then

$$f_Y(y|x) = f_N(y - x)$$

Accordingly that,

$$\int_{-\infty}^{\infty} f_Y(y|x) \log_2 \left[\frac{1}{f_Y(y|x)}\right] dy$$

$$= \int_{-\infty}^{\infty} f_N(y - x) \log_2 \left[\frac{1}{f_N(y-x)}\right] dy = \int_{-\infty}^{\infty} f_N(n) \log_2 \left[\frac{1}{f_N(n)}\right] dn \quad ...(3)$$

$$= h(N)$$

where, in the second line, we have used $n = y - x$ and $dn = dy$ for a given x. Substituting eq. (3) in (2), we get,

$$h(Y|X) = h(N) \int_{-\infty}^{\infty} f_X(x)\, dx = h(N)$$

Problem 9.12: A voice-grade channel of the telephone network has a bandwidth of 3.4 kHz.

(*a*) Calculate the information capacity of the telephone channel for a signal-to-noise ratio of 30 dB.

(*b*) Calculate the minimum signal-to-noise ratio required to suport information transmission through the telephone channel at the rate of 9600 b/s.

Solution: (*a*) Given channel bandwidth $B = 3.4$ kH.

and received signal-to-noise ration SNR = 10^3 = 30 dB

Then, the channel capacity is expressed by

$$C = B \log_2 (1 + \text{SNR})$$

Substituting the given values, we have

$$= 3.4 \times 10^3 \log_2 (1 + 10^3)$$

$$= 33.9 \times 10^3 \text{ bits/second}$$

(*b*) Now, given, information transmission ratio = 4800 b/s

then, $C = 4800 = 3.4 \times \log_2 (1 - \text{SNR})$

Solving we have

$$\text{SNR} = 1.66 = 2.2 \text{ dB}$$

Problem 9.13: A black-and-white television picture may be viewed as consisting of approximately 3×10^5 elements, each of which may occupy one of 10 distinct brightness levels with equal probability. Assume that (1) the rate of transmission is 30 picture frames per second and (2) the signal-to-noise ratio is 30 dB.

Using the information capacity theorem, calculate the minimum bandwidth required to support the transmission of the resultant video signal.

Solution: With 10 distinct brightness levels with equal probability, the information in each level is $\log_2 10$ bits. With each picture frame containing $3 \times 10^5 \log_2 10$ bits. Hence, the rate of information transmission of 30 frames per second corresponds to

$$30 \times 3 \times 10^5 \log_2 10 = 9 \times 10^6 \log_2 10 \text{ bits/second}$$

then, the channel capacity calculated is,

$$C = 9 \times 10^5 \log_2 10 \text{ bits/second}$$

From the information capacity theorem:

$$C = B \log_2 (1 + \text{SNR})$$

With a signal-to-noise ratio SNR = 10^3 = 30 dB, the channel bandwidth is therefore

$$B = \frac{C}{\log_2(1+\text{SNR})} = \frac{9\times10^6 \log_2 10}{\log_2 1001} = 3 \times 10^3 \text{ Hz}$$

Chapter 10

Error–control Coding

Problem 10.1: Consider a binary input Q-ary output discrete memoryless channel. The channel is said to be symmetric if the channel transition probability $p(j \mid i)$ satisfies the condition:

$$p(j \mid 0) = p(Q-1-j \mid 1), \quad j = 0, 1, \ldots, Q-1$$

Suppose that the channel input symbols 0 and 1 are equally likely. Show that the channel output symbols are also equally likely; that is,

$$p(j) = \frac{1}{Q}, \qquad j = 0, 1, \ldots, Q-1$$

Solution: The matrix of transition probabilities of a discrete memoryless channel with 2 inputs and Q outputs may be written as

$$p = \begin{bmatrix} p(0|0)\, p(1|0)\, p(2|0) \ldots p(Q-1|0) \\ p(0|1)\, p(1|1)\, p(2|1) \ldots p(Q-1|1) \end{bmatrix}$$

For a symmetric channel,

$$p(j \mid 0) = p(Q-1-j \mid 1), \quad j = 0, 1, \ldots, Q-1$$

Moreover, each row of the matrix p contains the same set of numbers, and each column of the matrix p contains the same set of numbers. For example, for $Q = 4$ we may write

$$p = \begin{bmatrix} a & a & b & b \\ b & b & a & a \end{bmatrix}$$

The sum of the element of each row of matrix p must add up to one. Hence, for this example,

$$2a + 2b = 1$$

The probability of receiving symbol j is

$$p(j) = p(j|0)\,p(0) + p(j|1)\,p(1)$$

For equally likely input symbols:

$$p(0) = p(1) = \frac{1}{2}$$

Hence,

$$p(j) = \frac{1}{2}\,[p(j|0) + p(Q-1-j|0)]$$

For the example of $Q = 4$, we have

$$p(j) = \frac{1}{2}(a+b) = \frac{1}{4}, \qquad j = 0, 1, 2, 3$$

In general, we may write

$$p(j) = \frac{1}{Q} \qquad j = 0, 1, \ldots, Q-1$$

Problem 10.2: Consider the quantized demodulator for binary PSK signals shown in Fig. P. 10.2 (*b*). The quantizer is a four-level quantizer, normalized as in Fig. P. 10.2 (*a*). Evaluate the transition probabilities of the binary input-quaternary output discrete memoryless channel so characterized. hence, show that it is a symmetric channel. Assume that the transmitted signal energy per bit is E_b, and the

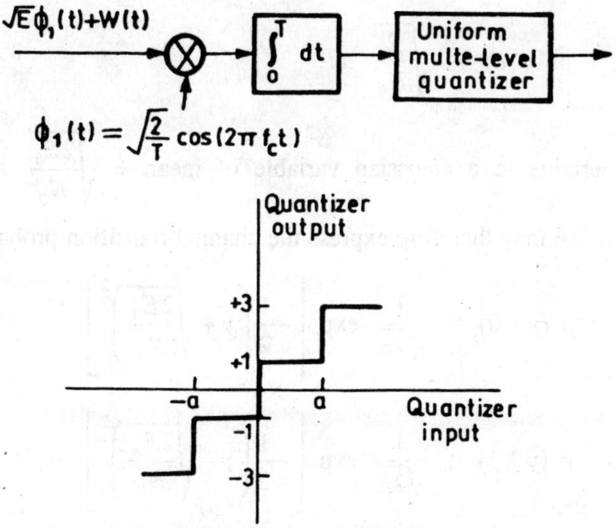

Fig. P. 10.2 and 10.2 (a)

additive white Gaussian noise has zero mean and power spectral density $\frac{N_0}{2}$.

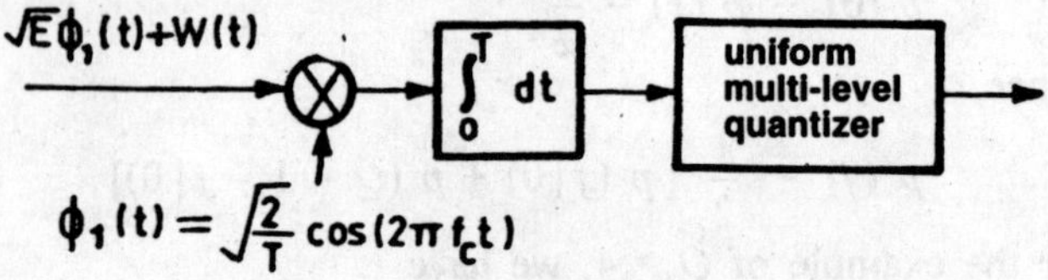

Fig. P. 10.2 (b)

Solution: For a binary PSK channel, the probability density function of the correlator output in the receiver is

$$f_x(x \mid 0) = \frac{1}{\sqrt{\pi N_0}} \exp\left[-\frac{1}{N_0}\left(x + \sqrt{E_b}\right)^2\right]$$

$$f_x(x \mid 1) = \frac{1}{\sqrt{\pi N_0}} \exp\left[-\frac{1}{N_0}\left(x - \sqrt{E_b}\right)^2\right]$$

Let $\quad y = \sqrt{\frac{2}{N_0}}\, x$

$$dy = \sqrt{\frac{2}{N_0}}\, dx$$

y pertains to a Gaussian variable of mean $\pm \sqrt{\frac{2E_b}{N_0}}$ and unit variance. We may therefore express the channel transition probability as

$$p(y \mid 0) = \frac{1}{\sqrt{2\pi}} \exp\left[-\frac{1}{2}\left(y + \sqrt{\frac{2E_b}{N_0}}\right)^2\right]$$

$$p(y \mid 1) = \frac{1}{\sqrt{2\pi}} \exp\left[-\frac{1}{2}\left(y - \sqrt{\frac{2E_b}{N_0}}\right)^2\right]$$

where $-\infty < y < \infty$

$$p(0 \mid 0) = \frac{1}{\sqrt{2\pi}} \int_{-\infty}^{\infty} \exp\left[-\frac{1}{2}\left(y + \sqrt{\frac{2E_b}{N_0}}\right)^2\right] dy$$

$$= \frac{1}{2} \operatorname{erfc}\left[\frac{a}{\sqrt{2}} - \sqrt{\frac{E_b}{N_0}}\right]$$

$$p(1 \mid 0) = \frac{1}{\sqrt{2\pi}} \int_{-a}^{0} \exp\left[-\frac{1}{2}\left(y + \sqrt{\frac{2E_b}{N_0}}\right)^2\right] dy$$

$$= \frac{1}{2}\, erfc\left[-\sqrt{\frac{E_b}{N_0}}\right] - erfc\left[\frac{a}{\sqrt{2}} - \sqrt{\frac{E_b}{N_0}}\right]$$

$$p(2 \mid 0) = \frac{1}{\sqrt{2\pi}} \int_{0}^{a} \exp\left[-\frac{1}{2}\left(y + \sqrt{\frac{2E_b}{N_0}}\right)^2\right] dy$$

$$= \frac{1}{2}\left[erfc\left[\sqrt{\frac{E_b}{N_0}}\right] - erfc\left(\frac{a}{\sqrt{2}} + \sqrt{\frac{E_b}{N_0}}\right)\right]$$

$$p(3 \mid 0) = \frac{1}{\sqrt{2\pi}} \int_{a}^{\infty} \exp\left[-\frac{1}{2}\left(y + \sqrt{\frac{2E_b}{N_0}}\right)^2\right] dy$$

$$= \frac{1}{2} \operatorname{erfc}\left[\frac{a}{\sqrt{2}} + \sqrt{\frac{E_b}{N_0}}\right]$$

We also note that

$$p(3 \mid 0) = p(0 \mid 1) \qquad p(2 \mid 0) = p(1 \mid 1)$$
$$p(1 \mid 0) = p(2 \mid 1) \qquad p(0 \mid 0) = p(3 \mid 1)$$

Hence, the channel is symmemntric.

Problem 10.3: Consider a binary input AWGN channel, in which the binary symbols 1 and 0 are equally likely. The binary symbols are transmitted over the channel by means of phase-shift keying. The code symbol energy is E, and the AWGN has zero mean and power spectral density .... Show that the channel transition probability is given by

$$p(y \mid 0) = \frac{1}{\sqrt{2\pi}} \exp\left[-\frac{1}{2}\left(y + \sqrt{\frac{2E}{N_0}}\right)^2\right], -\infty < y < \infty$$

Solution: From the solution to problem 10.2 we readily note the following:

$$p(y \mid 0) = \frac{1}{\sqrt{2\pi}} \exp\left[-\frac{1}{2}\left(\gamma + \sqrt{\frac{2E_b}{N_0}}\right)^2\right] \quad -\infty < y < \infty$$

$$p(y \mid 1) = \frac{1}{\sqrt{2\pi}} \exp\left[-\frac{1}{2}\left(\gamma - \sqrt{\frac{2E_b}{N_0}}\right)^2\right] \quad -\infty < y < \infty$$

where E is the code symbol energy.

Problem 10.4: In a single-parity-check code, a single parity bit is appended to a block of k message bits ($m_1, m_2, \ldots, m_k$). The single parity bit b_1 is chosen so that the code word satisfies the even parity rule:

$$m_1 + m_2 + \ldots + m_k + b_1 = 0, \qquad \text{mod } 2$$

For $k = 3$, set up the 2^k possible code words in the code defined by this rule.

Solution:

Message Sequence	*Single-parity-check code*
000	0000
001	0011
010	0101
011	0110
100	1001
101	1010
110	1100
111	1111

Problem 10.5: Compare the parity-check matrix of the (7, 4) Hamming code shown below with that of a (4, 1) repetition code.

Hamming code

Consider a family of (n, k) linear block codes that have the following parameters

Block length	$n = 2^m - 1$
No. of message bits	$k = 2^m - m - 1$
No. of parity bits	$n - k = m$ where $m \geq 3$

Solution: For the (4, 1) repetition code, the parity check matrix is

$$H = \begin{bmatrix} 1 & 0 & 0 & \vdots & 1 \\ 0 & 1 & 0 & \vdots & 1 \\ 0 & 0 & 1 & \vdots & 1 \end{bmatrix}$$

For a (7, 4) Hamming code, we have

$$H = \begin{bmatrix} 1 & 0 & 0 & \vdots & 1 & 0 & 1 & 1 \\ 0 & 1 & 0 & \vdots & 1 & 1 & 1 & 0 \\ 0 & 0 & 1 & \vdots & 0 & 1 & 1 & 1 \end{bmatrix}$$

For the Hamming code, the parity check matrix H is more structured than that for the repetition code. Indeed, the matrix H for the Hamming code include that for the repetition code as a sumbatrix.

Problem 10.6: For an application that requires error detection only, we may use a nonsystematic code. In this problem, we explore the generation of such a cyclic code. Let $g(X)$ denote the generator polynomial, and $m(X)$ denote the message polynomial. We define the code polynomial $c(X)$ simply as

$$c(X) = m(X)\, g(X)$$

Hence, for a given generator polynomial, we may readily determine the code words in the code. To illustrate this procedure, consider the generator polynomial for a (7, 4) Hamming code:

$$g(X) = 1 + X + X^3$$

Determine the 16 code words in the code, and confirm the non-systematic nature of the code.

Solution:

$$g(x) = 1 + X + X^3$$
$$c(X) = m(x)\, g(X)$$

hence, we may construct the following table:

Message word	*m (X)*	*e (X)*	*code word*
0000	0	0	0000000
0001	X^3	$X^3 + X^4 + X^6$	0001101
0010	X^2	$X^2 + X^3 + X^5$	0011010
0100	X	$X + X^2 + X^4$	0110100
1000	1	$1 + X + X^3$	1101000
0011	$X^2 + X^3$	$X^2 + X^4 + X^5 + X^6$	0010111
0110	$X + X^2$	$X + X^3 + X^4 + X^5$	0101110
1100	$1 + X$	$1 + X^2 + X^3 + X^4$	1011100
0101	$X + X^3$	$X + X^2 + X^3 + X^6$	0111001
1010	$1 + X^2$	$1 + X + X^2 + X^5$	1110010
1001	$1 + X^3$	$1 + X + X^4 + X^6$	1100101
0111	$X + X^2 + X^3$	$X + X^5 + X^6$	0100011
1110	$1 + X + X^2$	$1 + X^5 + X^6$	1000110
1011	$1 + X^2 + X^3$	$1 + X + X^2 + X^3 + X^4 + X^5 + X^6$	1111111
1101	$1 + X + X^3$	$1 + X^2 + X^6$	1010001
1111	$1 + X + X^2 + X^3$	$1 + X^3 + X^5 + X^6$	1001011

Comparing the code word to the message word, we see that the cyclic code generated by multiplying $g(x)$ and $c(x)$ is not a systematic code.

Problem 10.7: Consider the (7, 4) Hamming code defined by the generator polynomial

$$g(X) = 1 + X + X^3$$

The code word 0111001 is sent over a noisy channel, producing the received word 01011001. Determine the syndrome polynomial $s(X)$ for this received word, and show that it is identical to the error polynomial $e(X)$.

Solution: The error polynomial is

$$e(X) = r(X) + c(X)$$

we are given

$$e(X) = X + X^2 + X^3 + X^6$$
$$r(X) = X + X^3 + X^6$$

The error polynomial is therefore

$$e(X) = X^2$$

Consider next the syndrom polynomial $s(X)$. The syndrome calculator for the generator polynomial

$$g(X) = 1 + X + X^3$$

is shown in Fig. 10.7, this calculator is reproduced here for convenience of presentation:

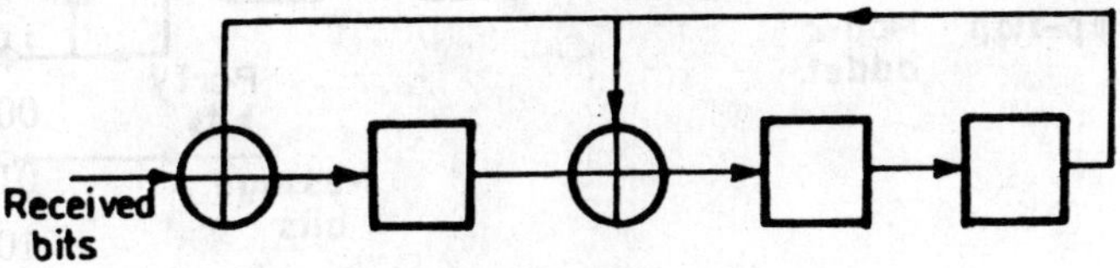

Fig. P. 10.7

Circulating the received bits through the syndrome calculator, we may construct the following table:

Initial state	000
	100
	010
	001
	010
	001
	010
	001

Here, the syndrome polynomials is

$$3(X) = X^2$$

which, for the problem at hand, is the same as the error polynomial. This result demonstrates the property of the syndrome polynomial, stating that it is the same as the error polynomial when the transmission errors are enfixed to the parity-check bits.

Problem 10.8: The generator polynomial of a (15, 11) Hamming code is defined by

$$g(X) = 1 + X + X^4$$

Develop the encoder and syndrome calculator for this code, using a systematic form for the code.

Solution: The encoder structure is

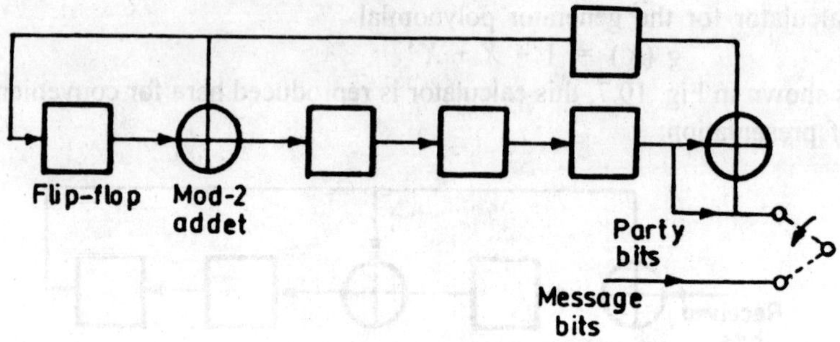

Fig. P. 10.8 (a)

The syndrome calculator is

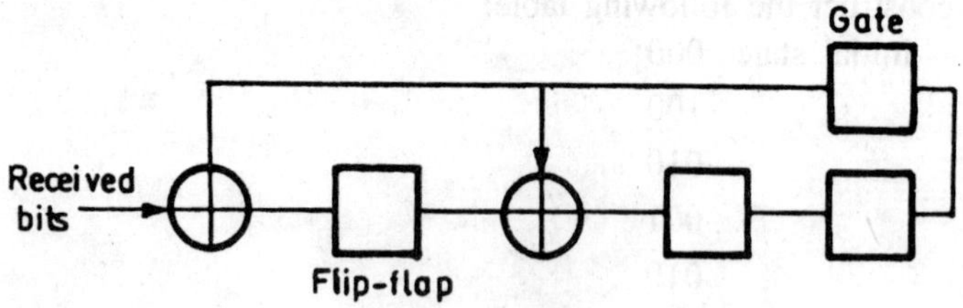

Fig. P. 10.8 (b)

Problem 10.9: Consider the (15, 4) maximum-length code that is the dual of the (15, 11) Hamming code of previous problem. Do the following:

(*a*) Find the feedback connections of the encoder.

(*b*) Find the generator polynomial $g(X)$; hence, determine the output sequence assuming the initial state 0001. Confirm the validity of your result by cycling the initial state through the encoder.

Solution: (*a*)

$$g_1(X) = (1 + X)(1 + X^2 + X^3)$$
$$= 1 + X + X^2 + X^4$$

The parity-check entries for the generator matrix G are

$$1 + X + X^2 + \dots X^4$$
$$X + X^2 + X^3 + \dots + X^5 \text{ cyclic shift by } X$$
$$X^2 + X^3 + X^4 + X^6 \text{ cyclic shift } X^2$$

Hence

$$G = \begin{bmatrix} 1 & 1 & 1 & 0 & 1 & 0 & 0 \\ 0 & 1 & 1 & 1 & 0 & 1 & 0 \\ 0 & 0 & 1 & 1 & 1 & 0 & 1 \end{bmatrix}$$

Adding row (1) to row (3), we get the generator matrix G in systematic form:

$$G = \begin{bmatrix} 1 & 1 & 1 & 0 & \vdots & 1 & 0 & 0 \\ 0 & 1 & 1 & 1 & \vdots & 0 & 1 & 0 \\ \underbrace{1 \; 1 \; 0 \; 1}_{p} & & & & \vdots & \underbrace{0 \; 0 \; 1}_{I_k} & & \end{bmatrix}$$

with $c = mG$, we may thus construct the code:

Message	*Code word*	*Hamming weight*
000	0000000	0
001	1101001	4
010	0111010	4
011	1010011	4
100	1110100	4
101	0011101	4
110	1001110	4
111	0100111	4

Since the minimum Hamming weight of the non-zero code words is 4, it follows that

$$d_{\min} = 4$$

(*b*) Since

$$1 + X^7 = h(X)\, g(X)$$

we have

$$h(X) = 1 + X + X^3$$

The easiest way to get the parity-check matrix is to use the relations:

$$G = [p \,\vdots\, I_k]$$
$$H = [I_{n-k} \,\vdots\, p^T]$$

$$\text{Hence,} \quad H = \begin{bmatrix} 1\,0\,0\,0 & \vdots & 1\,0\,1 \\ 0\,1\,0\,0 & \vdots & 1\,1\,1 \\ 0\,0\,1\,0 & \vdots & 1\,1\,0 \\ \underbrace{0\,0\,0\,1}_{I_{n-k}} & \vdots & \underbrace{0\,1\,1}_{P^T} \end{bmatrix}$$

(*c*) So construct the encoder, we use $g(X)$; thus

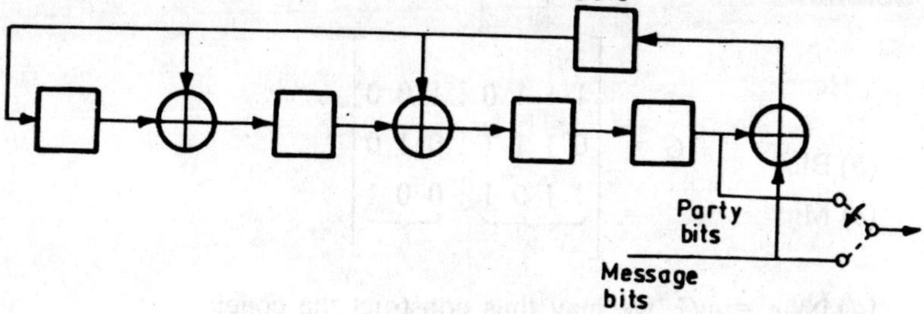

Fig. P. 10.9 (a)

For the syndrome calculator, we also use $g(X)$; thus

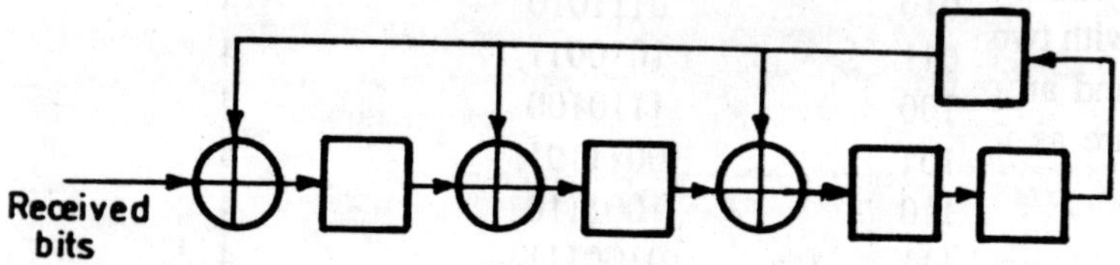

Fig. P. 10.9 (b)

Shift	*Input*	*Register contents*
		0000
1	0	0000
2	1	1000
3	1	1100
1	1	1110
5	1	1111
6	1	0001
7	0	1110

The syndrome is therefore 1110, indicating an error pattern (since the received word 0111110 is not a code word, the syndrome must be non–zero.)

Problem 10.10: Consider the (31, 15) Read-Solomon code.

(*a*) How many bits are there in a symbol of the code?

(*b*) What is the block length in bits?

(*c*) What is the minimum distance of the code?

(*d*) How many symbols in error can the code correct?

Solution: (*a*)

$$n = 2^m - 1 = 31 \text{ symbols}$$

Hence, the number of bits per symbole in the code is

$$m = 5 \text{ bits}$$

(*b*) Block length $= 31 \times 5 = 155$ bits

(*c*) Minimum distance of the code is

$$d_{\min} = 2t + 1 = n - k + 1 = 31 - 15 + 1 = 17 \text{ symbols}$$

(*d*) Number of correctable symbols is

$$l = \frac{1}{2}(n - k) = 8 \text{ symbols}$$

Problem 10.11: A convolutional encoder has a single-shift register with two stages, (i.e., constraint length $K = 3$), three modulo-2 adders, and an output multiplexer. The generator sequences of the encoder are as follows:

$$g^{(1)} = (1, 0, 1)$$
$$g^{(2)} = (1, 1, 0)$$
$$g^{(3)} = (1, 1, 1)$$

Draw the block diagram of the encoder.

Solution: The encoder is realized by inspection:

$$g^{(1)} = (10, 1)$$
$$g^{(2)} = (1, 1.0)$$
$$g^{(3)} = (1, 1.1)$$

For the Hamming code, the parity check matrix H is more structured than that for the repetition code. Indeed, the matrix H for Hamming code includes that for the repetition code as a submatrix.

Problem 10.12: Consider the rate $r = 1/2$, constraint length $K = 2$ convolutional encoder of Fig. P. 10.12. The code is systematic. Find the encoder output produced by the message sequence 10111....

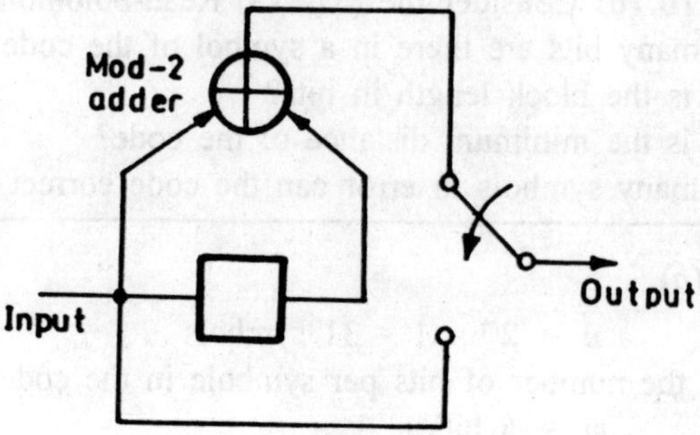

Fig. P. 10.12

Solution: Using this encoder, we may construct the following table by inspection:

Massage	1	0	1	1	1	1	...
Output	11	10	11	01	01	01	...

original massage

The code is in fact systematic.

Problem 10.13: Fig. P. 10.13 shows the encoder for a rate $r = 1/2$, constraint length $K = 4$ convolutional code. Determine the encoder output produced by the message sequence 10111....

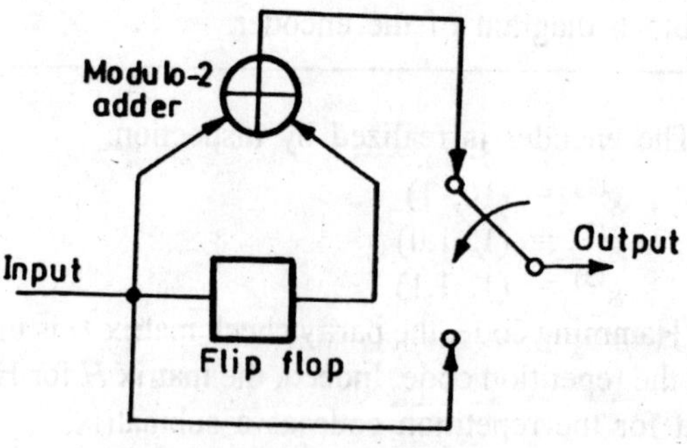

Fig. P. 10.13

Solution: The generator polynomials are

$$g^{(1)}(X) = 1 + X + X^2 + X^3$$
$$g^{(2)}(X) = 1 + X + X^3$$

The message polynomial is

$$m(X) = 1 + X^2 + X^3 + X^4 + \ldots$$

Hence,

$$C^{(1)}(X) = g^{(1)}(X)\, m(X)$$
$$= 1 + X + X^3 + X^4 + X^5 + \ldots$$
$$C^{(2)}(X) = g^{(2)}(X)\, m(X)$$
$$= 1 + X + X^2 + X^3 + X^6 + X^7 + \ldots$$

Hence,

$$\{C^{(1)}\} = 1, 1, 0, 1, 1, 1, \ldots$$
$$\{C^{(2)}\} = 1, 1, 1, 1, 0, 0, \ldots$$

The encoder output is therefore 11, 11, 01, 11, 10, 10

Problem 10.14: Consider the encoder of Fig. P. 10.14 for a rate $r = 2/3$, constraint length $K = 2$ convolutional code. Determine the code sequence produced by the message sequence 10111....

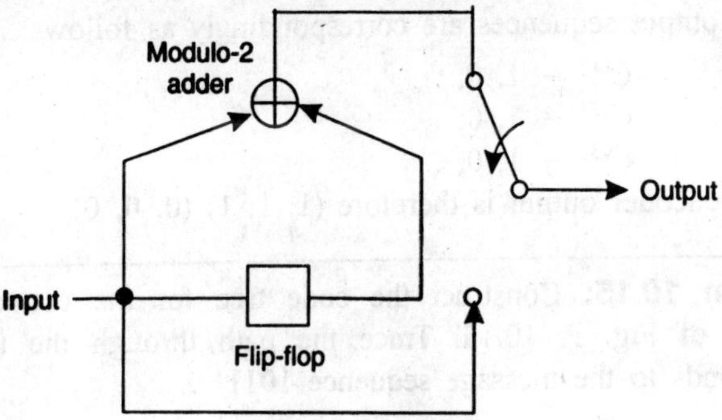

Fig. P. 10.14

Solution: The encoder of Fig. 10.14 has three generator sequences for each of the two input paths; they are as follows (from top to bottom)

$$g_1^{(1)} = (1, 1) \qquad g_1^{(2)} = (1, 0)$$
$$g_1^{(3)} = (1, 1) \qquad g_2^{(1)} = (0, 1)$$
$$g_2^{(2)} = (1, 1) \qquad g_2^{(3)} = (0, 0)$$

Hence,

$$g_1^{(1)}(X) = 1 + X, \qquad g_1^{(2)}(X) = 1,$$
$$g_1^{(3)}(X) = 1 + X, \qquad g_2^{(1)}(X) = (X),$$
$$g_2^{(2)}(X) = 1 + X, \qquad g_2^{(3)}(X) = 0$$

The incoming message sequence 10111 ... enters the encoder two bits at a time; hence

$$m^{(1)} = 11 \ldots$$
$$m^{(2)} = 01 \ldots$$

The massage polynomials are therefore

$$m_1(X) = 1 + X + \ldots$$
$$m_2(X) = X + \ldots$$

Hence, the output polynomials are

$$\begin{aligned} C^{(1)}(X) &= g_1^{(1)}(X)\, m_1(X) + g_2^{(1)}(X)\, m_2(X) \\ &= (1 + X)(1 + X + \ldots) + X(X + \ldots) \\ &= 1 + \ldots \end{aligned}$$

$$\begin{aligned} C^{(2)}(X) &= g_1^{(2)}(X)\, m_1(X) + g_2^{(2)}(X)\, m_2(X) \\ &= (1)(1 + X + \ldots) + (1 + X)(X + \ldots) \\ &= 1 + X + \ldots + X + X^2 + \ldots \\ &= 1 + X^2 + \ldots \end{aligned}$$

$$\begin{aligned} C^{3}(X) &= g_1^{(3)}(X)\, m_1(X) + g_2^{(3)}(X)\, m_2(X) \\ &= (1 + X)(1 + X + \ldots) + 0\,(X + \ldots) \\ &= 1 + X^2 + \ldots \end{aligned}$$

The output sequences are correspondingly as follows: .

$$C^{(1)} = 1, 0, \ldots$$
$$C^{(2)} = 1, 0, \ldots$$
$$C^{(3)} = 1, 0, \ldots$$

The encoder output is therefore (1, 1, 1) (0, 0, 0), ...

Problem 10.15: Construct the code tree for the convolutional encoder of Fig. P. 10.15. Trace the path through the tree that corresponds to the message sequence 10111...

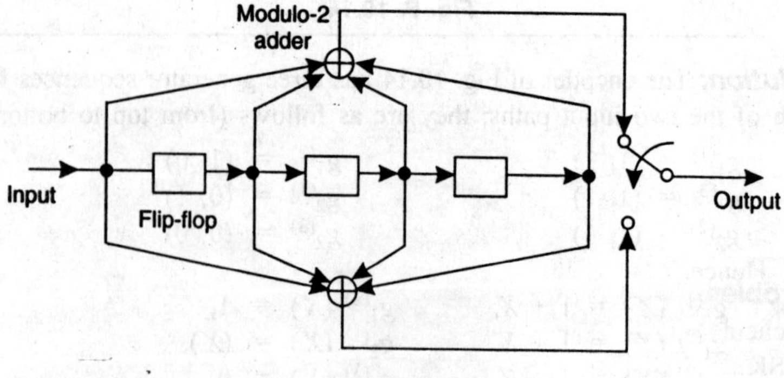

Fig. P. 10.15

Solution:

1 If the input sequence is 00, the encoder output is 00, 00, 00, 00.

2 If the input sequence is 11, the message polynomial is

$$m(X) = 1 + X$$

The two generator polynomials are

$$g^{(1)}(X) = 1 + X + X^2$$
$$g^{(2)}(X) = 1 + X^2$$

Hence,

$$C^{(1)}(X) = (1 + X)(1 + X + X^2) = 1 + X^3$$
$$C^{(2)}(X) = (1 + X)(1 + X^2) = 1 + X + X^2 + X^3$$

The encoder output is 11, 01, 01, 11

3 If the input sequence is 01, the message polynomials is

$$m(X) = X$$

Hence,

$$C^{(1)}(X) = X(1 + X + X^2) = X + X^3 + X^2$$
$$C^{(2)}(X) = X(1 + X^2) = X + X^3$$

The encoder output is 00, 11, 10, 11

4 Finally, if the input sequence is 40, the message polynomial is

$$m(X) = 1$$

Correspondingly,

$$C^{(1)}(X) = g^{(1)}(X) = 1 + X + X^2$$
$$C^{(2)}(X) = g^{(2)}(X) = 1 + X^2$$

Hence, the encoder output is 11, 10, 11, 00.

The encoder outputs calculated above are in perfect according with the entries of the code tree:

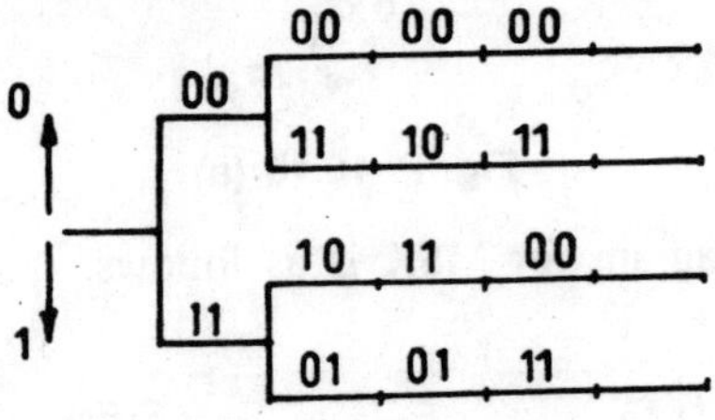

Fig. P. 10.15 (a)

Problem 10.16: By viewing the minimum shift keying (MSK) secheme as a finite-state machine, construct the trellis diagram for MSK.

Solution: An MSK system has two distinct phase states

State	Phase redians
a	0
b	π

The transmission of a 1 increases the phase by $\frac{\pi}{2}$, whereas the transmission of a 0 decreases the phase by $\frac{\pi}{2}$. Correspondingly, the transmission of dibit 10 or 01 leaves the state of MSK unchanged, whereas the transmission of dibit 00 or 11 moves the system from one state to the other. For the output, we have

Input dibit	Output frequenceis
11	$f_1 f_1$
01	$f_2 f_1$
10	$f_1 f_2$
00	$f_2 f_2$

We may thus construct the following state diagram for MSK.

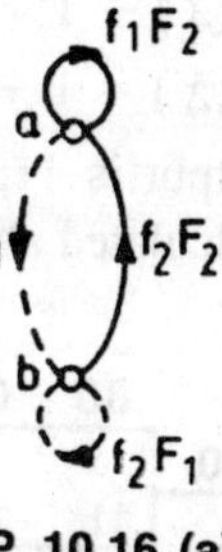

Fig. P. 10.16 (a)

The trellis diagram for MSK is as follows:

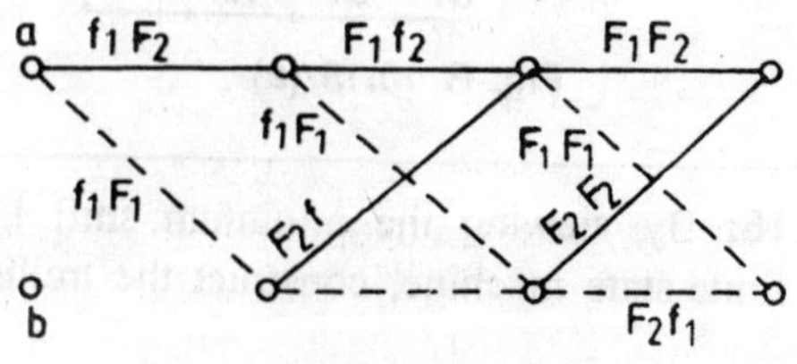

Fig. P. 10.16 (b)

Since $d_{min} = 5$ and the number of errors in the received sequence is 2, it should be possible to decode the correct sequence. This is readily demonstrated by applying the viterbi-algorithm.

Problem 10.17: Construct the code tree for the encoder of Fig. P. 10.17. Trace the path through the tree that corresponds to the message sequence 10111.... Compare the resulting encoder output with that found in Problem 10.13.

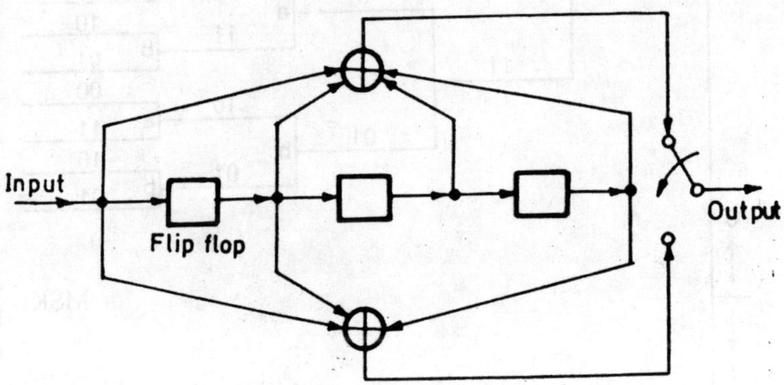

Fig. P. 10.17

Solution:

The output sequence is 11, 10, 11, 01, 01.

[see Fig. 10.17 (*a*)].

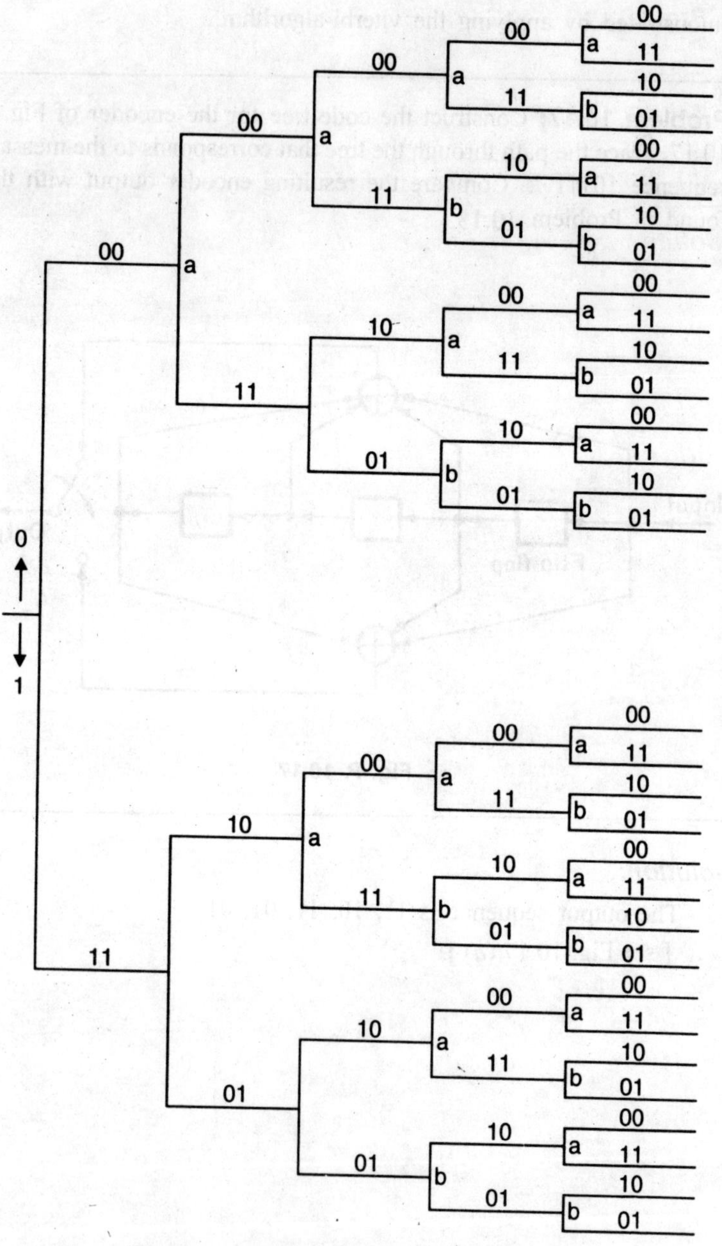

Fig. P. 10.17 (a)

The output sequence is 11, 10, 11, 01, 01

Problem 10.18: Consider a rate-$\frac{1}{2}$, constraint length-7 convolutional code with free distance $d_{\text{free}} = 10$. Calculate the asymptotic coding gain for the following two channels:

(*a*) Binary symmetric channel

(*b*) Binary input AWGN channel

Solution: (*a*) coding gain for binary symmetric channel is

$$G_a = 10 \log_2 \left(\frac{10 \times \frac{1}{2}}{2} \right) = 10 \log_{10} 2.5 = 4 \text{ dB}$$

(*b*) Coding gain for additive with Gaussian noise channel is

$$G_a = 10 \log_{10} \left(10 \times \frac{1}{2} \right) = 10 \log_{10}{}^5 = 7 \text{ dB}$$

Reader's Notes

Reader's Notes

Reader's Notes